GW00937951

LAGONDA
4½ Litre & V12

In Detail

LAGONDA
4½ Litre & V12

In Detail

BY ARNOLD DAVEY

H&S

Herridge & Sons

Published in 2004 by
Herridge & Sons Ltd
Lower Forda, Shebbear,
Beaworthy, Devon EX21 5SY

© Copyright Arnold Davey 2004

Designed by Ray Leaning
Special photography by Simon Clay

All rights reserved. No part of this publication may
be reproduced in any form or by any means
without the prior permission of the publisher.

ISBN 0-9541063-5-0
Printed in China

Picture Acknowledgments
Unless otherwise stated all photographs are from the
Lagonda Club Heritage Trust

Contents

Foreword

The public's conception of "Lagonda" varies from vague thoughts of funny lopsided boats in Venice to a recently-introduced family hatchback from Renault (the Laguna). Only the enthusiast will have heard of the Lagonda car make, even though it is one of the longest lived in the industry. It was founded in 1899 by Wilbur Gunn to make steam engines for Thames riverboats. He made his first motorcycle for sale in 1900 and grew steadily more ambitious. The company's finest period was in the 1930s, culminating in the large, powerful and expensive 4½ litre and V12 models which are the subject of this book.

During the period 1933-1940 the nature of the car industry underwent a huge amount of change, not only in the products themselves but also in the way they were made. Lagonda was not rich enough - was in fact perpetually short of money - to invest heavily in the expensive plant needed to mass-produce cars, and anyway the number of likely customers for so upmarket a vehicle was not enough to justify a change in the traditional way of making a car: a separate steel chassis on which was mounted a wood-framed, metal panelled body. But the nature of the cars so produced did change to meet the growing demand for more comfort and refinement, coupled with less maintenance, and all without any loss of performance. The same period also saw the decline of the open tourer body in favour of closed cars that did not require special clothing. As a halfway house, the drophead

coupé became popular, openable, but only rarely. Each of the five models of Lagonda covered here has its own character and we will trace the development of each in turn.

Considering the limited funds available, Lagonda had a continuing and successful involvement in competition at the highest level. Indubitably its finest hour was the win in the 1935 Le Mans 24-hour race, one of only four British makes to do so. That the company was in Receivership at the time and due to be auctioned the following day makes the story seem more like fiction, where the author is pouring on the drama. Yet that is what happened. Each of the models we are examining spawned a competition version and their exploits are given a separate chapter in order to cover them fully. Not that only factory or factory-backed entrants were in the competitive field at the time, but reports of the minor events of the period tended to be sketchy and are frequently vague, as they relied on outsiders supplying the information to the motoring magazines.

During the war there was a considerable debate within the company as to a postwar model: should the V12 be re-introduced or should it make way for a smaller, cheaper, car aimed lower in the market ? The latter view prevailed, but the introduction of the LB6, later the DB 2.6 litre, was held up by upheavals in the industry and political thinking that deprived the company of a steel allowance. Eventually the company was bought by David Brown, princi-

Wilbur Gunn, taken towards the end of his life. Before 1914 he sported a waxed "Kaiser Bill" moustache which became bad taste after war broke out.

pally for the advanced double overhead camshaft engine that he wanted to put into the Aston Martin, a company he already owned. The Aston transformation took time and for some years Lagonda sales kept the Aston Martin Lagonda concern afloat, until the DB2 got under way.

The same kind of story was repeated in the late 1970s when the William Towns designed V8 Lagonda, with its space-age styling, sold over 600 examples, many to Middle East sheikhs, and kept the company going while a revised Aston Martin was produced. Aston Martin Lagonda is now part of Ford and the last Lagonda was produced in 1990, apart from a few one-off, four-door Astons badged as Lagondas. But the name persists and every now and then a prototype emerges with the hallowed badge. We live in hope.

Arnold Davey
June 2004

Chapter One

The Background

The first thing you have to do when writing about Lagonda's history is to explain the origins of the strange name. The founder of the company, Wilbur Adams Gunn, was American, born in Troy, Ohio, in 1860 and growing up in Springfield, Ohio. Wilbur was the second child of Rev. James Wynn Gunn, a clergyman who had a day job as postmaster and ran a bookstore. On leaving school, Wilbur was apprenticed at Singer's, the sewing machine firm, and eventually became a sewing machine repairer in Springfield. In 1885 he married the girl next door, Bertha Myers, and three years later they moved to New York, where a daughter, Marjorie, was born.

In the spring of 1891 Wilbur came to England, leaving his wife and child in New York, and set himself up as a freelance consulting engineer, specialising in hydraulic power plants, then extremely popular as being reliable and easier to understand than electricity. As a hobby he tinkered with steam engines and was an accomplished amateur opera singer.

One of his hydraulic sites was miles from any railway station and Wilbur took to cycling to it until a bad winter made the roads "heavy", a Victorian term describing a top three-inch layer of mud and horse droppings. So he made a small petrol motor, about a half horsepower, and fixed it to drive the front wheel through a set of gears, later replaced by a belt. The date of this is not recorded, but he was undoubtedly a pioneer motorcyclist.

Some time in the mid-1890s, perhaps through a common interest in opera, he met Constance Grey, who lived with her husband Charles in The Cottage in Thorpe Road, Egham, Surrey. Charles and Constance were well connected, he being a brother of Lord Grey and Constance the daughter of a cavalry officer. Charles died in 1896 and by the middle of 1898 Wilbur Gunn had divorced Bertha (or been divorced by her) and married Constance. Once installed in The Cottage, he set up a small workshop in the greenhouse and started to make small compound steam engines to sell to the owners of steam launches on the Thames. In 1899 he set up a company called the Lagonda Engineering Company, the name being that of a district in Springfield, which itself was a French corruption of the Native American name for the stream now called Buck Creek. He wasn't alone in using the Lagonda name as his brother-in-law had also founded a Lagonda company in Springfield , making tube cleaning machinery for boilers and other steam-related plant. Lagonda tube cleaners were still being made in the USA and in Britain in the 1970s, but there was no commercial connection between the two companies.

In 1900 Wilbur Gunn made his first motorcycle for sale, a photograph of which survives. The bicycle parts were made by a Staines firm, Knights, and Wilbur made the engine and fitted it, driving the rear wheel by belt. At this time cycling clubs admitted motorcycles and the club connection led to orders by word of mouth. In November 1902 Gunn registered the trademark "Lagonda" and in 1903 he became a founder member of the Auto-cycle Club. In that year he took part in the 1000

The first motorcycle of 1900. Gunn had made himself one before that, but this one was made for sale. Motorcycles were produced for about four years, getting steadily more powerful, until overtaken by the popularity of the tricars.

Miles Trials, riding one of his own machines and thus bringing it to national attention, since the event was very widely reported in the motoring press. Gunn achieved a second-class award but the publicity led to several orders and to his taking on employees, the first of whom were Bert Hammond, recruited from Knights, and Alfie Cranmer. Not long after, Bill Amiss and George Wise joined. All these gentlemen stayed with the company until the 1930s and Bill Amiss was there throughout the Second World War.

By 1904 tricars were beginning to take the place of the unpopular trailers for motorcyclists who wanted to take a passenger. Gunn's friend G W Manning, who combined being secretary of the Thames Valley Motor Cycling Club with being Engineer and Surveyor to the Staines Rural District Council, ordered a tricar from Gunn, who fitted a 3½hp engine and belt drive, just as on his motorcycle. This equipmentment proved to be inadequate, and the engine had to be enlarged to 5hp, with chain drive, to get the machine up the Surrey hills. To accommodate the new production Gunn roofed over part of his garden, extending the Thorpe Road boundary wall upwards and cutting a wider gate in it to allow the finished machines out.

From 1904 to 1907 these tricars grew larger and heavier, eventually reaching 12hp, with water cooling and wheel steering. But they had become unwieldy beasts and in 1908 the market for tricars suddenly collapsed, being replaced by sidecars and cyclecars. The Lagonda Engineering Company, which had become the Lagonda Motor Company Ltd in May

1904, went into Receivership in April 1907 but carried on trading, and Gunn found it quite easy to add a fourth wheel to his giant tricar and thus make a "proper" car in 1908.

Once established as a car maker, Lagonda grew rapidly. The 12hp car of 1908 was replaced by a 14/16hp using a bought-in four-cylinder engine by Coventry Simplex, then by a 16/18hp model, also powered by Coventry Simplex. Next a 20hp engine of Lagonda's own make was installed in the 16/18 chassis and finally there was a 30hp six-cylinder, also Lagonda-powered. The bodies were built by

10/12hp air-cooled twin tricar of 1905, photographed in Thorpe Road outside the works. You can see in the brickwork where Gunn's original garden wall has been extended upwards to make a tricar factory. A wider gateway was needed too.

Bert Hammond in the 1909 lightweight 18hp racer at Brooklands after winning the Summer Handicap

Lagonda's next door neighbour, Warmingtons, on the corner between The Causeway and Thorpe Road.

Wilbur Gunn was a great believer in competition as an aid to sales. In the motorcycle era a Lagonda had formed part of the Great Britain team in the 1904 International Cup race held in France, and Gunn drove one of his own products in all the important reliability trials of the tricar period from 1904 to 1907. Similarly, in 1909 a stripped 18hp

two-seater had a series of successes at Brooklands driven by Bert Hammond, who was now the firm's tester. In 1910 Gunn and Hammond took part in a 2000-mile reliability trial in Russia which was so over-regulated by the organisers that no clear result emerged. But a special award was offered to any competitor who could achieve Moscow to St Petersburg in one day and Gunn won this, was in fact the only entrant, but completed the run in 12 hours and got a gold medal and a certificate from the Tsar. The Russians were so impressed that he was able to set up a Russian subsidiary that took virtually all the output for the next two years.

Gunn was a great admirer of Henry Ford and shared his view that the future of the motor industry lay in simple cars for the masses. In 1912 he set about designing a revolutionary cheap car and simultaneously sought the necessary capital and premises to build it in. A complicated deal with a car repair and cab company in Hammersmith resulted in the setting up of Lagonda Limited in March 1913 to make the new model, with world selling rights going to Tollemache & Griffin Ltd, itself a re-structure of the Montague Garage Company of 195 Hammersmith Road. For premises, Gunn bought out two of his neighbours, Philip Head, a furniture store that also acted as undertakers, and Henry Warmington's coach-building workshop. Both were then totally rebuilt by Gunn's staff using the cheapest materials avail-

Wilbur Gunn and his crew at the start of a stage in the 1910 Russian rally. Gunn is driving the 16/18hp car, with Hammond behind him. The front-seat passenger is Thornton, Gunn's Russian agent, and the official observer, complete with sword and spurs, is in the other rear seat.

able - corrugated iron on timber frames and earth floors - since the newfound capital, already eaten into to settle Gunn's debts, was barely enough (it was about £9000) to get his revolutionary new design into production.

The Lagonda 11.1hp of 1913 foreshadowed modern unitary construction by 20 years or more. There was no chassis as was then the norm. Instead, a "hull" made up from angle steel strips and tinned steel sheet had several large sub-assemblies fixed to it: an engine/clutch/gearbox unit, the front suspension (a transverse leaf spring and radius arms), and the rear axle/transmission (called the "road unit"). In detail, the body unit contained the coachwork, the quarter-elliptic rear springs, the radiator and the interior. The power unit was the combined engine, clutch, transmission brake and gearbox, with all pedals and the handbrake attached. These four large assemblies came together at a very late stage in building the car, and for subsequent servicing could easily be detached.

The engine was a four-cylinder overhead inlet, side exhaust (ioe) design with dimensions of 67x77.8mm, giving 1099cc. Its power output has never been established. It drove a three-speed gearbox through a cone clutch and a feature of it, shared with Ford's Model T, was that the sump was a massive aluminium casting which held everything together and encompassed the flywheel and clutch. The combined block and head was bolted

to it. The worm rear axle was located by an A-frame pivoted on a balljoint just to the rear of the gearbox.

It really was tiny, only 10ft 3in (3.1m) overall and weighed only 9cwt (457kg). Only one body style was offered, a little two-seater coupé with a rounded rump and a matching bullnose radiator. Alfie Cranmer did much of the detailed design and it incorporated lots of his little weight-saving ideas. For example, there was no steering box. Instead, an arm was fitted at right angles to the steering column and this worked the track rod directly, giving 1 to 1 steering, as on a bicycle. The bevel gears for the differential were cut on to an upset on the inner ends of the halfshafts, avoiding a bolted joint there, and a short remote gearlever in the centre of the car changed the gears (probably a world first). The fact that the driver had to use his left hand to work this was regarded with great suspicion when the car came to be tested by the motoring magazines.

Gear ratios were widely spaced, as was normal then, but were cunningly selected by Cranmer so that only three sizes of cog were needed, with a fourth for reverse. The overhead inlet valves were worked by pushrods and, unusually, the rockers were very short and were longitudinal, not transverse. They gave trouble at once and early cars had to be recalled. The solution was to fit much longer rockers, so that the pushrod by number one

An 11.1hp two-seater of 1913, probably taken at Runnymede, close to the works. The driver is W H (Bill) Oates and the passenger is believed to be Wilfred Denison, a director of the company.

Munitions work in 1917. The little trolley being pushed by the woman on the right was made up from 11.1hp parts to avoid females having to lift heavy metal products. Note the forest of flapping belts.

cylinder worked number two inlet valve and vice versa. 1913 cars had no battery and no instruments, with oil sidelamps and acetylene headlamps. The complete car sold for £150.

It was October 1913 before a production car was available for magazines to test and they were generally very enthusiastic, but then they always were in those days. In June 1914 a cheaper two-seater was introduced with more primitive weather equipment than the glass windows and rigid windscreen of the coupé.

Immediately after the outbreak of war in August 1914 the War Office commandeered every carthorse in the land, instantly creating a brisk market for motor vans. Lagonda obliged and by mid-September had one on offer, based on the coupé and at the same price, but featuring lower gearing to cope with the 5cwt (254kg) payload. Hot on its heels, in November 1914 a four-seater appeared, built on the same principles but with a 15-inch longer wheelbase. It cost £7 10s more than the coupé but you got no tyre on the spare wheel for this. Car production was legal but slow until November 1916 when it was stopped by the government, but Lagonda was by then heavily involved in munitions work, principally shell production, where its reputation for precision machining carried great weight.

The factory expanded rapidly and the Gunns left their house, which was pulled down, the whole site at the corner of The Causeway and Thorpe Road becoming the Lagonda works. The Gunns

took a lease on Hythe House, only a few yards away on the other side of Thorpe Road, facing Staines Bridge. Wilbur never seemed to sleep throughout the war, appearing in the factory at all hours of the day and night. Three shifts were being worked and at its peak there were 1600 employees, of which 800, mainly women, were in the main machine shop alone. There were a series of financial reconstructions during the war, which saw Tollemache & Griffin disappear and capital raised to buy all the machinery the company needed to fulfil its munitions contracts. By October 1917, when an engineering journal visited the place and wrote it up, there was a foundry and a free canteen, and the works had extended on to the neighbouring property called The Chestnuts. That house itself was still standing, and was in fact to become the home of a future Managing Director in the 1920s.

All munitions work stopped overnight at the Armistice in November 1918 and Wilbur Gunn, now 59 and ailing, had to start to convert a factory designed to mass produce millions of shells back into a car plant. Fortunately his key personnel had been exempted from conscription, had in fact been "fetched back" as Bert Hammond put it, and were available for the rebuild. Timber frames and corrugated iron proved to be extremely versatile and an improved 11.1hp was offered for sale in May 1919, with delivery by July. The old Tollemache & Griffin depot in Hammersmith was now part of the Lagonda empire and was used as a London sales office and service garage. The coupé and four-seater were offered at 275 and 285 guineas respectively. Changes from pre-war versions included proper geared steering, a dynamo and electric lighting (actually available as an extra in 1915), a starter motor and a Panhard rod added to the front axle to control the rather approximate steering that followed from an axle shackled at both ends. All these extras meant that the formerly frugal 11.1hp, which had achieved 51mpg in 1913, had grown from 9cwt (457kg) to 12.7cwt (647 kg), to the detriment of its performance and fuel consumption.

In November 1919 Lagonda made its first appearance at a London Motor Show since the Tricar days, showing a coupé with a new flat radiator and a four-seater still carrying the bullnose radiator and looking a trifle Edwardian as a result. Prices were rising rapidly and the 335 and 355 guineas were said to be "provisional", which they were, growing to over £400 in March 1920. All cars were still painted green, one of Mr Ford's money saving dodges that Gunn had copied, but wings and wheels were stove enamelled black and nickel plating had spread from just the radiator to a number of other fittings.

Needless to say, Lagondas began to appear in competitions just as soon as they started up again after the war, and Wilbur Gunn, despite his ill-health, was as keen as ever on reliability trials. His main companion was W H Oates, a member of staff since 1910, who had risen to be a Major and been awarded the OBE during the war and was now sales manager of the company. In 1915 Oates had built himself a highly tuned 11.1 competition two-seater but had had few chances to exercise it. Now he took on the combined job of competition driver and product developer so that, for example, the car he drove in the 1920 London to Land's End Trial was the prototype of the 11.9 and later the press car.

Wilbur Gunn's health deteriorated rapidly in 1920 and despite gaining a gold medal in the London to Edinburgh Run at Whitsun, he died of lymphatic cancer on 27 September. His death rather threw the company, which had relied on him totally for direction and ideas. The result was to split the engineering and the management, with Alfie Cranmer in charge of technical matters, although not becoming a director until 1923, and Colin Parbury becoming managing director. Poor Constance Gunn found herself leasing the rather

grand Hythe House but without Wilbur's salary. She retired to a nearby hotel and finally became a boarder with a family in Wimborne, Dorset, dying in 1930.

All cars were in brisk demand in 1920 and Lagonda was selling 15 a week by October. It was a good moment to introduce a new model, the 11.9hp, even if, at £495, the price was double that of the 1919 car. The 11.9 was clearly a development of the 11.1, using the same chassisless

Tyre and wing store in 1921. The trolleys are still in use, and were so useful they stayed in the factory throughout the Lagonda era, the Maclaren era and the Petter period. They were still there when the factory was demolished in 1989, except that the wheels were given to a Lagonda 11.9 owner.

A 1921 11.9 coupé with dickey seat. Extending the wheelbase to 9 feet made the former two-seater look a bit odd.

Bert Hammond in Major Oates's single-seater racing 11.9. There isn't a crease in the scuttle: the original photograph has been damaged.

construction principles, but the engine had grown to 1420cc (69x95mm) and the block and crankcase were now separate items, the latter being of aluminium. The shorter wheelbase was dropped, so all cars now had the 9ft version, which on the coupé meant that the stumpy rounded tail was replaced by a long flat sloping one which incorporated a dickey seat. The flat radiator was standardised and both axles were strengthened. However, the 1920 boom fizzled out in 1921, and prices were steadily reduced. Meanwhile the new management had carried out another financial restructuring, paid off all the wartime mortgages

and taken on a new one with Barclays Bank.

Wilbur Gunn's competitive spirit lived on and as well as entering all the major reliability trials, which were very extensively reported in the motoring press at the time, the company helped Bill Oates when he decided to build himself a single-seat racing version of the 11.9. This was a tiny thing, only 28in (71cm) wide and very sleek, with body sides coming up to the driver's neck. The engine was bored out from 69mm to 70.5mm, giving a capacity of 1483cc. It must have been sensationally tuned, because once he had got it running properly Oates was lapping Brooklands at speeds well into the 80s, virtually double the standard car's top speed. Oates had considerable success with his single-seater and company advertising managed to convey the impression that the ordinary 11.9 was a potential racer. At the end of 1921 Oates succeeded in capturing five light car records at Brooklands, ranging from the flying mile at 86.91mph to 100 miles at 80.19mph, this last showing that the car was no one-lap sprinter, but had serious stamina as well. Inspired by this the factory had built two two-seater versions of Oates's car to contest the JCC 200 Mile race of 1921. This was the first long-distance race to be held in Britain for light cars of up to 1½ litres and was a big contrast to the majority of Brooklands races, normally little more than two or three laps of the track. Oates was to drive one car and Bert Hammond the other, each with a riding mechanic.

Major Bill Oates, taken at the wheel of his single-seater. As well as his motoring, he was a radio ham and had constructed a television set by 1930.

The engines had a special long stroke, giving 1496cc with the normal 69mm bore. The race was regarded as so important and testing that practice was permitted for three weeks beforehand. Both cars ran faultlessly non-stop but were overwhelmed by the unexpected speed of the opposition and came in 11th and 13th, Hammond beating Oates by 4min 13sec and averaging 76.9mph. This act of insubordination raised something of a furore at Staines and Hammond did not get another works drive.

Oates's records only lasted over the winter and were all beaten by AC in March 1922, but he carried on with the single-seater with occasional wins and a huge number of second places, which became a bit of a joke. He used the car for hill-climbs too in 1922. The 200 Mile race was brought forward to August in 1922 and only one of the two-seaters was entered, for Oates to drive. It went a great deal quicker than before but the tuning had been at the expense of reliability and the engine expired after 17 laps. Throughout the year Oates and others had been entering all the big trials and only rarely got worse than a gold medal.

Other features of 1922 production were the introduction of a cheap two-seater K model and a relaxation of the "green only" rule, so that coupés became blue and four-seaters grey. Only minor bodywork changes marked the 1923 year cars, but the weight was steadily growing as more equipment was added. The four-seater now weighed 14.5cwt (737kg) and top speed was only 46.7mph, making it slower than the 1913 11.1hp's 48mph and thirstier at 30mpg against 51. Prices were dropping too and the cheapest 11.9, what we would call nowadays the entry level car, was only £265. For that you got no starter and few were sold, but it looked good on the price list.

The post-Gunn management had kept to his policy of making everything in-house, even nuts and bolts, and when in April 1923 The Motor visited the factory the output was up to 25 a week from a workforce of 500. It was remarked that "a famous Italian make" had followed Gunn's principles of construction recently. This must refer to Lancia and the Lambda. Just as this distinguished make was starting on unitary construction, Lagonda was contemplating abandoning it. A new model, the 12/24, was being developed and was announced at the end of 1923, although the actual process was rather piecemeal, with a series of changes, starting with the rear axle in June. A month later the new engine was announced. For the first time the valves were concealed under a cover and all the auxiliary drives were rearranged to give better accessibility. The transmission brake

Bert Hammond and Glen Logan in the second "works" 11.9 two-seater for the October 1921 200 Mile Race at Brooklands.

was dropped and the much larger rear brake drums now contained two pairs of shoes each, one pair worked by the handbrake, the other pair by the pedal. But the really major change was not pointed out to journalists and went unremarked. This was the reduction in distance apart of the body main longitudinal members, which was now down to about six inches. Although the construction didn't change in principle, the reduction would enable conventional separate coachwork to be fitted, hitherto impossible. Not that there is any record of this happening, but it was now possible.

To begin with, the 11.9 and 12/24 were made in parallel, but the later car soon began to drift upmarket with more equipment and different body styles, including a domed radiator bought in from Gallay, a nail in the "everything in-house" policy. The 12/24 new models started with the R-type "All-weather" with wind-up glass windows, introduced at the end of 1923, followed by the LC tourer at the 1924 Wembley Exhibition, which for the first time offered low-pressure tyres and front-wheel brakes as an option, necessitating a stronger front axle.

Of course, Bill Oates drove 12/24s in the trials of the day and we learn from the entry sheet for the RAC Six Day Light Car Trial of 1924 that his R-type had a compression ratio of 4.76:1 and weighed 17.25cwt (883 kg) at the kerbside, information never made available by the factory. Over the whole trial it averaged 34.88mpg, running with the hood up to compete in the saloon class.

Yet another body type appeared at the 1924 Motor Show: the first full saloon on the 12/24 chassis. It had six lights and was four inches wider than the R-type, weighed 18cwt (914kg) and was lavishly equipped by 1924 standards. It was clear where the company was positioning itself in the market. Unable to compete on price with Austin or Morris and lacking the financial resources to expand, the only remedy was to pile on the luxury and charge accordingly. Prices in the industry were still dropping and the prices of the existing models were lowered at this time, with some compensating reductions in cost, for instance leathercloth instead of leather upholstery.

When *The Light Car* tested an S-type saloon it came out only 21lb short of the ton. The engine's 24bhp was not much to propel this sort of weight, over double that of the 11.1, and to get reasonable acceleration the rear axle ratio had been altered to 5:1. However, this meant that top speed was down to 48mph again, so nullifying any power gains the 12/24 had over the 11.9. The low gearing meant that first gear, at 4.7mph per 1000rpm was virtually never used. One proud owner who wrote to the factory remarked that he had only once ever used first gear and that was on the hairpin of Sutton Bank near Thirsk, a well-known trials hill. Things got worse when the saloon axle ratio was changed to 5.5:1 for the 1925 Show, but this was overshad-

A 12/24 R-type "All-weather". This is the car Hamish Moffat drove across the Sahara to Capetown in the 1950s. On the way he had to burn the floorboards at the roadside to melt bearing metal after a companion ran a big end.

owed by the appearance of Lagonda's secret weapon, the 14/60, an entirely new model from stem to stern.

With hindsight, many observers see the introduction of the 14/60 as one of the abrupt changes of policy that have peppered Lagonda history. This is not entirely true and comes from comparing the 11.9 with the Speed Model 2 Litre. Chalk and cheese indeed. But the steady upgrading of the 12/24 in the 1923-25 period makes the contrast less glaring and in fact the saloon bodies on the last 12/24s and early 14/60s have a great deal in common. Nevertheless, the 14/60 was indeed a change of policy. Any semblance of unitary construction had been abandoned and a conventional channel-section chassis frame with beam axles on semi-elliptic springs took its place, upon which separate tourer and saloon bodies were built.

Consultant designers had been hired for this important new model, Arthur Davidson to do the engine and Eddie Masters the chassis. Bodies were to be the responsibility of Walter Buckingham, who had designed the later 12/24s. The 14/60 was completely new and no parts were carried over from the preceding models. The engine was Lagonda's first with a detachable cylinder head and its dimensions were 72x120mm, giving 1954cc. It drove the four-speed gearbox through a short shaft and a further cardan shaft drove the spiral-bevel rear axle. The engine was fitted with twin camshafts, mounted in extensions of the block above the block/head face. These operated the valves, which were inclined at a 90-degree included angle, by rocking fingers adjusted by eccentric fulcrums. The combustion chambers were hemispherical. This arrangement allowed the head to be lifted without affecting the timing in any way, a great selling point in a period when the owner expected to do this twice a year. Throughout the car there was a huge emphasis on ease of maintenance, and Lagonda Club members say that there is little point in removing any component to work on it as it is just as accessible where it is. Unfortunately the emphasis on ease of maintenance had perhaps gone too far in that the ingenious camshaft drive design had placed the shafts just where the inlet and exhaust ports ought to be, resulting in very tortuous routes with several right-angle bends.

The chassis frame was conventional for the period. Channel-section members parallel beside the engine widened out at the clutch level to become parallel again to the rear. All the greasing

points were linked by a series of little pipes to a row of nipples on the chassis either side of the scuttle. The braking system was very powerful for the period and initially offered full compensation both front to rear and across the car, but this changed over the years to a simpler system. The 12/24 arrangement of four shoes in each rear drum continued.

Three body styles were offered: a six-light saloon, a full five-seat tourer and the "semi-sports", a refreshingly honest term for a narrower four-seat tourer with an optional vee windscreen and, commonly, wire wheels instead of the steel artillery wheels of the more conservative models. The semi-sports was also higher geared.

The 11.1 and its descendants had gone on so

A catalogue illustration of a 1925 14/60 saloon.

Interior of the 14/60 saloon, showing the amazing amount of legroom in the rear of these early saloons. At the price of no exterior space for luggage, of course, but then the servants would bring that.

A 14/60 "semi-sports" tourer, with vee windscreen and wire wheels. The body is perceptibly narrower at the rear than the full 5-seater tourer.

The only known picture of Brigadier-General Francis Metcalfe, who ran Lagonda from the late 1920s until his death in 1934.

long that this completely new model was seen as a sensational change, driving Lagonda several stages up the market, and this was reflected in the prices at £570 for the two open cars and £720 for the saloon. In 1925 the 12/24 saloon had been £370, so the price had nearly doubled. It was almost logical to assume that the new model should go at double the speed and the firm took to claiming an 80mph maximum in their advertising. It was a bit of a disappointment, when the 14/60's first road tests appeared, to find a top speed of only 64.8mph. Another two years would pass before the magic 80 was attainable.

The 12/24 remained in sporadic production for a further year, continuing a noble Lagonda tradition of using up all the parts, and as this was the first time two very different models had been in production at the same time, it was decided to call the new model the OH, for overhead valve, and to start the engine number sequence all over again with the first 14/60. But the "car number" sequence that had started with the Tricars carried on as before, with the result that from 1925 to 1935 all Lagondas have an engine number approximately 8250 less than the car number, although there are a few small variations.

Having broken the mould in 1925, there was a further shock in 1926 when another new model appeared, the 16/65. At a casual glance it looked like a six-cylinder version of the 14/60. The chassis was a similar shape, though nine inches longer in the wheelbase , deeper in section and made of thicker metal. But the engine bore no resemblance, having one low camshaft with pushrods prodding

valves all in a line and operating in combustion chambers nowhere near hemispherical. While the 14/60 had a water pump but no fan, the 16/65 had a fan but no water pump. With tiny inlet ports and carburettor, this was clearly not a sporting engine. It was smaller than you might expect, too, its 65x120mm bore and stroke giving 2389cc, only 400cc larger than the four-cylinder but in a car weighing 35cwt (1778 kg) to the earlier car's 29cwt (1473 kg).

Initially only a saloon was on offer, and since the engine was considerably longer much of the extra nine inches of wheelbase was taken up by it. Passenger accommodation was not much greater, although perceptibly more luxurious to justify the price of £795, rising soon after to £860. Performance of the 16/65 was almost exactly the same as the 14/60 saloon's and contemporary road tests are silent about the fuel consumption, leading one to suspect the worst. Coincidentally with the arrival of the 16/65 (which was certainly a 'sixteen' and may have developed about 65 horsepower) the 12/24 was dropped, and to distinguish the new model on the car's identity plate the code letter Z was brought in, perhaps because this was regarded as the last word. All subsequent 10ft 9in wheelbase Lagondas have a Z code, later extended to the 10ft 3in wheelbase cars.

At some point in 1926 a new managing director was appointed, 48 year old Brigadier-General Francis Metcalfe. He wrought several important changes in the way the place was run, the type of car the firm produced and the way the cars were sold. All the dealerships were reorganised and the Hammersmith Road property was leased to Bill Oates to use as a service enterprise. General Metcalfe's influence became very obvious at the August 1927 Lagonda Fete at Brooklands when the 2 Litre Speed Model was introduced and demonstrated. This was a true sports tourer and 80mph was guaranteed. It represented a painstaking development of the 14/60 which transformed it from a competent, reliable but unexciting car into a real star, with stunning good looks and offering almost Bentley performance and handling for a fraction of the price. Although basically unchanged, the chassis had been stiffened and simplified, with rods replacing some of the cables in the braking system. The engine had been upgraded by introducing drilled oilways instead of external pipes, stronger pistons, drilled crankshaft and a higher compression ratio. It was set back about nine inches in the chassis to give more

A 1928 high-chassis Speed Model 2 Litre, Car Number OH8985. This pre-war picture was taken in a London square in the early morning. Black lamps were quite common but have all been plated by now. Note that the bonnet is not shiny but is fabric covered, by the secret Buckingham method, and matches the fabric of the body.

Cross section of the 2 Litre engine, showing the unusual valve gear operation, which permitted a combination of a hemispherical combustion chamber and the ability to lift the head without disturbing the timing. This is actually a supercharged engine, with bolt-on balance weights and a mechanical fuel pump.

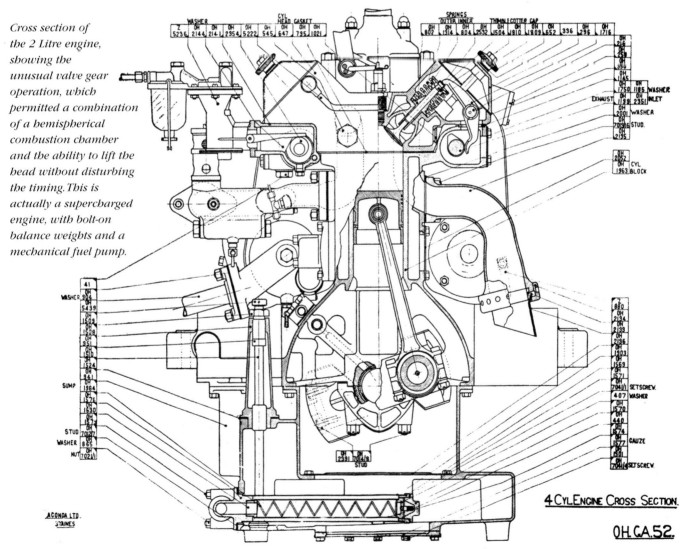

LAGONDA 4½ LITRE & V12

sporting handling, and gearbox internal ratios were changed to give higher speeds in the intermediate gears.

The tourer body was far lighter than the semi-sports and remains one of the most handsome cars of its era, owing something perhaps to the Vauxhall 30/98 and VdP Bentleys, but much less massive. It was no wider than the chassis frame at the bottom and in production form had only two tiny doors on the nearside. Almost all of it was panelled in aluminium and covered in cellulosed fabric over kapok padding. Only the bonnet top and wings were steel. Much larger headlamps, by Rotax, were mounted in a higher position so that their centres aligned with the sidelamps, and a rod-operated Barker dipping system was fitted, whose lever was confusingly like the gear lever and rather close to it.

All the changes, many of which found their way on to the 14/60 in due course, meant that the Speed Model tourer weighed the same as the semi-sports, but the engine modifications allowed higher revs, so that Lagonda could guarantee an 80mph top speed and 70mph in third. At road test time, none of the magazines actually achieved these figures but said they thought they might be possible given a long enough straight.

Throughout the second half of 1927 the Metcalfe influence made itself felt. Speed Model-type modifications were made to the 16/65, including boring the engine out to 69mm, which gave a capacity of 2692cc. A fabric-covered Weymann saloon version of the Speed Model was produced, and the warranty system was overhauled to give a series of five two-year periods. At the end of each, the warranty could be renewed, provided the owner

paid the factory to do any necessary repairs. Very few owners kept a car that long in those days, but it was a valuable selling point and the factory did honour it when required to.

The Speed Model was an ideal trials and rally car and successes soon came in. These encouraged Frank King, the sales manager, and General Metcalfe to launch a racing programme subsidised, probably not voluntarily, by the dealers. A team of four special light Speed Models was prepared for long-distance racing in 1928. Somehow, Bertie Kensington-Moir was lured away from Bentley to run the team. Le Mans was the ultimate target, but the reserve car was first tried out in the Essex MC's 6-Hour race at Brooklands in May, where it demonstrated it could lap at 70mph but went out with a fuel pipe blockage (which was not correctly diagnosed at the time). In practice at Le Mans all three cars lapped at 69mph and hopes were high for a class win. In the race itself things started well, with all three cars in the top ten, but on lap 12 Samuelson's car flew off the track at Mulsanne, hit the fence and bounced back into Baron d'Er-langer's path. The resulting delays put one car out and severely damaged the other, although it limped to the finish. The third car went out with a cracked radiator when lying eighth overall and leading the 2 Litre class. Not dismayed, the team was entered for the revived Tourist Trophy race on the Newtownards circuit in Ulster, but the bumpy track put out two cars with mechanical troubles, and the other was flagged off after falling seven laps (96 miles) behind the class leader.

Back at Staines, concern was growing over the lack of sales of the 16/65, now available in tourer form as well as the saloon. The upshot was a new

A high-chassis Speed Model saloon.

Known as a "Close coupled saloon" to the factory, but as a "Honeymoon coupé" to everyone else, only two of these attractive and practical bodies are known to have survived, perhaps because the very heavy doors broke the "A" post.

model, the 3 Litre, using the 16/65 chassis, but with a heavily revised engine, bored out to 72mm, the same as the 2 Litre, and giving a capacity of 2931cc. The new engine looked similar to the old one, but in fact both block and head castings were different and the valve actuation was much simplified. A second, longer, wheelbase of 11ft 6in was added, to accommodate the bulky family limousines that were also offered. Soon after the introduction, the additional power began to show up the shortcomings of the 16/65 gearbox and a new heavier one, using roller rather than plain bearings, was substituted. Rather oddly, the 3 Litre

didn't take the place of the 16/65 and the latter was a listed model for another seven years, although few were sold.

After the disappointing results of the 1928 racing team, with one finish out of seven starts, Lagonda had doubts about carrying on with the enterprise, but the corporate mind was made up after an approach from the PERR Syndicate, a party of amateur racing enthusiasts from Hertfordshire which included Bill Edmondson, General Metcalfe's lawyer. The syndicate bought two special 2 Litres, forerunners of the Low Chassis model. Arthur Fox of Fox & Nicholl bought

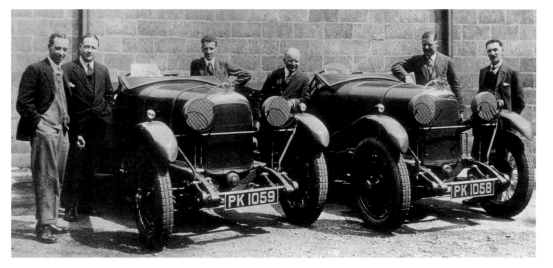

Two of the four 1928 Team 2 Litres at the factory with key personnel. The cars have low-chassis engines (you can see the dynamos peeping out from under the radiators). The people are (left to right) Ted Bolton (Works Manager), Walter Buckingham (Body designer), Eddie Masters (Chassis designer), Alfie Cranmer (Technical Director), Bertie Kensington-Moir (Racing Manager) and Bert Hammond (Chief Tester and reserve race driver).

The 1929 Team cars outside Fox & Nicholl at Tolworth on the Kingston Bypass. Numbers 24 and 25 are the PERR Syndicate cars, 30 is Fox's own and 31 the Robin Jackson car. These cars are in fact rebuilds of the 1928 ones and all still survive. Car numbers OH 9411 to 9414.

another and all three were to race as a team under Fox's direction. A fourth car was bought by Robin Jackson. The programme was to race in the Double Twelve in May, Le Mans in June and the 6 Hours a fortnight later. Eventually, the Irish GP and the TT were added. Unknown to the Syndicate, what they got were rebuilds of the 1928 cars which, by the end of that season, were pretty dilapidated. However, they did feature the new lowered chassis that would become a listed model later in 1929.

The Syndicate was in for a nasty shock at Brooklands in the Double Twelve, when their team were all outrun by Mike Couper in PK 2339, last year's high chassis 2 Litre, which had gained a number of distance records in the autumn of 1928 and was in fact a disguised factory entry. Couper went on to win his class and come ninth overall. One Syndicate car broke its crankshaft, the other came second in class and Fox's car sixth in class. A row ensued and as a sop to the disgruntled Syndicate the General lent them his brand new model, the 3 Litre "Special", for the 6 Hour race. The Special bore the same relationship to the standard 3 Litre as the Speed Model did to the 14/60, being a markedly more sporting open version, complete with set-back engine and lightweight tourer body.

Only Fox's 2 Litre went to Le Mans, where it went out on the 28th lap with head gasket failure,

but the entry list for the 6 Hour race contained eight Lagondas, two 3 Litres and six 2 Litres. At the end, the 3 Litre had proved to be slower than the 2 Litre, but nevertheless won its class, while the Fox team of 2 Litres (his own plus the two Syndicate cars) won the team prize and was awarded the Mobiloil Trophy, today one of the Lagonda Club's annual prizes.

The summer of 1929 saw the rather muted introduction of the low chassis 2 Litre, still called the Speed Model. Minor changes to the chassis frame and a new, more deeply dropped front axle enabled the whole car to be lowered by some inches, while under the bonnet some simplification of the auxiliary drives followed the moving of the dynamo to the nose of the crankshaft, where it had always been on the 16/65 and 3 Litre. Performance was unchanged, but the car looked more modern. It was a further year before the saloons got the same treatment.

Arthur Fox entered a 3 Litre and two 2 Litres for the Irish Grand Prix (which was for sports cars) in July 1929. All three finished, but unplaced. The Tourist Trophy in August was no better: three 2 Litres started, one retired and the other two were unplaced.

The year 1929 was in many ways the high point for the original company. The factory was extended to 125,000 square feet and employed 500 people, turning out eight cars a week in the winter and 16 a week in the summer. There were three drawing offices, a main one with separate smaller ones for jig and tool design and works operations. The business was highly seasonal with hardly any cars sold before Easter, increasing interest up to the end of July, and then nothing until the October Motor Show sparked a short boom from customers wanting the latest model, this boom fizzling out as Christmas loomed.

By Motor Show time in 1929 the Depression was beginning to make itself apparent and Lagonda offered little in the way of novelty. Cycle-type wings were the new fashion and these were offered as an option, attached to the front brake back plates, so that they turned with the steering, keeping mud out of the driver's eyes on right turns. However, they also added substantially to the unsprung weight and were liable to exacerbate axle tramp when components wore.

From the sales point of view 1929 had been a very successful year – sales in fact had been limited by the factory's production capacity – but it all collapsed in the autumn, and in quest of more customers the number of models on offer multiplied to the extent that the catalogue listed 24 different types on five different chassis, with prices ranging from £495 for a bare 14/60 chassis to £1100 for a Weymann saloon on the 3 Litre.

Lagondas continued to be prominent in reliability trials. For example, the 1929 London to Exeter Trial had eight Lagonda starters and is notable for the inclusion among them of Lord de Clifford, whose gold medal was a result of his first appearance in the make in competition. For the next five years or so he was to become one of the Lagonda "stars".

For 1930 the factory launched its own racing team and the PERR Syndicate had to turn to MG Midgets. For the Double Twelve the factory entered three 3 Litres and a 2 Litre, plus a dealer entry that was very much factory backed. This was the year of the Talbot crash, which eliminated the 3 Litre's principal class rival, but mechanical bothers put out two of the 3 Litres and the factory 2 Litre. By some sort of natural justice, the PERR Syndicate, having been spurned by Lagonda, won the team prize.

The complicated inlet passages of the 2 Litre engine had always limited its power output and the principal development of 1930 was a supercharged version with dramatically increased performance. It was first shown at the Lagonda Fete at Brooklands in July and featured the latest version of the tourer body, designated T2, which widened out to hide the chassis frame and looked, remarkably, better with the cycle wings. Development was full of setbacks and the first car reappeared over the next four months with a bewildering variety of blowers, axles and gearboxes. None seems to have been sold until September, by which time the 3 Litre's heavier rear axle and stronger gearbox had become standard. The price, at £775 for the tourer, was higher than expected, allegedly to allow for two replacement superchargers in the first warranty period.

Supercharged 2 Litre, shown outside the paint shop in 1930. Specifications of blown cars vary widely but few, if any, others had the large sidelamps and the majority had cycle wings. This is the T2 body, which conceals the chassis sidemembers.

*Supercharged
2 Litre engine. At
least three different
superchargers were
fitted by the factory,
finishing with the
Zoller, probably
chosen since they
were allowed to
make these at
Staines.*

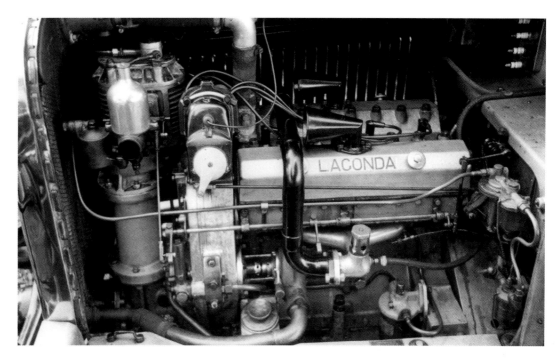

The rest of 1930 was very quiet as the Depression tightened its grip and customers shied away. At the Motor Show all the Weymann saloons gained aluminium lower panels as the all-fabric version had shown a distressing tendency to rot, and a separate boot became an option on all saloons, its drop-down boot lid carrying the magnificent tool kit, a Lagonda speciality which featured about 30 items.

The next year, 1931, was Britain's year in the Monte Carlo Rally, which was won by Donald Healey in an Invicta. Lord de Clifford came fourth in a blown 2 Litre and Conrad Mann in another won his class in the Mont des Mules hillclimb as well as the Condamine Cup in the driving tests.

Most of the first half of 1931 was devoted to modernising the 3 Litre, whose sales had dropped off from the original level, where they had equalled those of the four-cylinder cars. The Z gearbox was not the car's most endearing feature, although examples did vary enormously in ease of use. Lagonda, in common with much of the motor industry, was investigating making gearchanging easier and after a number of experiments settled on the Maybach Doppelschnellgang (dual overdrive) system, in which, apart from moving off from rest, the clutch was not required, the changing of the gears being done by vacuum servo cylinders actuated by inlet manifold depression. This gearbox gave eight forward speeds and, should you feel so inclined, four reverses. But it

was immensely weighty and bristling with ancillary bits and bobs, so fitting it into the 3 Litre chassis presented all sorts of difficulties. When they did get the gearbox in, its weight caused cracks in the sidemembers, so additional bracing was welded in, resulting in two cracks instead of one. The extra weight also began to worry the brakes, so Cranmer finally grasped the nettle and designed an entirely new chassis for this "Selector" model.

The new frame had sidemembers much straighter in plan view and of deeper section. They were parallel from the front to the clutch and then diverged at a slight angle to be as wide as possible at the rear. The massive weight of the Maybach gearbox was taken by two 4in (100 mm) tubular crossmembers. New axles were designed, the front one much straighter than the low chassis axle and the rear axle with only a single pair of brake shoes each side. All the brake drums were larger and stiffer, being cast rather than pressed, and the mixed rod and cable braking system was replaced with a much simpler all-rod system with Perrot shafts at the front. The complications of trying to compensate the brakes side to side and front to rear were abandoned. Instead it was expected that the system, once installed properly, would need no attention.

Testing the Selector took most of 1931, and since upward gearchanges on the Maybach 'box took so long the Lagonda clutch brake had to be re-installed to speed things up, rather making a nonsense of the clutchless change idea. The Selector was finally announced just before the October Motor Show and with it came the first tourer body to have a boot, designated T3. The presence of the boot drove the spare wheel to live beside the scuttle and the extra length made the hood arrangements rather complicated. It was to be available only on the Selector and supercharged 2 Litre. At the other end of the car a new radiator design and a new winged badge distinguished the Selector. For the first time the radiator had a separate shell. For the saloon version a version of cycle wings called "helmet" wings was offered which did not turn with the steering and could carry the side-lamps, which on cycle-winged cars had retreated to stalks growing out of the scuttle.

At last the 14/60 had been dropped and although the 16/65 was still listed there is little evidence of any being made this late. Nevertheless, the 1931 catalogue still lists 17 models on three chassis, among them the 3 Litre Special, which carried on at least until the stock of old chassis frames was used up. All prices for the older models were reduced. When road tests appeared for the Selector it became obvious that it was 3.75cwt (190kg) heavier than the previous model and its top speed 2mph less. Fuel economy was unchanged, so for the extra cost the buyer only got better brakes and the rather daunting complexity of the Maybach gearbox. To correct this, the

answer was to bore out the 3 Litre engine to 75mm, giving 3181cc and 79bhp at 3800rpm. At Lagonda's request Ricardo had designed an inlet-over-exhaust cylinder head which gave 100bhp, but Lagonda could not afford to put it into production and it remained a one-off.

It had become very fashionable to have six-cylinder engines and some as small as 1100cc were

The rear view of the T3 tourer body is not its most attractive and the erected hood shows how little rearward vision the driver was allowed in 1932. This is a "works" 3 Litre Selector, driven by Lord de Clifford in the 1932 Monte Carlo Rally.

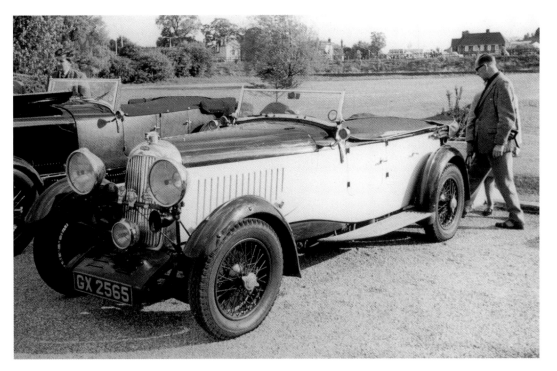

The Continental 2 Litre of 1932 was short-lived in production - only four months - but long-lived since, in part owing to its steel bodywork.

A 1934 Abbott tourer on the Rapier chassis. The design closely resembles that of the bigger Lagondas.

engine, Lagonda arranged to buy a Crossley engine as used in that firm's Shelsley model. At 1991cc it was closer to two litres than the four, but neither then nor since has it been called a two litre. It was announced as the "Special Six" and featured the Continental chassis with the Crossley engine installed. Nowadays we call it the 16/80, its factory name, and for once it was a "sixteen" and probably would do 80mph. I doubt it had 80bhp though.

Lagonda had to do quite a bit of modification to get the engine in and several versions of the induction side were tried before settling on a final one. Crossley sent completely assembled engines up to Staines but Lagonda insisted on stripping them down and reassembling. It was probably at this point that the Lagonda-inspired parts were added. After one year's production a second version which incorporated even more Lagonda parts was introduced. 16/80 bodies closely resembled the Continental and in addition to the steel tourer (T5) and Weymann semi-panelled saloon (W24P) a sporting 2-seater by Vanden Plas was added. These cars were partly built by Vanden Plas and then sent for finishing at Staines. They were mechanically identical to the other models, so no quicker, but at least looked more sporting. Most, but not all, had a dickey seat for fine weather outings.

The 16/80 was perceptibly lower geared than the four-cylinder cars, so its acceleration figures compared quite well to the blown 2 Litre, rather than the unblown one, but it suffered on top speed

on sale, with the result that Lagonda's big-four 2 Litre was losing sales rapidly. In April 1932 a new model called the Continental was a stopgap intended to rouse interest. It had an all metal panelled body with a sloping radiator and better brakes using cast instead of pressed drums, but retaining the 2 Litre layout. The new body was designated the T4 and 18in wheels replaced the former 21in ones, with a larger section tyre to keep the gearing much the same and add to comfort Within four months it had been replaced with the "six" the firm so desperately needed. Unable to afford to develop their own two-litre six-cylinder

The 16/80 eventually acquired the T7 tourer body as on the M45, but it is narrower and retained the 2 Litre dashboard. This is a 1934 car.

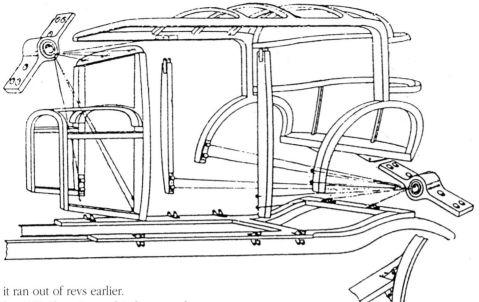

The principles of the Silent Travel body system, built to Daste patents.

since it ran out of revs earlier.

At the 1932 Show Lagonda's long attachment to the Weymann saloon was terminated and bodies built to Silent Travel principles took their place, giving pillarless saloons with much easier access. Silent Travel were holders of the Daste patents and each car produced meant a royalty to Silent Travel. Whereas the Weymann principle was that each timber was separated from its neighbour, attached only with metal tongues which allowed the body to flex, the Daste principle was to make the body up from three large rigid sections and attach them to each other and to the chassis with Silentbloc rubber joints. Elsewhere at the Show there were three new developments that were to affect Lagondas in the following year. These were ENV's intention to go into production with car-sized epicyclic gearboxes to the Wilson patents, Smiths' introduction of their "Jackall" system of built-in jacks, and the André company's launch of their Telecontrol system for controllable damping of road springs. But 1933 was going to be a very momentous year in Lagonda affairs.

The 3½ Litre shared the T9 body with the M45 Rapide. Only the radiator differed but various items of equipment were omitted, such as the built-in jacks.

Chapter Three

Four and a half litres – the M45

Roger Firth's 1934 M45 pillarless saloon. The metal spare wheel cover was standard equipment when new but vulnerable to mishandling and is now very rare.

Despite its apparent replacement by the 16/80, Lagonda continued to play with the supercharged 2 Litre in early 1933, the car now on its second camshaft, third cylinder head and third make of blower. All prices had to be raised in April. Despite the hard times, or perhaps because of them, the revised price list quoted 20 separate models on six distinct chassis, since the ordinary 3 Litre survived alongside two types of Selector and both Speed Model and Continental 2 Litres were still quoted, even though the 16/80 was in full production. In June some changes to the 16/80 made the ENV epicyclic gearbox available as an option for an extra £25, while it was a free option on the Selector. At the same time a revised tourer body, the T6, with a swept tail incorporating a substantial boot replaced the T5. Normally the spare wheel was mounted on the bootlid, although a number of owners preferred and got the side-mounted position. Under the 16/80 bonnet, even more Lagonda modifications were made.

At this point the PERR Syndicate re-enters the story. They had been racing MGs since 1930 with no little success, but Bill Edmondson had retained his 2 Litre that he had bought from the Syndicate at the end of 1929. He was also still General Metcalfe's lawyer and in constant contact with him. There must have been a hankering for a return to the heavy metal for in the spring of 1933 we find the whole Syndicate having a meeting at Staines, the result of which was the General sending them a draft proposal for the Syndicate to submit as if it was their initiative. Under its terms the Syndicate would place an order for two 9hp chassis and a 3 Litre chassis fitted with a 4½-litre engine. The bill would be £800. If the company proceeded to production with the 9hp, the company would buy back both chassis for £130 each and pay the Syndicate £1 per chassis royalty for three years. Similarly with the 4½ Litre, the figures here being £100 and £5 respectively. There followed a complicated legal clause, the effect of which was that if Lagonda went broke in the middle of the exercise, the Receiver would gain no benefit from the experi-

mental cars. Clearly the General was more worried about finances than he appeared to be in public. In his covering letter, Metcalfe said that both experiments are well under way and that so far no snags had revealed themselves. The proposal was accepted by the Board on 1 May and although a formal contract was intended, none ever materialised. But work went ahead anyway.

The Syndicate stood to gain three racing cars for £800, to which they had only to add skimpy racing bodies. Lagonda stood to gain most of the £800 as cash up front to underwrite the development costs of both new models, the 9hp which was to become the Rapier, and the 4½ Litre which was to become the M45.

It is not clear from the papers of the Syndicate whether the £800 was actually ever paid. Since they never got their cars, one suspects it was not. In June 1933 the General went into hospital for a serious operation and Sir Edgar Holberton, the Chairman, in taking over the reins, wrote to the Syndicate on 21 July saying pay up or else. It seems they did not do so, and when the General emerged right at the end of July, it was too late for the 1933 season anyway. The PERR Syndicate then disappear from the story

The Rapier was of course a totally new model. To design it Lagonda hired Tim Ashcroft and allocated him one draughtsman and a space in the drawing office. Alf Cranmer took on the 4½ himself, as it was "merely" a shoehorn job to fit a Meadows engine into the Selector 3 Litre chassis. One fancies he examined and rejected any idea of boring out the Lagonda 3 Litre engine to the new size. It would have required 14mm extra on each cylinder and that was probably impossible. Coincidentally, at this time Invicta collapsed and their supply of 4½-litre Meadows engines became available. So, just as in the previous year Lagonda had given up making 2 Litre engines in favour of buying in Crossleys, now they were going to buy in from Meadows, but there was no intention to

Roger Firth's M45 has the ST34 body built by Lagonda to Silent Travel patents. This is Car Number Z10695. The indefinable "greyhound" look of the early 4½ saloons was to disappear as refinement took pride of place over sporting performance.

This drawing of the 3 Litre Selector chassis if anything oversimplifies the maze of pipes and cylinders associated with the Maybach gearbox. This chassis was the basis of the M45 and few changes were needed: an extra tube joining the dumb-irons, a crossmember to take the back of the Meadows gearbox, and some surgery to the massive front crossmember tube to clear the clutch brake.

Michael Drakeford's 1933 M45 tourer, Car Number Z10477, wears Lagonda's T7 body. This view exemplifies the good looks of Lagonda bodywork.

stop production of the 3 Litre model.

Henry Meadows Ltd of Wolverhampton had been building proprietary engines since 1921, and by 1933 had built up a good reputation for supplying reliable and robust engines of all sizes at reasonable prices. The 1½-litre four of 1922 had been joined by a six-cylinder of 2.2 litres in 1925, and this had been progressively enlarged to 2.5 litres, 3.3 litres and finally 4.5 litres. The 4.5-litre version involved considerable internal rearrangements and appeared in 1928. Apart from Invicta, users included the army, whose Vickers Carden-Loyd light tanks used various versions from 1931 onwards. There were marine versions too.

By 1933 the 4½-litre 6ESC Meadows was a well-tried unit of straightforward design and with no nasty habits. The head and block were of chromidium cast iron, the separate crankcase and sump

of aluminium. The forged crankshaft ran in four main bearings of which the rearmost had a four-bolt cap. The crankpins were of 2in diameter and a Lanchester-type torsional damper was fitted to the crankshaft nose. The valve gear was operated by pushrods and rockers from a four-bearing camshaft located in the crankcase, and the valves were vertical, in-line and supplied mixture to bathtub-shaped combustion chambers. As a result of the various enlargements only the exhaust rockers of numbers 1 and 6 cylinders worked at right angles to the rocker shaft, all the others being at varying and rather haphazard-looking angles to it. The pistons were of aluminium with split skirts and four rings, two compression and two scrapers. To accommodate the half-inch extra bore of the larger engine, the centres of the bores were offset in relation to the crankshaft and also shuffled along a bit

so that the water spaces between cylinders 1 and 2, 3 and 4 and 5 and 6 disappeared and asymmetric connecting rods were called for. These were of H-section steel, split at 90° at the big end, and located the gudgeon pin by a split and locking bolt at the small end. The inlet manifold was partly cast in the head and had the other half formed by an aluminium cover plate of half-round section. It led to six inlet ports on the offside of the head and on the opposite side were six exhaust ports, coupled to an exhaust manifold whose design owed more to symmetry than to gas-flow studies.

At the time this engine was designed, aluminium was regarded as "trouble metal", so it is not surprising that cast iron was used for the head and block, but the aluminium bits did reduce the weight a bit. This kind of construction was commonplace in the 1920s, but had become rather dated by 1933. It gives rise to a tendency for the nuts holding the block to the crankcase to work loose, leading to an oily engine. The other bugbear that the designer, Mr Crump, tried to avoid was gasket trouble, and to this end there were no water passages through the head gasket, the water transfer being effected by three aluminium transfer passages bolted to the outside of the exhaust side of the engine.

Although the 3-litre engine is believed to have had only one plug per cylinder, the 4½-litre had two, the exhaust side ones fired from a coil and distributor, driven by the dynamo, and the inlet side ones fired from a horizontal magneto, BTH CE6/S to begin with, driven from the same shaft as the water pump. There was a large cast fan driven by Whittle belt from the dynamo, itself driven by a double inverted-tooth chain from the crankshaft. Another of these chains, triple this time, drove the camshaft and magneto/water pump shaft.

As befits a Vintage engine the oil filtration was primitive, consisting of a coarse gauze round the oil pump pickup in the sump and a slightly finer one in the delivery gallery to the crankshaft, the filter housing having "Clean Often" cast on its lid as a prominent reminder. In this sense the Meadows engine was a retrogression from the 3 Litre and 16/80 engines which by 1933 had the "Autokleen" system of full-flow filtration, operating automatically by being linked to the pedals. This could have been added to the Meadows as there was a housing for it, but for some reason Lagonda chose to ignore it.

Meadows made gearboxes and clutches to go with their engines, and it was possible to have the

gearbox either attached to the clutch or separate. Lagonda, to begin with, intended to use their own Z-type gearbox, which had recently been modified to a "Silent Third" design incorporating double-helical gears and dog engagement. This ZE/S3 design cost more to make than its predecessor as outside contractors had to make the expensive double-helical gears, chosen to eliminate end thrust and possible resulting noise. A second drawback proved to be that a badly missed gearchange was liable to cause far more damage than on the earlier designs as the gearchange yoke acted on the layshaft but the engaging dogs were on the mainshaft.

The first batch of 30 or so M45s were fitted with the ZE/S3 gearbox but adverse comments from the motoring press and mounting warranty claims

Inlet side of the early M45 engine, showing the twin SUs and the magneto which fired the inlet-side spark plugs.

Exhaust side of the same engine, with the other set of spark plugs, the distributor which served them and the back-to-back SU fuel pumps.

Power and torque curves for the 4½ litre Meadows engine, taken at Staines and dated 4 July 1933. They show peak power of 108bhp at 3150rpm and peak torque of 216.7lb ft at 1600rpm. See the chart in Chapter 5 for the extra power Lagonda later managed to wring out of this engine.

The M45 was the "in" car of 1934. An advertisement in Vogue *features the prototype (Car Number Z 10419) which, having started life as a 3 Litre, retained its T6 body and 3 Litre radiator with its cutout for the dynamo.*

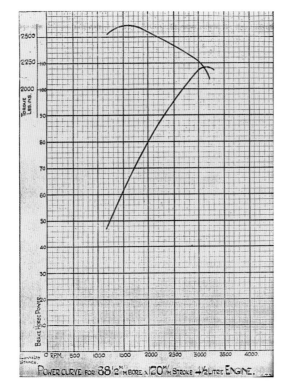

POWER CURVE FOR 88½ ᴹ/ᴍ BORE × 120ᴹ/ᴍ STROKE 4½ LITRE ENGINE.

forced a resort to the Meadows T8 unit, which had the added advantage of an easier to learn change, important in this market. All, or nearly all, the early cars had the Meadows gearbox fitted when they came in for service

The Meadows clutch was used from the outset, but with Lagonda's own clutch brake added.

This enabled drivers in a hurry to change up instantaneously instead of waiting for the driven plate and front propeller shaft to slow down. It was adjustable both for how hard it came on and also when.

The weight of the complete Meadows engine with flywheel and clutch was 5¾ cwt (292kg), no heavier than the 3 Litre Lagonda engine, but it produced something like 30bhp more than the 3 Litre's 79bhp, and this nearly 40 per cent increase in power had an electrifying effect on the performance. Not only that, but the Meadows engine's peak torque was 215lb ft (158Nm) at 1500rpm and over 200lb ft (148Nm) from tickover to 2300rpm, rendering the gearbox nearly superfluous if the spark control was used with discernment.

The prototype car, APJ 367 (Z10419), was clearly a converted 3 Litre and still sported the 3 Litre radiator with its inverted U-shaped cutout in the bottom of the radiator to accommodate the dynamo, even though this was not needed with a Meadows engine. A certain amount of butchery was requires to get the longer engine into the chassis, and a slice had to be cut out from the forward tubular crossmember to clear the clutch stop mechanism; a vertical plate was welded in to restore the strength. A tiebar was added to the extreme front of the frame to link the dumb irons and another crossmember was added to the chassis between the two massive tubes that were such a prominent memento of Mr Maybach. This new one was only about half the diameter, but was sufficient to support the rear end of the gearbox. Invicta had specified a special domed rocker cover but Lagonda were content with Meadows' normal rectangular one, into which they cut "Lagonda, Staines", soon shortened to just "Lagonda". The Meadows name did not appear anywhere, although they did stamp their own serial number on the rear engine mounting, starting at around 7880 for the first M45s and proceeding in small batches as orders were received.

The prototype, APJ, was fitted with a standard T6 tourer body in green with brown wings, but it was the intention to modify this for production to produce the T7, which had the bonnet extended back towards the windscreen so that its rear edge was at a similar angle to the screen and the bonnet louvres were angled to match. But the biggest change was to do away with the two tiny doors on the nearside and replace them with a single large one which occupied the whole side from windscreen to rear wheel and had a deep cutout in its

APJ 367

Lagonda
BRITAIN'S THOROUGHBRED CAR

Coat of grey krimmer as expressed by Isobel. 89 gns

AUL 720 is one of the very first M45 tourers and has some early features that were altered later. For example, the frame that supports the headlamps was designed for cycle wings that moved with the wheels. Later cars had the frame extended each side to brace the fixed "long" wings.

top matching the driver's side. The small door on the offside rear compartment was retained, but deepened by about six inches.

The dashboard was radically changed too, the first substantial revision since 1929. The oval metal panel which held most of the instruments vanished and a small trapezoidal one replaced it, containing only the electrical gear. The speedometer, having grown somewhat, being moved to the timber part of the board to join the equally large rev-counter. A clock and a reversing lamp became standard and the saloon shared a similarly equipped dashboard, but with a horizontal top and a small shelf for oddments next to the screen. Tourer passengers got a grab-rail, but saloon passengers did not, presumably since the closed door should offer sufficient support in enthusiastic cornering. The cast aluminium bulkhead first seen on the low chassis 2 Litre was still in use, but had timber side extensions added to widen the body.

For the new model the Silent Travel pillarless saloon body (ST24) of the 3 Litre was modified quite considerably. The peak over the windscreen disappeared and the boot was made 3¼in longer

Rear vision was slightly better in the saloon than in the tourer, but not much. This car has been modified to take Morris Minor rear lamps after the original stalks snapped off.

This rear view of the tourer shows filler panels between the rear wings and the body, later deleted.

by stealing some rear seat legroom; the joint between it and the main body was now a smooth curve rather than a pronounced beaded joint. The removal of the peak over the windscreen was said to be an "eddy-free front" and much play was made of this phrase. The peak disappeared from the 3 Litre too, its ST24 body now being designated ST24A. There were other detail changes: the glass rain louvres over each window lost their chromed frames and were set directly in the bodywork, and although it is by no means obvious the ST34 is an inch lower than its predecessor. Swept wings were standard, but cycle wings, which had gone out of fashion as abruptly as they had come in, were an option. The brake backplates continued to be made massive enough to take the loading these produced and indeed some cars, even some saloons, were built with cycle wings. The first few cars had the same "goalpost" arrangement of tubes to mount the headlamps as the 3 Litre had used, but, probably because the new heavy front wings, which were of steel with inner aluminium liners to stop stone pitting, had begun to work loose, an additional horizontal tube was added each side which braced the wing supports to the headlamp support framework.

The Meadows engine was the first fitted to a Lagonda to have its carburettors on the right-hand side. All previous engines, designed in the 1920s,

had had to avoid the massive steering box and column beloved of the make by mounting the inlet side on the left and exhaust on the right, resulting in hot feet for the driver. The M45 exhaust being on the left, where there were no pedal slots, should have made the car more habitable in hot weather than its predecessors. But not much, for the 4½ produced more heat anyway, so a system of cold air vents were added to the inside of the front wings (unless they were cycle ones) which led via

ST34 Silent Travel saloon on the M45 chassis. The last of the lean and hungry look in saloons, soon to give way to more sober designs. A very few were built with cycle wings, which look very odd.

The early Meadows had a low-set oil filler which can result in a very messy engine when the spring closing the lid weakens, since the filler is directly in line with the timing chain.

Lagonda had to pay a royalty to Silent Travel Ltd for every ST24 and 34. Each body bore a little plate with its licence number stamped on it, fixed to the offside body valance below the driver's seat.

Control wheels for the Telecontrols mounted on the floor to the driver's right. Later cars had these below the dash, next to the relevant pressure gauges.

metal pipes to outlets by the crew's feet. Unfortunately they don't work, probably because there are several right angle turns on the way in. A flap on the wing closed the vents when not needed.

The suspension of the M45 was made more sophisticated than the 3 Litre's by adding André Telecontrol adjustable dampers to the ordinary Hartfords. These worked by means of liquid-filled rubber bags attached to each damper. The pressure in each axle pair of these bags was controlled by the driver, who had a pair of tiny pressure gauges in front of him and a pair of handwheels to alter the pressure. On the prototype and very early

tourers the handwheels were on the floor behind the driver's legs, but this awkward location soon gave way to a steering column position where the driver would not tread on them when leaping in.

The rear axle of the Selector had had to be made very strong to cope with the very low gearing in the Maybach gearbox and little attention was needed to cater for the Meadows, but the splines were strengthened at the half shaft/differential joint. To begin with a 3.67 (12 x 44) ratio was used for all M45s but later on a 3.31 (13 x 43) option was offered for tourers to give quieter cruising. Buyers opting for a drophead coupé, which would mean going to an outside coachbuilder, got the saloon ratio.

Although photographs and details of the 4½ Litre and Rapier were released to the press, there is some evidence of the customary Staines rush to get the new model to Olympia, one piece of evidence being that there isn't a true photograph of it in the catalogue issued at the Motor Show. The photograph which purports to be of the 4½ Litre chassis is in fact a 3 Litre with the Meadows engine drawn in; the tourer photograph is a 3 Litre with the T7 body but retaining the oval panelled dashboard, carefully posed to avoid showing the radiator which would give it away, and the saloon illustration is only a profile drawing. That 3 Litre tourer had to work for its living in this catalogue, as it also illustrated the 16/80 as well as itself. In fact the photograph of it masquerading as a 16/80 is the same one as is used for the 4½ Litre.

Another error in the 1933 catalogue was the stated engine capacity, given as 4429cc, a figure widely quoted thereafter. Henry Meadows was a very English firm which worked solely in inches, and their engines at the time were the 6EPC with a 3in bore and the 6ESC with a 3½in one. These were quoted by themselves as 76mm and 88.5mm, with a common stroke of 4¾in, also quoted as 120mm. The Meadows catalogue then goes on to convert these figures to capacities, arriving at 3301cc and 4467cc, this last figure being used by Invicta. Now if one multiplies up six 88.5mm bores by a 120mm stroke you get 4429cc, as Lagonda must have done. To confuse it further, Meadows made a marine version of the 6ESC, given in the catalogue as 3½ x 4¾in, and this time they got 4422cc. For the first year of production, Lagonda stuck to 4429cc, but then, perhaps as a result of actually measuring an engine for the TT, a revised stroke of 120.65mm (exactly 4¾in) was quoted, giving a capacity of 4453cc, a figure always used

The hood is a replacement, only to be expected after over 70 years, and has a much larger rear window than the pair of tiny letterbox-like slots used in 1933. The T7 body had a small door to the rear seat on one side only.

thereafter. The puzzle remains why, with all these Imperial dimensions, the bore was 88.5mm, which it undoubtedly was. Three and a half inches inches is 88.9mm, and although the author has speculated in the past that this might have been the correct dimension, the discovery in the 1980s of a brand new unused 6ESCengine confirmed the smaller figure. It must have been that in enlarging the bore to get 4½ litres the designer reached the limit of how thin he was prepared to accept the metal between the pairs of cylinders.

The same sorts of confusions, brought about by too many rather than not enough figures, beset the question of the power output of the standard, unmodified Meadows engine. Their catalogue quoted 103bhp at 3000rpm, running on a 6:1 compression ratio. In fact curves for bhp, bmep and torque were provided, albeit for the earlier 6EST engine. The marine version, running on 5.75:1 with very non-sporting looking breathing and only one 46mm carburettor, produced 80bhp at 2250rpm. The slightly more ambitious 6ESTB

The trim on the tourer's front passenger door, emphasising the deep cutouts in the door tops.

Invicta results of 115 at 4000rpm, which may not necessarily be at variance with 108 at 3000, but 4000rpm is very much on the high side for an untuned Meadows and in fact the car's rev-counter was red-lined at 3800, only being lifted to 4000 after substantial Lagonda-sourced modifications in later years.

Having said all this, it is salutary to look at a surviving works testbed result for the special Rapide engine fitted to the 1935 Monte Carlo Rally car. This had a 7:1 compression ratio and had been very carefully assembled from hand-picked and matched parts. It gave 105bhp at 3200rpm. Adding 30 per cent Benzol and advancing the ignition 6½° produced 109.25bhp at 3400rpm - this was a very special engine. But before dismissing all published figures as rubbish, we will have to consider whether the Lagonda testbed was giving accurate answers. It probably wasn't if the experience of developing the Sanction 3 LG45 engine is anything to go by. We will come to that in due course

Both the M45 and the Rapier were finally announced to the world in the middle of September 1933, at roughly the same time as the 3½ Litre Bentley. Even a journalist could see that the 4½ Litre was an updated 3 Litre, especially

used in the Vickers light tanks turned out 88bhp at 3000rpm. Invicta had claimed 115bhp for their version, but to begin with Lagonda issued no figures at all. They never had issued power figures and saw no need to now. But of course they had run tests, and a surviving chart from July 1933 shows 108bhp at 3000rpm. When the firm was prodded to produce figures for the motoring magazines they issued the

The number plate swivelled to allow access for the starting handle.

with APJ's body and radiator being from the earlier model, so the smaller Rapier, brand new from front to back, naturally captured all the column-inches. However, the autumn passed with no further Rapiers forthcoming, since the company was busy lengthening the chassis to accommodate four normal-sized occupants and at the same time casting about for a body-building firm after their own bodyshop had refused to take on the extra load. As a result, press attention switched to the M45.

There were two M45s on Stand 143 at Olympia in the end, a tourer and a pillarless saloon, together with a prototype Rapier on the shortlived 7ft 6¾in wheelbase. There were also the latest versions of the 16/80 and 3 Litre saloons, plus a 3 Litre coupé by Martin Walter. Freestone & Webb were also showing a huge limousine on the 11ft 6in 3 Litre chassis. There were minor changes to the older models, the ENV epicyclic gearbox becoming standard on the 16/80, for example.

The prices announced for the M45 were surprisingly low at £675 for the bare chassis, £795 for the tourer and £895 for the saloon. These were below the prices then existing for the smaller cars, so these had to be cut too. By the following February

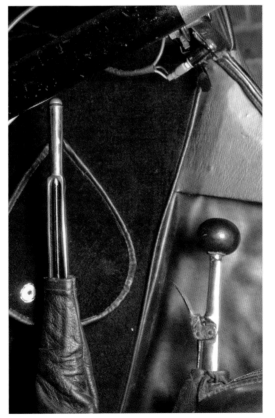

Most Lagondas had chrome-plated bezels to their instruments, but an owner could specify black. As was common in the 1930s, the rev-counter is in front of the driver and the passenger gets to look at the speedometer.

Gearlever and handbrake live together on the right, which doesn't make getting in or out any easier for the driver.

all prices were raised again.

The Autocar had a quick drive in APJ in September, but the first full road test appeared in mid-November in *The Motor*. Until then then there had been a lot of speculation about a possible 100mph maximum speed, but Lagonda had never claimed this. In fact they hadn't claimed anything and in the advertisements had poured scorn on "the 100mph fallacy", saying that the 4½ Litre "touches something very near that figure". In their test *The Motor* got 92 mph, with 82 in third gear and 50 in second. The 0-60mph time was 14.2 seconds. Although vacuum servo brakes using a Dewandre servo had been the intention from the outset, APJ had been lent to the press without them, causing some reservations about the braking from high speed, but by the time of *The Motor*'s test they had been fitted and were acclaimed. The gear ratios quoted in the statistics are those of the T8 Meadows 'box, but this was yet to be fitted (early the following year) so promises must have been made about replacing the rather wayward Z3. The second press car, ALU 803, based at Warwick Wright's, had the production bodywork. When Tommy Wisdom tested it for *Sporting Life* he was not too keen on the Z gearbox, although otherwise full of praise.

At the end of 1933 M45 tourers and saloons began to be delivered to early customers. The car was competing head-on with the new Bentley, whose bare chassis was £1100, to which had to be added a further £300-400 for the bodywork. Not only was the Lagonda much cheaper but also it was available from stock if the customer wasn't too fussy about colour - and in only a few weeks if he was. Lagonda, alone among quality car manufacturers, had a large and competent bodyshop, a relic of the 11.1/11.9 era, while the body designs, under the supervision of Walter Buckingham, were as good as anyone else's and better than most. The advantages to Lagonda were control over the weight of the body and a possible price benefit in there being only one firm taking a profit, not two. Possible drawbacks included increased overheads when trade was slack. Control of weight was important and stringent limits were laid down in the guarantee document, exceeding which nullified the warranty.

As with any coachbuilder, the customer could dictate all sorts of extras and special requirements, some of which were eccentric in the extreme. Some build sheets ran to several pages, and there was one which read, under "colour", "Blue, to match eiderdown supplied by customer". One can just imagine the state that eiderdown got into after weeks in the paint shop. Later on, in the LG era, when the company was offering drophead coupés, one customer demanded a hood in patent leather. On being told that such a hood could not be folded without cracking, he expressed himself content never to open it, so one is forced to wonder why he chose a drophead. Yet another customer had a flight of ducks in cast aluminium attached to the side of the car, with the beak of the leading duck forming the side of the peak over the windscreen.

In the Buckingham era the company did not offer a drophead coupé and customers wanting one had to buy the bare chassis and seek another coachbuilder. The objection to the drophead was the weight of the huge doors that a two-door four-seater demanded. These tended to overstress the windscreen pillar if the door was front-hinged or tear out the B-post by the roots if rear-hinged. In 1932 and 1933 there had been a short run of dropheads on the 16/80 and 3 Litre chassis, but these had been built by Vanden Plas, although sold as a Lagonda model.

As well as making tourer and saloon bodies the Staines bodyshop also revived the CCS (Close coupled saloon), usually known as the "honeymoon coupé", an elegant fixed-head body with two normal front seats and two smaller rear ones which folded up to provide additional luggage space. This type never found its way into the catalogue, but a small number were built on the M45 chassis.

The central accelerator pedal was to remain a feature of Lagondas until the V12 arrived.

In keeping with the new model, publicity arrangements were taken away from Lagonda staff and the work given to an associate company of Warwick Wright called Woodwright Publicity and Press Service Ltd. It was run by J Stanley Woodward from Warwick Wright's premises in Bond Street. Woodward compiled a press cuttings file during the period 1933 to 1935 which has survived and is one of the Lagonda Club's cherished archives. Frank King remained as Sales Manager at Staines and the new model and livelier publicity meant that sales improved dramatically, leading to a rearrangement of the dealerships. Warwick Wright took over from Henlys as London Distributor, Patrick Motors in Birmingham became the Midlands Distributor and a new firm, Carr, Gallagher Ltd in Belfast became Distributor for the province. In Scotland, Burton & Tweedy were the Distributor, feeding cars to Bass Rock Motor Co. in Edinburgh and A D Grassick in Blairgowrie. Old faithful, Central Garage in Bradford, stayed on and was joined as a Distributor by Westover Garage Ltd in Bournemouth. Below the Distributors in the pecking order were the dealers, like Gaffikin Wilkinson and Carr's in London.

In mid-November the Scottish Motor Show opened at Kelvin Hall and Bass Rock showed a silver and black M45 saloon as well as one of the Rapier prototypes. The Scottish Show was for dealers, not manufacturers, and C S Grant showed a 16/80 but neither of the latest models. Further south, the M45 press cars were having a busy time as all the daily and Sunday papers borrowed them, producing generally glowing reports. H E Symons in *The Sunday Times* probably had APJ, since he complained about the brakes and admitted he had started his journey from the factory. Tommy Wisdom wrote to Woodward after returning the car, saying it was the best over-3-litre car he had ever driven - and that included a certain excellent sports car that cost twice as much. *Country Life, The Sketch, Britannia & Eve,* and so on, all queued up to print eulogies and marvel at the low price. No doubt about it, Lagonda really had got a winner and M45s began to dominate the workshops. There was still production of 16/80s and 3 Litres, but now only in small batches.

With the introduction of the 4½ Litre the numbering of the cars, never straightforward, grew more confusing still. It has never been established at what stage in a car's construction the "Car Number" was assigned to it. The author suspects it was at order stage, or perhaps when work started.

Until 1933 the Car Numbers, still following the sequence started with the Tricars and now carrying a prefix - S for 16/80, Z for 3 Litre and OH for 2 Litre - had been issued in roughly chronological order, bearing in mind that we now only have the date of first registration to go by and if a car proved difficult to sell this could be months later than the construction date. In the case of dealers' demonstrators they were normally kept for a year on trade plates and only registered when sold, usually when the following year's model was announced. The engine number, now without a prefix, followed the same pattern and was about 8251 less than the car number, reflecting the decision to start again with the first 14/60 in 1925. In keeping with the liberal warranty arrangements,

Most unusual: the Telecontrol damper system pressure gauges showing some pressure at rest. Many, or even most, of these systems are empty nowadays.

Twin 6-volt batteries lie on either side of the rear axle. Moving them to under the bonnet enabled Frank Feeley to lower the rear roof line of the later Sanction 3 LG45 model.

on the ID plate. As the 4½ Litre had a virtually unchanged 3 Litre chassis, the Z prefix was retained for the Car Number and the code M45 was evolved. It is anybody's guess whether the M stood for the Maybach chassis or for Meadows, but at least the 45 is clear. The "plate" engine number continued in the (Car Number minus 8251) series, but a further series was started, actually stamped on the engine this time and starting at M45/1. As ever, these engines were issued to chassis in entirely random order, so that the tenth car had M45/27 and the fifth car M45/32. Not only that, but the batches of cars were not sold in order, so that a batch carrying engine numbers in the M45/120 to 140 range were sold in March 1934 but carried Car Numbers 40 or so lower than the M45/10 to 40 range that had been sold the previous October.

this number did not actually appear anywhere on the engine, only on the identity plate on the bulkhead. Then, if a car came back for serious repairs, the engine could be replaced without the owner being any the wiser, and repaired at leisure, while the owner got his car back very quickly. Only when the works were making two versions of the 3 Litre did a practice start of stamping the engine number on the engine mount, the 75mm version being christened ZM (probably for "Maybach"). But this number, running in a series confined to 3 Litres, bore no relationship to the "Engine Number"

Lord de Clifford now re-enters the story, as Woodward conceived the idea of lending him APJ 367 to do a well-publicised reconnaissance of the 1934 Monte Carlo Rally route from the Athens start point. He took with him Humfrey Symons, motoring correspondent of *The Sketch* and *The Sunday Times*, and Jack Ridley, competitions manager of Triumph. It was an adventurous run; they did Dieppe to Brindisi in 44¾ hours, an average of 38mph, and this included a delay to repair the petrol tank after hitting a kerbstone lying in the road in Naples. This time was 14 hours quicker than the express train schedule despite

Meadows T8 gearbox, very accessible once the floorboard has been removed. The large ribbed cylinder to its right is the brake servo.

using a much longer route. They then caught up on their sleep as the car was transferred by ship from Brindisi to Athens. At Athens they had to fit two new rear tyres before setting out for Bulgaria as part of the Rally route. At Thebes another rock was hit, which broke the front brake cross-shaft and cracked the sump. The former was noticed and could not be repaired, so the other front brake was disconnected to balance the braking. The other fault was not noticed until a horrible engine rattle started in the Pass of Thermopylae. Fortunately they had supplies of oil on board and were able to carry on. In the Pass of Phourka they got involved in a landslide (one hesitates to suggest that the 2-ton Lagonda had anything to do with this). After this they finally became completely bogged down in the World War 1 battlefield that the Greek government had deliberately left untouched near the Bulgarian border to discourage invasions. A team of oxen pulled the car out and the weary rallyists returned to Salonika where they put the battered APJ on the train for London, returning themselves on the Orient Express and reaching London just before Christmas.

Lord de Clifford was not put off by these adventures, and in the next chapter we will cover his subsequent attempt at the Monte Carlo Rally proper, driving AMT 77 (Z10605), another of the factory's demonstrators.

The 1933 version of the annual return of share capital and shareholdings that had to be sent to Companies House under the terms of the 1929 Companies Act still survives in the Public Records Office, despite Board of Trade "weeding" of the papers. It shows that Lagonda's authorised share capital was only £50,000, which isn't very much for a company whose products retailed at nearly £1000 each. So it is no surprise that each winter saw periodic cash crises. One such, possibly 1933 or 1934, resulted in there being not enough in the bank to pay the wages one week, even though a fat cheque from a large dealer was on its way. One of the older employees, who was reputed to have a "long stocking", was politely asked to meet the directors and cards were put on the table. With X's cheque in the post, could he help the firm out by paying one week's wages ? It is a mark of his loyalty that he could and did, and heartening to record that he got his money back, for there was little security to offer him. It was a long way from the motor industry of the 1960s and 1970s. This was a period, of course, when there were half a dozen unemployed skilled men available for every

A popular option in the 1930s, these metal spare wheel covers rarely survived long, being prone to mishandling. "Ace" wheel discs reduced the task of cleaning wire wheels; they didn't stop the dirt but you couldn't see it. The asymmetric wing nut holding the spare wheel was a Lagonda speciality. If it works loose, the heavy end stops in the six o'clock position and it won't loosen any further.

job and when the long grassy bank of The Causeway, which faced the factory and was a relic of the time when this area flooded every winter, would be lined with men hoping to see a board go up seeking hands.

In February 1934 the sales office, perhaps reluctantly, agreed to put the prices that had been lowered the previous autumn back up again, adding £30 to the tourer and £75 to the saloon. Production of the M45 was in full swing now and the supply of unused 3 Litre chassis had been used up, but in order that production should be not disrupted by a design change, new ones were ordered exactly the same, including the "cut out and replate", dodge at the rear of the engine. The early cars had had engine mounts made up as fabrications but now proper castings were available. Similarly, early cars had made do with a single SU petrol pump, but a second was available as an extra and proved so popular that it became standard, even though it is doubtful that it ever was really necessary. On the other hand, the short life and patchy reliability of early SU pumps made a second pump a useful precaution against breakdowns.

In February 1934 General Metcalfe died, never having properly recovered from the previous year's serious operation. His place was taken by Sir Edgar Holberton, who added the post of Managing Director to his Chairmanship. No Rapiers had appeared yet, and it was becoming clear that in order to get the numbers produced up to a profitable level Lagonda was going to be an assembly plant rather than a manufacturer. Engine production had been given to Coventry Climax with an order for 500 engines, gearboxes and rear axles were to come from ENV, clutches from Roper & Wreaks, front axles from Alford & Alder and coachwork from A N Other.

There was speculation in the motoring press that the RAC was going to ban superchargers from the Tourist Trophy race, and that if it did Lagonda might enter since they had the fastest car in current production. Invicta had already demonstrated that the Meadows engine could make a satisfactory racing power plant.

Road Tests of the M45 were still appearing. *The Autocar* had tested a tourer in December 1933 and found it faster than *The Motor* had, at 95.7mph, though less accelerative. Their acceleration figures were the best the magazine had ever achieved from a production car and they emphasised their remarkable consistency, which was a product of the Meadows engine's tractor-like torque curve. The gear ratios quoted are those of the T8 gearbox, but the gearshift pattern shown was for a Z gearbox, with top nearest the driver, leaving one to wonder just which gearbox was actually fitted. This car, or at least the illustration shown, was Warwick Wright's demonstrator. *Motor Sport* tested APJ 367 in January and despite its Balkan adventures got it up to 96mph. They were the only magazine to even mention that the engine came from Meadows and had a few criticisms, some of which, like the low height of the windscreen threatening to separate a tall driver from his hat, had already been rendered out of date by the adoption of the new T7 body. At the other extreme, *The Times* tested a saloon and took it up Dashwood Hill, near High Wycombe, romping

over the summit at 74mph. Less than 30 years before that, Wilbur Gunn had publicly congratulated himself that his Tricar was one of the few able to climb this hill without pedal assistance. The tester from *The Times* then descended the hill and tried again from a standing start in top gear. The Lagonda managed this with no trouble and accelerated to 29mph by the summit, probably trailed by smoke from a baked clutch lining.

Suddenly the Lagonda was the fashionable car to have. Its nearest rival, the 3½ Litre Bentley, was faster in top speed but less accelerative and twice the price. Sir Malcolm Campbell bought a tourer, AYU 1 (Z10993), painted blue "to customer's pattern", and in it he transported the Emir of Transjordan around Brooklands at the British Empire Trophy meeting. Later in 1934 a nightclub called The Lagonda opened in Denman Street, London - it had no connection with the car firm and in fact rather embarrassed them, bringing forth a tetchy disclaimer. Even in fiction Leslie Charteris's hero The Saint drove a Hirondel, which was a thinly disguised M45, based on the author's own car. The coachbuilders had noticed the absence of a drophead from Lagonda's range and hastened to fill the gap, such models being offered by Freestone & Webb, Carlton and Lancefield.

No fewer than 14 Lagondas were entered for the 1934 RAC Rally in March, eight of them M45s including a "works" team of three entered by Warwick Wright. We will cover their adventures in the next chapter. By now the redesign of the Rapier was finished and a contract was let to E D Abbott of Farnham to supply most of the bodies, although a substantial number of bodies were built at the customer's request by other builders. The occasion of the RAC Rally finishing at Bournemouth was seized on by the factory and a special display of Rapiers was laid on at Westover Garage Ltd, the Hampshire Distributor.

Despite the show at Westover's the Rapier was still not yet really ready for production and the factory was concentrating on trying to make 4½ Litres quickly enough to satisfy demand. In April *The Autocar* tested a pillarless saloon and headed the report " A car so fascinating that to overrate its virtues is hardly possible". The saloon was very little slower than the tourer despite its extra 3cwt. In fact the 0 to 60mph times were identical, and the 10-30mph times in third and top fractionally quicker. Probably the tourer had been a bit tired by the time it came to be road tested. The saloon's top speed of 90mph was very creditable for a luxurious and fully equipped saloon and it even used less petrol: 17mpg against the tourer's 16. Both cars were geared exactly the same, although later the tourer was offered with a taller rear-axle ratio as an option.

The saloon definitely had the Meadows gearbox fitted and the testers remarked what an improvement it was. It was also clear that the Lagonda bodyshop had been quietly improving the car's finish to go with the market the company were now selling to, with pewter inlays in the mahogany trimming rails, ladies' and gents' companion sets, driver-operated rear window blinds and a host of detailed refinements. On the outside too, refinements were apparent. The spare wheel, nearly always carried on the bootlid, could now be fitted with a metal case with a chromed band round it to keep it clean. On the first cars the rear lamps had been attached to the rear number plate, itself screwed to the spare wheel by the central wingnut. After the testers had dropped this a few times and tripped over the flex, a neater arrangement was evolved. The legal requirement that the rear lamps be only so many inches from the rear of the car precluded fixing the lamps directly to the wings so cast mazak stalks were interposed, borrowed from the contemporary Buick, and these rather vulnerable stalks were modified on the offside to carry a square number plate. At the same time the nearside lamp was altered to include a reversing lamp. A stop-lamp had appeared, operated by the brake rods.

Lord de Clifford had embraced the Rapier ever since its first prototype appearance and was about to launch his own special "de Clifford" model, with the engine capacity reduced to just under 1100cc, instead of Lagonda's quirky 1104cc, which put the car into the 1½-litre class in most competitions. He had joined forces with Charles Dobson, who ran a garage next to Staines Bridge, but on the opposite side of the river to the factory, the new venture being called Dobson & de Clifford Ltd. The aim was to take bare chassis from the Lagonda factory and construct Rapiers to one of three stages of tune, normal, sporting and full-racing. Dobson also had a useful sideline in disposing of the cars Lagonda had taken in as part-exchanges. As a first step, Lord de Clifford had bought an early Rapier, fitted it with a skimpy racing body and a short-throw crankshaft and was preparing it for Le Mans. On test at Brooklands it was found to be capable of lapping at 90mph, not that much slower than a 4½ Litre.

By July, when entries at single fees closed, there was no sign of M45 entries for the Tourist Trophy, even though, as predicted, superchargers had been banned. Lord de Clifford had entered his Rapier, but there were no other Lagondas until right at the last minute, when Arthur Fox of Fox & Nicholl entered three M45s. Fox's blown Alfas were ineligible now and he wasn't going to pit his Singers against factory ones. The actual ownership of these Lagondas has always been obscure. They were ordered by Warwick Wright and delivered to Fox & Nicholl as bare, very special chassis. Lightweight, doorless bodies were put on them by Fox, who ran

Two views of the author's M45 pillarless saloon, Car Number Z10932, shot in 1992. The car has since been returned to its original black colour scheme.

The T8 tourer body, introduced on the M45 at the end of 1934 for the 1935 model year, had two large front doors instead of one large front and one small rear door. Otherwise it was similar to the T7.

the team throughout their racing career in 1934 and 1935. Nevertheless, these cars were widely regarded as "works" entries and certainly Fox was given free access to the testbed and other facilities at Staines. Their competition history must wait for a later chapter.

In the middle of 1934 Woodward must have decided that the introduction of the Rapier had been so slow and so muddled that a proper launch was needed, which he duly organised on 19 July at Great Fosters, an Elizabethan country house near Egham in Surrey which had become a hotel. On the off-chance that potential Rapier customers might be persuaded to lift their sights a little, a full complement of M45 demonstrators was also present, including the author's own, resplendent in black with a chrome waistband and cadmium-plated brake drums. Lagonda certainly got the publicity they sought, even though Woodward was less than pleased when first a formation of more than 20 aeroplanes started "stunting" overhead and then a film crew turned up with a squad of bathing beauties to make a film based on the hotel's swimming pool. Both these events distracted the pressmen from the serious business of appreciating

the Lagondas, but they responded in the end and Woodward's press cuttings book has pages of references to the occasion, gleaned at times from some most unlikely sources.

The summer selling season tended to end abruptly in August as the customers rushed off to the grouse moors, and at this time the firm placed discreet adverts in *The Motor Trader* hinting that they wanted to expand the number of dealers, but only to firms used to dealing with the well-heeled. This must have worked, for when in September the 1935 model year products were announced, *The Motor* needed six pages to accommodate all the Lagonda dealers' advertisements. The pride of the 1935 year was going to be the Rapide version of the M45, plus its downmarket cousin the 3½ Litre, which used a simplified version of the same chassis and a bored-out version of the 3 Litre engine. The 3 Litre was to disappear after eight years in production, but the Rapier, 16/80 and standard M45 were to carry on with only minor modifications. For example, M45s would now have semaphore indicators as standard. Both the principal motoring magazines devoted several pages and an art-paper supplement to the new range.

M45 SUMMARY STATISTICS

Engine

configuration	6 cylinders in line, overhead valves, pushrods
capacity	4453cc
bore	88.5mm
stroke	120.65mm
RAC rating	29.13hp
compression ratio	6:1
firing order	1 4 2 6 3 5
valve timing	io 10° btdc, ic 50° abdc, eo 60° bbdc, ec 15° atdc. Inlet opens for 240°, exhaust for 255°
tappet clearances	(hot) 0.006in (0.15mm)
brake horsepower	118 @ 4000rpm (claimed) 108 @ 3130rpm (measured)
crankshaft	
no of bearings	4
main bearing	2in (50.8mm) diameter
big end	2in (50.8mm) diameter
oil capacity	2 galls (9.1 litres)
cooling system	Water pump, thermostatic radiator shutters, capacity 6 galls (27.3 litres)
ignition system	Two spark plugs per cylinder. 12-volt coil and Rotax distributor on exhaust side, BTH CE6/S horizontal magneto on inlet side
ignition timing	42° btdc fully advanced. Both plugs fire at same time.
contact breaker gap	Coil: 0.012-0.016in (0.3-0.4mm) Magneto: 0.012in (0.3mm)
sparking plugs	18mm Champion 16, gap 0.019in (0.48mm)
carburettors	Twin SU HV5 1⅝in Jets 0.100. Needles KT (standard), C1 (weaker), K (richer)
fuel pumps	Two SU type L, mounted back to back.
dynamo	Lucas, RJF control box
starter motor	Lucas M45A
clutch	Meadows
engine number location	Lagonda number on offside of timing case Meadows number on offside of flywheel housing
batteries	Two 6v 90Ah in series under rear seat

Chassis

wheelbase	10 ft 9in (3277mm)
track, front	4 ft 8¾in (1441mm)
track, rear	4 ft 9¼in (1467mm)
overall length, tourer	14 ft 8in (4470mm)
overall width, tourer	5 ft 8in (1727mm)
kerb weight	Chassis 27cwt (1372kg), Tourer 32½cwt (1651kg), Saloon 35½cwt (1804kg)
turning circle	43ft (13m)
wheels and tyres	Wire spoked, Rudge splined hubs, 3.62in rims, 6.00 x 19 Dunlop Fort tyres
tyre pressure, front	32-34psi
tyre pressure, rear	32-34psi
brake drums	16in x 1⅝in (406 x 41mm)
brake servo	Clayton Dewandre vacuum
steering box	Cam Gears, 14:1 ratio
propeller shaft	Hardy Spicer with needle roller UJs
rear axle	Lagonda spiral bevel. semi-floating
ratios	Tourer 12 x 44/3.67:1, Saloon 10 x 41/4.1:1, Limousine 4.6:1, Optional tourer ratio 13 x 43/3.31:1
mph @ 1000rpm in top	24.4 (3.67:1), 26.9 (3.31 to 1)
oil capacity	3.5 pints (2 litres)
shock absorbers	4 Andre Hartfords + 4 Andre Telecontrols with dashboard control
fuel tank capacity	20 galls (91 litres)
chassis number location	Brass identity plate on engine side of bulkhead

Gearbox

type	Meadows T8 four speed non-synchromesh
internal ratios	Top direct, third 1.3:1, second 2.012:1, first 3.148:1
oil capacity	4.5 pints (2.5 litres)

Prices

Chassis	£675 (1933)
Tourer	£795 (1933)
	£825 (1934)
Saloon	£895 (1933)
	£970 (1934)

Number produced

(estimated)	345

Chapter Three

The M45 in Competition

Lord de Clifford's experiences on his December 1933 reconnaissance for the Monte Carlo Rally were put to good use when the factory prepared a car (AMT 77, Z10605) for the rally itself. The springs were given extra camber to produce a nine-inch ground clearance and all the brake gear was gaitered. On the tail a vast wooden chest carried shovels and other de-ditching gear and completely obscured the rear view. De Clifford's original choices for crew were T G Moore, the proprietor of *Motor Sport*, and H B (Bertie) Browning, then secretary of the Monte Carlo Rally British Competitors Club. Even the drive to the start was not without incident, involving rebuilding the steering after an accident in Vienna and having to be dragged out of mud three times in Bulgaria. Then, after arriving in Athens, there was a sudden thaw and all the snow melted. Ted de Clifford, himself a very fast driver indeed, reckoned neither Tom Moore nor Bertie Browning was fast enough to keep up the schedule he wanted in the dry(ish) conditions, and arranged for Charles Brackenbury to come out on the Orient Express. Tom Moore needed the story for Motor Sport and refused to leave, so Bertie had to return by train since the fourth seat was occupied by winter equipment. After all these travails it is a bit of an anticlimax to record that Lord de Clifford hit an even bigger rock before they left Greece, broke the crankcase and had to retire. There were two other Lagondas in the event, both blown 2 Litres, and both starting from John o'Groats. Neither was placed but in the driving tests at the finish Roland Gardner won his

class and J Charters was second to him.

The RAC Rally for 1934 had nine starting points which converged on Bournemouth after about 1000 miles of road sections. Fourteen Lagondas were entered, eight of them M45s. The three "works" cars started from London and Lord de Clifford, in one of the prototype Rapiers, from Newcastle. The weather was unexpectedly foul for March, with heavy snowstorms, worse for the later starters. Despite this, virtually everyone got to Bournemouth unpenalised, so that the whole rally depended on the split seconds won or lost in the wiggly driving tests on the front. Here the M45 proved too much of a handful and none of the Lagonda entries did well. Roland Gardner (2 Litre supercharged) was the best, coming tenth in his class. They did better in the coachwork competition, in which W A Fitzgerald, in a cream and green Lancefield-bodied M45 saloon, came second in his class.

The Eastbourne Concours d'Elégance was at this time attracting an enormous entry (185 in 1934) and commensurate publicity. The organisers had banned trade entries but had not really been able reliably to sort out which they were. Major Cohn, a keen Lagonda owner for many years, had bought himself a dark red Lancefield drophead M45 (AUF 77, Z10746) and contrived to win his class as a saloon with the hood up and come second in the tourer class with it down. The winner in this class was R C Fish in a Freestone & Webb drophead M45. Fish also won the class for an Eastbourne resident and Cohn the class for a Sussex resident. There were 24 classes in all and the seriousness

T C Mann in his M45 (Car Number Z10691) competing in the RAC Rally of 1935. He got a First Class Award. This car has been in the Mann family from new and is still rallied by the family of the original owner. At his request it was fitted with a T5 (16/80 type) body instead of the normal T7. For no clear reason the offside headlamp has its bulb support tripod upside down.

The Fox & Nicholl M45 Team cars before setting off for Ulster in August 1934. John Hindmarsh is the balding man seen above the aeroscreens of BPK 202. The tall man on the extreme right is Donald Wilcockson, Fox & Nicholl's chief mechanic.

with which the event was taken can be gauged by looking at the names of the judges, who included Lord Howe, The Earl of March, Brian Lewis, George Eyston, Selwyn Edge and Donald Healey.

After Mike Couper's success in the 1932 Alpine Rally, Lagonda interest in this event had been awakened and Arthur Dobell had entered his M45 for the 1934 rally, scheduled for 7-12 August. Dobell was remembered by old Staines hands for not liking the standard Lagonda dashboard layout and for having enough pull with the management for him to be given a drawing board and space in the drawing office to design his own, which was subsequently put on the car. Unfortunately, in the rally he misunderstood the rules on the timed climb of the Stelvio Pass and lost a Glacier Cup by three marks.

It was noted in the previous chapter that Fox &

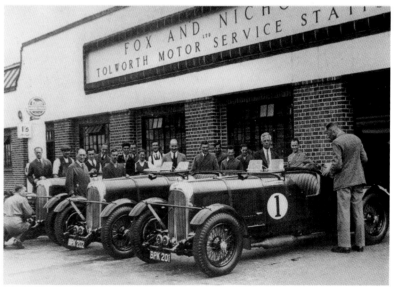

Nicholl came to run three special M45s ordered by Warwick Wright and entered in the 1934 Tourist Trophy. Technically, these cars were so special they should not have been eligible for a race theoretically restricted to standard production cars. They used the 10 ft 3in wheelbase and Girling brakes of the M45 Rapide, a model not yet announced as a production model, although if the Car Number can be taken as a guide the factory had already made two prototypes. Lagonda were not alone, of course, in liberally interpreting the rules: the special Bentley of Eddie Hall was even more special and never did result in a production model.

The 4½-litre Meadows engine had never been conceived as a racing unit and it was uphill work to make it one. On the other hand its reliability and vast torque were great assets. For once it can be stated unarguably that racing improves the breed, since most of the modifications first introduced by the racing team found their way on to production cars later. Both Arthur Fox and Alfie Cranmer were worried by the flexibility of the crankcase and for the racing engines had them cast in RR50 alloy, asking Meadows to strengthen them around the main bearings. It is not recorded how this was done but a later development involved holding the bearing caps with four bolts instead of two, and I dare say this was Meadows' approach too. They also increased the size of the studs holding down the cylinder block, which had been known to snap at high revs. Meadows supplied special connecting rods without a split at the small end, while the big ends, one-eighth of an inch larger than standard, were metalled directly, without the normal shell. The valves were special, too, without the normal slot and held by split collets. All the usual cleaning up and polishing of ports and cylinder head took place, while the valves were slightly smaller to avoid masking. The oil pump on the Meadows is right at the back, giving rise to oil starvation under braking, so additional sump baffles were provided. The BTH magneto was replaced by a Scintilla, although this was probably a personal preference of Fox's since it had no effect on power, but the coil and distributor on the nearside were replaced by a Vertex magneto. The ordinary radiator shutters had their thermostatic control replaced by a Bowden wire that the driver could operate, and the big cast fan was removed. Four SU fuel pumps were fitted, wired up as two pairs.

Inside the engine, special Martlett pistons gave a 7:1 compression ratio (6:1 was normal) using the standard copper gasket. The three special engines, M45/269 to 271, were ready for test in mid-August, rather late for a race on 1 September. M45/271, with the above modifications, gave 120bhp at 3400rpm and 112.5bhp at 3800 - rather disappointing. A thinner gasket raised the compression ratio, producing an increase to 120.75bhp at 3400rpm and 122bhp at 3600. This last speed was important: it was the one Fox was telling his drivers not to exceed since he believed it could be sustained indefinitely. The cars were scrutineered at Staines on 16 August and set out for Ulster on the 27th, although work continued on them even on the ferry to Belfast.

A special straight-bevel rear axle with a 3.14:1 ratio was fitted and the gearbox had different internal ratios, so that 3800rpm in each gear would produce 38, 59, 84 and 110mph using 6.00 x 19 tyres. The Telecontrol dampers were removed and vane-type hydraulic ones by Luvax took their place. Fox designed and built simple doorless bodies and since the rules called for a hood to be fitted but did not require it to be erected while running, he devised a tonneau cover for the rear seats that could be raised on an arrangement of tubes to become the "hood" and snapped down in seconds to resume its tonneau duties. An example of Fox's attention to detail, aside from split-pinning virtually every nut on the car, was to reverse the left-hand bonnet catch on the nearside and the right-hand one on the other side. These Amal catches were normally opened by a half-turn anticlockwise on one side of the car and a half-turn clockwise on the other. Reversing one of each pair meant that the bonnet could be released on either side with a clockwise twist of one hand and an anti-clockwise twist with the other – a much more natural movement and easier under pressure.

The cycle-type wings were the minimum size allowed by the regulations but were well braced by extra tubes at the front to prevent them working loose in a race. Most of the tail was occupied by a 27 gallon (123 litre) petrol tank with a little "manhole" on the top to give access to the two fillers. Fox had devised a huge square funnel with four legs which fitted the tail of the car and held a five-gallon can for refuelling stops. The spare wheel was carried inside the tail on a cradle which swung out. The lid which gave access to it had a little vertical fin formed in it, the only touch of nonsense in the bodywork. A standard M45 radiator was fitted, sloped to the rear. For the TT no

lights were required, so none were fitted.

As the largest cars in the race the Lagondas were to carry numbers 1 to 3, drivers being The Hon. Brian Lewis in 1 (BPK 201, Z11118), John Hindmarsh in 2 (BPK 202, Z11078) and John Cobb in 3 (BPK 203, Z11079). Lewis and Hindmarsh were Fox & Nicholl regulars but Cobb was not and in fact was rather scathing. He wrote to Rex Mundy, the Competitions Manager of KLG, late in July seeking his OK to drive for another make, saying: "Although I am in receipt of a princely retainer from your good firm I trust you will not be very angry if I drive a Lagonda for Arthur Fox in the TT. I have not got any mount of my own for the race, so it is the Lagonda or nothing. In any case I don't think they are any good, but it makes a holiday". Hardly a race-winning attitude.

Cobb's car, which had been the last to be finished, proved to be slower than the other two when practice started on 29 August. Lewis did only three laps on the first day, the best 11min 10sec. Hindmarsh managed 11min 18sec and Cobb 11min 23sec. Cobb then asked Lewis to take No. 3 round to see if it was the car or the driver that was at fault, and as Lewis could only record 11min 16sec it looked to be a bit of both. Midnight oil was then burnt in abundance. On the following day Lewis got down to 10min 45sec and Hindmarsh to 10min

47sec, but Cobb was still stuck on 11min 13sec. Eddie Hall in the equally untried 3½-litre Bentley was fastest in the class with a lap in 10min 36sec, equal to 77.36mph. As the race was a handicap, which had already been determined, there was no point in breaking records in practice and only enough laps were done to familiarise the drivers

Close-up of BPK 201 in practice for the 1934 TT shows some of Fox's little dodges. The front bonnet catches have been reversed, for example, and little levers have been fixed to the front damper bodies so that they can be quickly tightened without tools at a pit stop. This is Brian Lewis's car. No lamps were carried in the TT.

Arthur Fox (left) at the 1934 TT. The other man is unknown and may be the owner of the garage used by the team in Belfast.

with the circuit and its very long laps. And of course to calculate fuel consumption and tyre wear rates, this last proving very important since the circuit had been resurfaced in places with an extremely abrasive stone.

There was a magnificent entry of 41 cars, including nine teams of three entered for the team award. Everyone was complaining about the handicapping, which had been calculated by "Ebbie" and seemed extraordinarily harsh but proved , in the event, to be uncannily accurate. On the second day of practice some of the drivers began to be very worried about the rate of tyre wear and got up a petition to allow them to have their wings removed so that wear could be observed from the cockpit. (Racing tyres had a white breaker strip incorporated so that it was obvious when all the tread had gone). The Lagonda team, having every confidence in Arthur Fox, declined to sign this and the RAC wouldn't hear of it anyway, as they were determined to attract manufacturers to the TT by making the cars look normal, even if, as with most of the entries, they concealed mechanics some distance from the norm.

The morning of the race was fine and cold and the expected hordes eventually arrived at the circuit, mostly by tram, but it was 10am before they really represented a crowd. At half past ten the Prime Minister arrived, followed by a string of notables, working up to the Governor, for the TT was a big social occasion in Ulster. The cars were despatched in groups, according to the handicap, smallest first. The last group consisted of the Lagondas, the Bentley, the Talbots and a team of Irish V8s whose light weight and good torque gave the others some cheeky competition on initial acceleration. Hall, in the Bentley, nearly ended his race on the first lap with a spin at the Moat, but he recovered and carried on at undiminished speed. In a long handicap race like the TT the positions on the road in the early stages meant little and it was accepted that the only way to keep track of the race was by checking the positions on handicap at, say, half-hour intervals. At the end of the first half hour it was seen that Hall was nearest to his handicap speed, having averaged 77.87mph and "overtaken" all the MGs. Lewis and Hindmarsh were fifth and sixth on handicap. Not long after this came the first serious incident when H B Prestwick (Riley) made up for the non-appearance of Freddy Dixon by leaping his car over the famous hedge at Quarry, injuring himself and removing the number 2 Riley team from the team contest.

Brian Lewis was now getting his eye in and as the fuel load lightened the Lagonda was speeding up so that, whereas in the early stages Hall had been gaining 9 or 10 seconds a lap, Lewis gradually whittled this down to zero. Hall responded with two consecutive laps at 79.31 and 79.83mph. At noon, Lewis had worked up to third on handicap, with Hall still leading from Fotheringham (Aston Martin). Hall's average, at 78.89mph, demonstrated his consistency. From about this time Charles Dodson (MG) began to speed up and make his ultimately successful attempt for victory, climbing from sixth place at noon to third at 12.30 and second by one o'clock. This new threat brought a further response from Hall in the form of a lap at 80.48mph.

Arthur Fox had planned to run through with only one stop for fuel and tyres for each car, but this plan began to fall apart just before one o'clock when Hindmarsh called at the pits to have the brakes adjusted as the pedal travel had got ridiculous. There was a hurried debate as to whether, while he was there, the tyres should be changed and fuel topped up. They decided not to, but nevertheless this stop dropped him out of the first half dozen on handicap. At 1.20 Hall made his first pit stop, which took 2min 48sec, dropping him from first to sixth, there being a considerable delay getting the steel brake drums off, the need to do this suggesting that new brake shoes were called for. For the following year's races alloy ones were to be specified to overcome this problem.

At two o'clock Dodson was leading by 25sec from Lewis, whose average of 78.76mph was now faster than Hall's. About 3.30 Lewis came in for his planned pit stop, which took 2min 44sec, just as long as Hall's and including an adjustment to the brakes. He was followed in by Hindmarsh, and among a great flurry of pit stops Hall worked his way up into the lead again, with Dodson second 81sec behind him and Lewis and Hindmarsh third and fourth. Throughout the race Cobb had been lapping 25sec or so slower than his team mates, bearing out the impression from practice that number 3 was a slower car than the other two. Also at around 3.30 Hall came in for his second stop, which again took approximately 2½ minutes. It was followed by instant drama, for as Hall pulled away from the pits Lewis's scarlet Lagonda came flying up the road from Dundonald and passed the Bentley as they disappeared into Quarry and up Cree Hill. The duel that followed, albeit for second place, brought the race to life and the crowd to their feet as Lewis and Hall repeatedly swapped the lead in a six-lap tussle. The cars were well matched, the Bentley undoubtedly the faster overall as it was more nimble on the twisty bits, but the Lagonda more accelerative and faster in a straight line. Six laps represented over an hour on the long Ards circuit and for all this time the two cars were rarely more than 10 yards apart, with full use of pavements and shopfronts necessary on the narrow Irish roads for either large car to pass the other.

It is probably true to say that Hall had realised that two stops were going to be needed and had carried only enough fuel to get him to his first stop, whereas Fox had filled his cars right up in order to run through with a single stop. The duel started when the Bentley had just refuelled and the Lagonda was half way through its tankful, so that they were more closely matched than usual. Ironically, as is often the way, the thrilling cut and thrust actually slowed both drivers down, for Lewis's fastest lap of the race was the one on which he caught Hall, taking 10min 8sec. His later ones were slower than this but he managed to pull a little way ahead of Hall who, on lap 31, got round in 10min 6sec (81.15mph) the fastest lap of the day. This got him clear, just, of Lewis and he set off after Dodson, now three minutes ahead. He could gain nearly 30 seconds a lap but were there enough laps left to catch him? Lewis now had to slow down as the fierce battle had wrought havoc on his tyres and the white breaker strip was showing. There was a debate in the Fox camp whether to bring Lewis in, knowing that the stop would take him out of contention totally. Then Fox's hand was forced when a thunderstorm broke at Comber and Lewis had to come in only two laps from the end. On the last lap it still was not clear if Hall was going to catch Dodson, Hall being 42sec behind at Newtownards, 35sec at the Moat, 31 at Comber, 26 at Ballystockart, 22 at Dundonald and 17sec at the finish. Had the pit stops been quicker, Hall could have won easily. Lewis eventually came in fourth, nearly four minutes behind Hall, followed by Hindmarsh in fifth place and Cobb eighth, their speeds being, respectively 77.57, 77.38 and 74.58mph.

The race naturally had a tremendous press, the RAC were congratulated on the new rules that had

Hindmarsh's car crosses Conway Square at Newtownards in the 1934 TT. For once the crowd seems well back. Although the square is large, both entrance and exit were narrow and tricky at racing speeds.

been so savagely mauled in the same columns a few weeks earlier, and Hall, Lewis and Dodson were the heroes, with dozens of photographs and drawings of the epic Hall/Lewis duel. A lot of the "if only" post mortems centred on Hall's 2½-minute pit stops, when Grand Prix teams achieved half this, and it is an amusing indication of the different standards of the day to discover that the Prime Minister of Northern Ireland, Lord Craigavon, took a spin round the track while the race was in progress. Mind you, he was in a quick Bentley and he was chauffeured by Algernon Guinness, reaching 90mph on the run down to Comber, but nowadays VIPs are expected to confine their activities to the grandstand.

"Ebby" had predicted the winner's handicap time six months earlier to be 6hr 13 min 26 sec. Dodson actually took 6 hr 13 min 24 sec so the new rules had not overcome the Ebblewhite skill. Interesting comparisons have emerged since the race. The Fox & Nicholl M45s weighed 30.07cwt (1524kg), significantly lighter than a standard M45 tourer's 32.5cwt (1647kg). Hall's Bentley, admittedly a litre smaller, weighed in at 25.06cwt (1270kg), which probably explains its advantage on the twisty parts of the circuit. In retrospect it is marvellous that Lewis's engine survived the race, as afterwards he admitted he was doing 300 revs above the red line

during the duel and Meadows engines are very unforgiving about maximum revolutions. In fact, this engine was never afterwards the fastest of the three, but whether this was due to the pasting it had had in the TT, or merely because Lewis was never available a second time to drive it, one can only leave unanswered.

Woodwrights were quick to follow up the publicity value of the TT in their advertising and gave prominent mention of both Fox & Nicholl and Warwick Wright. Even though the Lagonda team had finished fourth, fifth and eighth they had not won the team prize, which went to Aston Martin for finishing third. Sixth and seventh. But the results were worth trumpeting, coupled with the assertion that there had been no mechanical trouble throughout the long race. Further, "You can buy an identical chassis". Well, not yet you couldn't, but the following week the Rapide was announced and then it was possible.

Not long after the TT, Alan Hess managed to borrow one of the racing engines and have it fitted to an M45 saloon in order to gain a sneaky advantage in club racing. Driving this car at an MCC meeting at Brooklands he hit a bird at speed on the railway straight, shattering the windscreen, which was of toughened glass. It is believed that this incident, which left him temporarily unable to

The Lagonda handbrake was perfectly placed to go up the driver's trouser leg in a Le Mans run-and-jump start. Hence on Fox's cars it was bent out of the way.

see through the screen, led to the banning of toughened glass in competitions.

The Motor Show in October 1934 saw the public's first glimpse of the M45 Rapide, which will be described in the next chapter, and also of the 3½ Litre to replace the 3 Litre, using a simplified version of the Rapide's 10ft 3in chassis. The Rapide did not replace the standard M45 but was sold alongside it at an elevated price. During the autumn Fox & Nicholl proudly exhibited the racing team cars in their showroom at Tolworth in Surrey and offered demonstration runs in them. One hopes they didn't pretend that a standard M45 tourer had the same performance, but of course it would be a sight more comfortable.

Lagonda's calendar for 1935 featured one of Bryan de Grineau's drawings of the Lewis/Hall duel in the TT and in keeping with the publicity value it was given a much wider circulation than usual, being offered free to all readers of *The Autocar* and *The Motor*. The response was so great that they ran out in a week and had to reprint.

From this point on the M45 and M45 Rapide stories combine, so I will jump forward to the 1935 Le Mans and continue the Fox & Nicholl saga up to the time when the cars were sold off at the end of that year, and will relate the later Rapide achievements in the next chapter.

True to his own traditions, Arthur Fox announced his entry for Le Mans at the last possible moment, and it was for just one car, not three. It transpired that he had bought BPK 202 from Warwick Wright. Lagonda Ltd by then was not only in Receivership but actually up for sale by tender, the tenders due for return by the Monday after the race. So there was no chance of factory involvement at this time. Not that this stopped a large party from the works making their way there. Fox's drivers were to be the reliable Fox veteran John Hindmarsh and the rising star of 1935, Luis Fontes. Fontes had sprung into the limelight by winning the 250-mile Silver Jubilee Day International Trophy Race at Brooklands in a three year old 2.3 Alfa Romeo, bought the previous evening, and beating Freddy Dixon and Eddie Hall. Within the month he had won his class at Southport and was placed third in the Mannin Moar. His name came from a Brazilian father, but he had been raised in England and was only twenty-one. Bespectacled and of studious appearance, he looked like a schoolboy in contrast with the breezy and now balding Hindmarsh. Fontes's driving style was spectacular and a forerunner of that employed

nowadays by rally drivers, in that he deliberately set the car swinging about a vertical axis so that he could use the rotational inertia to help him round the corners, assuming he got the timing right. To the uninitiated he appeared to teeter on the edge of disaster the whole time, and it was only when it was realised that each essay at a bend was exactly the same as the last that it became clear he was doing it deliberately.

Five days later, Fox entered another Lagonda for Dr Benjafield and Geoff Manby-Colegrave, but this entry over-subscribed the list and was only accepted as a reserve. In all there were 60 cars entered, 35 of them British, with a mathematical progression of one Lagonda, two Frazer Nashes, four Austins, six Rileys, seven Aston Martins, eight MGs and nine Singers. The MGs included George Eyston's all-women team. Having won the event four years in succession, the favourites were a quartet of supercharged 2.3 Alfas driven by Lord Howe/Brian Lewis, Raymond Sommer/De Sauge, Heldé/Stoffel and Chinetti/Castaud. (Heldé was a pseudonym adopted by Pierre Louis-Dreyfus, perhaps to avoid confusion with Rene Dreyfus, perhaps for family reasons). Chinetti, the winner in both 1932 and 1934, and second in 1933, was allowed the car with the new shape of radiator cowl and Lord Howe had painted his car blue to stifle in some way the criticism levelled at him for continually driving foreign cars. There was also a brace of 4.9-litre Type 50 Bugattis to give the Alfas a run for their money, one driven by Veyron and Labric and the other fated not to start after being crashed by de Valence in the last period of practice. The largest car in the race was a 7-litre Model J Duesenberg driven by Prince Nicholas of Romania, the same car as he had driven in 1934.

Fox's first entry was given number 4 in the engine size order normal at Le Mans. When his second entry was allowed in after someone dropped out, it could not be given the number 5 as that was already allocated, so the second Lagonda became number 14 but was allowed to start alongside its team-mate at 4 o'clock on Saturday 15 June. The 58 cars that actually started were a record entry. The line was so long that for the first time numbered circles had to be painted for the drivers to stand in and a relay flag system devised so that the higher numbers should see the flag fall at the right time.

In the nine months since the TT all three cars had been well used by Fox & Nicholl, and it is illuminating that Fox chose to purchase BPK 202. Dr

Benjafield had bought BPK 203, Cobb's car in Ulster, and by now presumably brought it up to the standard of the other two, which it manifestly was not in 1934. It was arranged that 203 would run as a team with Fox's car, and in the end the co-driver was Sir Ronald Gunter, Bart.

Lamps were essential at Le Mans and Fox had rigged up a pair of large cheap Rotax headlamps on brackets attached to the tube which joined the front wings together. This put them very high up, a good thing for the long straights at Le Mans, but also meant that the air pressure at speed tended to bend the framework, so a further strut was added each side, sloping back at about 45° to the bonnet boards and rather impeding access to the forward bonnet catches. An extra stay was added to the rear end of each front wing. Anticipating trouble at night distinguishing between the cars, he added a foglamp to each car, on the offside of number 4 and the nearside of number 14. Never a great believer in wire stoneguards, Fox had each lamp covered by a cloth and celluloid cover for the daylight part of Saturday's racing. A second bonnet strap was added at the behest of the organisers and Fox's opinion of this requirement was shown by his mounting it as close to the other one as he could get it. Anticipating trouble with roasted drivers if the weekend should be hot, he added

Le Mans 1935, the start. It rained for most of the race. Hindmarsh in number 4 (BPK 202) is away quickly.

small hinged ventilators to both cars, low down on the scuttle sides. There is no record of what extra tuning was done to the engines, but a small modification was the provision of a bulge in the offside bonnet panel which looks as if it hid some form of air gathering device, although it may merely have been to overcome the closeness of the bonnet side to the carburettors. As in Ulster the cars were to race with the wire mesh windscreen folded flat and a single aero screen for the driver. The second aero screen had now been removed.

Practice passed off without incident for the Lagonda team and they were encouraged to receive a telegram of good wishes from Basil Holden, the Receiver, clearly no stony-hearted accountant. The weather was miserable and Saturday dawned to a downpour that persisted, with a few breaks, up to just before the start. Charles Faroux flagged off the field on to roads swimming with water. The Hon. Brian Lewis in Lord Howe's Alfa was first away although Hindmarsh led him on the road due to his starting position. The monster Duesenberg was mixing it with them as the cloud of spray that was the field rushed off towards the Esses. By the end of the first lap the traditional lunatic sprint was on, led by Lewis and followed closely by Sommer, Chinetti, Prince Nicholas and Heldé. Hindmarsh was

seventh. The first eight cars had already opened up a perceptible gap between themselves and the 2-litre cars.

For the first few laps the order at the front changed back and forth between Sommer and Lewis, with Chinetti never far away. Then first Sommer and then Lewis came in with ignition bothers, both losing time, although Sommer retained second place. After an hour the Lagonda of Hindmarsh had worked up to fourth place behind the three Alfas. It had begun to rain again and with such a crowded course some of the bends, especially Arnage, became very tricky. Nevertheless, Chinetti was lapping at 85mph and Sommer even faster as he tried to regain lost time. The fastest Astons and Rileys were locked in a grim battle of their own, only one lap down on the leaders.

Sommer got back into the lead just after 5 o'clock and Lewis was going faster than anyone, though two laps down after a stop to rebuild the distributor. On the 16th lap both Heldé and Chinetti stopped at the pits to change to wet weather tyres as the rain had got heavier, their stops letting Hindmarsh up into second place. Chinetti's stop lasted 10 minutes after it was found that oil was leaking on to the rear brakes, and he was back again soon after with the same problem. The various pit stops had shuffled the order and by 6 o'clock, when the rain became even heavier, Sommer led by just over three minutes from Hindmarsh, with Veyron's Bugatti 32 seconds behind. Heldé was fourth, Prince Nicholas fifth and Dr Benjafield, in the second Lagonda, sixth. The worthy doctor, vastly experienced in the ways of Le Mans, had not indulged in any of the histrionics of the opening laps but had been driving steadily and picking up places as his rivals dropped back or dropped out. Hindmarsh, too, had been running absolutely steadily without ever losing touch with the leaders.

Around 6.30pm the leading cars had completed the regulation 24 laps and could start their pit stops for fuel, oil and water. At this point Sommer was told that his co-driver, taken ill the previous day, was too sick to drive and that he would have to drive the whole race himself. Lord Howe took over from Lewis, but not every team changed drivers. The Lagondas didn't even stop, as the vast fuel tank and high gears of the 4½ Litre allowed about 350 miles between stops and Fox was planning to run right through the 24 hours on the same tyres.

By 7 o'clock Dr Benjafield had picked off the Duesenberg and was now fifth, a lap behind Hindmarsh and two laps down on the leader. The heavy rain continued and the roads were breaking up in places under the combined attention of racing cars and water, so that flying stones became another hazard. Where it wasn't breaking up the alternative danger was the slipperiness, and there were lots of minor, and some not so minor, skids and spins. Just after 9 o'clock, when the light was fading but before lamps were much use, Fotheringham in the Aston Martin had a gigantic slide on the exit from White House and his car overturned. The driver was thrown out and luckily sustained only bad cuts, but Gardner's Aston and Hindmarsh, following close behind, had exciting avoidances and the Lagonda just clipped the tail of the stricken car, damaging the Lagonda's steering and knocking away the offside headlamp. The lamp was refixed, the cover was replaced to keep water out of the electrics, and the car soldiered on without losing a place, still running faultlessly.

By 10 o'clock, the quarter distance, it was remarkable how few of the entry had given up, despite the atrocious weather, or possibly because of it, since lap speeds were well down on the maximum in the bad conditions and this must have given the engines an easier time. Sommer was comfortably in the lead at an average of 81.87mph and the Hindmarsh/Fontes car was two laps behind and four minutes ahead of the Heldé/Stoffel Alfa. Benjafield and Gunter were back down to sixth now that Howe and Lewis had caught up and passed them. The Index of Performance was dominated by the Singers, holding first, second and fourth places. Although only six cars had gone out by 10 o'clock, there then followed a spate of retirements. Mrs Wisdom's Riley ran a big end, the Duesenberg went out with magneto troubles, the Newsome/McClure Riley crashed, a Singer and a Bugatti gave up - all in the space of a half hour or so. But at least the rain was stopping.

The race seemed to be settling down by 11 o'clock, with only the steady climb up the board of the Lewis/Howe car to arouse interest. Then, a sensation when Sommer failed to appear. His engine had died on him at Mulsanne with a blocked fuel pipe. Having already driven for seven hours unaided, he had now to start a nightmare struggle back to the pits using the starter motor, pushing and occasional hiccups from the engine as some drops of fuel got through. This took nearly half an hour and in this time the Lagonda caught up and roared into the lead. A Lagonda leading at

Le Mans – if only General Metcalfe had lived to see it! But fingers had to be kept crossed, for the accident with the Aston Martin had started severe tyre wear on the offside front and also unbalanced the brakes. Arthur Fox's plan to race right through on one set of tyres was endangered, as were the drivers' necks in their efforts to lead an important race in a car which would not pull up straight on the treacherous surfaces.

It took Sommer's pit crew ages to even partially clear the fuel blockage on his car and he restarted seven laps down on the Lagonda, the order being otherwise unchanged. Lewis was still lapping faster than anyone else and although still fourth at midnight, he passed the Veyron/Labric Bugatti as it refuelled in the next hour to gain third place. Before 1am he had taken second from the Heldé/Stoffel Alfa. On the 84th lap, at 1am, the order was Hindmarsh, Lewis, Heldé and Veryon, all on the same lap, and Chinetti back in fifth place after a fast but unspectacular drive. At 1.15 Sommer, now 20 laps down, had had enough and came in to retire. He had been driving for nine hours, the fuel starvation was not cured and the car was progressing in jerks that would have upset even a fresh driver. The French crowd wouldn't hear of it and cheered him into continuing, but after another two laps and cross-eyed with fatigue, he called it a day (or night).

Somewhere between 1 and 2am Lewis got past the Lagonda and retook the lead he had lost so many hours before, losing it again temporarily at his refuelling stop to Veyron. The Lagonda had stopped for a long time at the pits while something was done about the steering and braking. It is clear from the contemporary magazines that all the journalists were in bed, for nowhere in the dozen or so accounts published is there any reference to the timing or duration of this stop, but it was long enough to drop the Lagonda to fourth place by 4am. However, he was only one lap down on the leaders, for this was proving to be a grim battle of endurance between closely matched cars, with the Lagonda's speed and fortitude a revelation to the French crowd.

At the halfway point, 4am, Howe and Lewis had completed 113 laps at an average of nearly 79mph, with the 4.9 Bugatti 2 minutes behind and the Heldé/Stoffel Alfa and the first Lagonda both on the lap behind. Chinetti/Gastraud were four laps behind the Lagonda and Benjafield/Gunter two laps further back, only one lap ahead of the leading Aston Martin of Martin/Brackenbury.

Within the next hour Chinetti and Veyron were both out, both with broken transmissions, so that the English Alfa led the Franco-German one and the Lagondas were third and fourth. At 5.30 the Howe/Lewis Alfa went out with a broken piston after leading for four hours following an epic chase. Everyone moved up one place and the attentions to the faster Lagonda must have proved successful, for it began to overhaul the Heldé/Stoffel car until it was only one minute behind. It was a long drawn out struggle, the gap closing from 1min 50sec at 8am to 1min at 9am. Eventually, at 10am, the Lagonda got by and went back into the lead when the Alfa stopped at the pits. These two, the Lagonda and the Alfa, were now nine laps up on the Aston Martin, which had passed the second Lagonda but was still on the same lap as it. Fifth was a new name, the Delahaye of Paris and Mongin, coming up the field as the leaders destroyed themselves. Dixon's Riley caught fire at the pits and was burnt out, and Sébilleau's Riley overturned at Arnage without injury to the driver. Then the rain started again, but patchy this time, so that parts of the track were wet and others dry.

The second-place Alfa now entered a slow period with a few longish stops to try to cure a water leak, so that by 11 o'clock the Lagonda was two laps ahead and the Delahaye had climbed up to third from the Martin/Brackenbury Aston and the second Lagonda. All these three were on the same lap but seven laps down on the second place car. The Lagonda's average speed for the 19 hours was 78.75mph, a model of consistent driving, for Fontes had proved an admirable choice as team mate to Hindmarsh, with just the right blend of dash and steadiness required of a long-distance driver. At this point the Alfa was lapping about 4mph slower than the leading Lagonda and the Delahaye was in trouble, enabling Benjafield to pass it and set off after the Alfa. Not long afterwards Heldé's car started a misfire that led to a seven-minute stop to change plugs, and there looked to be a chance that the second Lagonda would overtake it. Lagonda first and second! In Ulster the year before Ted Bolton, the Works Manager, had bitten his fingernails far enough to draw blood during the Lewis/Hall duel and not noticed in his excitement. What was he like now? But things didn't work out like that. Just after passing the pits there was a nasty noise in Benjafield's gearbox and the transmission locked up solid, causing the car to skid to a halt. What followed would do justice to a Buster Keaton

movie, and is best described in the words of Randall Bell, Benjafield's timekeeper, who was an eyewitness.

"It was one of my relief periods, so I was able to accompany a mechanic, who was sent off to find out what had gone wrong. We knew roughly where he was. Benjafield was stopped, his back wheels locked up, and was waiting calmly by the car with no notion what to do. On our arrival he came to our side of the track – the mechanic was not allowed on the course - and then a pantomime incident ensued. The mechanic and Benjie having shouted to each other across the fence (it was very noisy), Benjie gathered that the tools he required were in the boot of the car and was told what it seemed he need do. Time was going on and the unhappy mechanic, aware that he could sort out the troubles almost in a trice, was gradually getting frantic, which Benjie's unruffled calm did nothing to dispel. Benjie proceeded to hold up the contents of the boot one by one in unhurried sequence to find which were the ones required – about which he himself had not a clue. This caused the unhappy mechanic to dance a jig with frustration, at which, I had to admit, I could only giggle. But having found out what tools to use, he

set to work with a will and presently got the car going again by rocking free the back wheels when one side was jacked up".

As soon as Benjafield got round to the pits again he stopped and it was found that one of the gears had broken up and, falling into the box, had caused havoc, so that only top gear now worked. A quick calculation showed that the car only had to do another four laps to qualify for the Rudge Cup next year so, once more blessing the Meadows' vast torque, he set off to run off the remainder of the race in top gear only.

At 1pm the leading Aston Martin moved up into third place overall, as well as leading the Coupe Bienniale and in due course the Delahaye and von der Becke's Riley passed the ailing Lagonda, which was eventually to finish well down but did get the sought-after qualification.

By three o'clock, with an hour to go, the whole Fox & Nicholl pit – which by then appears to have contained the firm's entire staff plus a sizeable chunk of the English population, was a mass of crossed fingers. Heldé and Stoffel seemed to have cured their water leak and the two cars were closely matched again, but with the Alfa two laps down. Then consternation when Fontes, who had

Le Mans 1935, with Fontes in number 4 rounding Mulsanne during one of the dry periods.

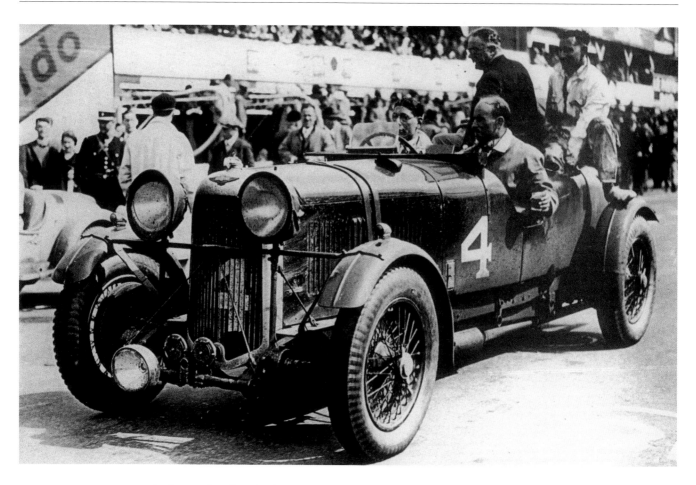

At the finish of the 1935 Le Mans: Fontes driving Hindmarsh, with Arthur Fox sitting on the tail. The foglamp glass is smashed and the offside front wing crumpled as a result of the accident during the night.

the last spell at the wheel, came in for an unscheduled stop to report that the oil pressure was wavering under braking. It took three minutes to discover a serious oil leak and to realise that they could not refill without being disqualified. Fox told Fontes to continue, but to accelerate very gently. The next lap he was back, more worried than ever, but Fox could only repeat his instructions. As Fontes trickled away from the pits, Stoffel brought the Alfa in to hand over to Heldé for the last spell. He was told that the Lagonda was clearly in trouble and set off like a bat out of hell to regain the two laps. Fontes wasn't going to give in without a struggle and with only about 20 minutes of the race left, Heldé got past Fontes to be only one lap in arrears.

At this point the loudspeakers produced the staggering statement that the lap scoreboard had been wrong for hours and the Alfa was now actually leading. This wasn't what Fox's charts, kept by Randall Bell, said, nor Alfa's either, come to that, but while the former protested vigorously and immediately, the Alfa team accepted it gleefully and told their driver to ease off lest he broke the

car in his enthusiasm. Fox's protest bore fruit, backed by Bell's charts which had recorded all the closer rivals as well as the Lagondas, and with only about five minutes to go the loudspeakers casually remarked that the previous announcement had been in error and the Lagonda still led after all. It was too late to tell Heldé and the race ran out with Fontes in the lead by 8.5km. It will be argued forever more whether the Alfa could have caught the Lagonda if Heldé's pit hadn't slowed him, and the incident does show how important it was (and is) to keep your own charts. The odd thing was that at about two o'clock the Alfa pit had asked Bell how many laps the Lagonda had done, and Fox was able to tell them the correct relative positions of both cars.

The winners had covered 3006.797km, which I make 1868.74 miles, an average speed of 77.86mph and faster than the previous year, although slower than 1931 and 1933. There was no comparison with the weather, though, for the previous three races had all been run in the dry and 1935 was very wet indeed. Of the 58 starters, 28 finished and of these 22 were British, the

Martin/Brackenbury Aston Martin coming third overall and winning the Rudge Cup at an average of 75.22mph. Fourth was the von der Becke/Richardson Riley. All the ladies of the MG team qualified for 1936 and the winning Lagonda also came seventh in the 1934/5 Biennial Cup as well as 13th on Index of Performance. Naturally, it won the 4-litre class as well. The second Lagonda finished after covering 2649.918km (1696.94 miles), an average of 68.61mph, to come 13th in the 13th Le Mans race. From noon to 4pm, while running in top gear only, its lap speed dropped by 31mph. Fox's principal prize was the eighth Coupe Annuelle, the Coupe de la Revue des Usagers de la Route, presented by a magazine for road users and now one of the Lagonda Club's sacred relics.

The finishing area was soon packed with delighted British spectators as the two muddy red Lagondas were lined up for photographs and the prize presentation. Arthur Fox and his team had been sure all along that the M45 was a possible winner but few people had shared their confidence. An hour's battle with the Bentley in Ulster was one thing, 24 hours at Le Mans quite another, but Fox had amply proved his point. *The Evening News* the following day described the win as being like a motor racing novel come true. It was too. The stock plot of such a novel has always been the last-minute winning of the big race by the car of a make in a bad way financially and thought to have little chance. The romantic story verged on the absurd when the real-life winning car was found to have scarcely a pint of Rimer's oil in its sump when inspected after the race. Notwithstanding this, Fontes had been lapping at 75mph at the end, aiming to avoid overmuch acceleration by not slowing for any but the sharpest corners. Apocryphal accounts that he was just touring after the discovery of the oil leak are disproved by Fox's lap times. Within hours the congratulatory telegrams began to pour in, including one from the Receiver and one from the Minister of Transport, Leslie Hore-

The usual mêlée at the finish. Wilcockson, Fontes, Hindmarsh and Fox are standing by their surrounded car. The man in the foreground is operating some mysterious apparatus mounted on two tripods, possibly an early sound recorder.

Tolworth, 1935. The two Le Mans cars, still with the scars of the race, on show at Fox & Nicholl. This firm was a very successful racing business, as shown by the big showcase of trophies between the cars.

Belisha, who cannot have been the ogre popular opinion made him out to be. A present day minister, if he took any notice at all of a British victory, would prate only about safety belts or the like.

Monday's papers were in no doubt that it was an overwhelming victory and every one carried a considerable story, lightened by the howlers that the dailies could be relied on to produce when talking about motor racing. *The Times* said that the Lagondas were "more lightly built than their Italian and French rivals" when even a Fox & Nicholl 4½ Litre scaled the thick end of two tons. They also produced an amazing variety of winning distances and speeds. The author has recorded 10 different ones as they grappled with unfamiliar kilometres. The irony of the fact that the tenders for the purchase of the company were due in on the same day was not lost on the journalists.

It should be added here that the above account of the race above was compiled from four eyewitness versions which differ on many vital points as well as in details. Fotheringham's crash, for example, is reported to have happened at various different times from 9pm on Saturday to the small hours of Sunday morning, while both Hindmarsh and Fontes are alleged to have been driving at the time and did or didn't hit the wreck. However it was, the car was undoubtedly damaged and can be

seen to be so in the photographs taken at the finish, with the foglamp smashed and the front wing mangled.

For some reason, perhaps because it was so unexpected, the legend has grown that the Lagonda victory at Le Mans was due more to luck than anything else. In their 50th-anniversary history of Le Mans even *The Autocar*, who ought to know better, said "the Alfas were miles ahead when they retired", which is manifestly untrue - the 1935 event was a classic case of an endurance race where the Lagonda, which had no mechanical trouble of any kind until right at the end, lapped at an absolutely consistent speed while the opposition tended to proceed in bursts of high speed, punctuated by lengthy spells in the pits to rebuild the cars. Tortoises and hares spring to mind. The following hourly averages bring out this point:

Time	Average speed
5 pm	75.42
6pm	81.23
7pm	81.38
12pm	78.94
4am	78.21
8am	78.87
11am	78.75
4pm	77.86

What's more, the Alfas and Bugattis were highly strung "racers", all light alloy and overhead camshafts, in chassis designed for racing, whereas the Meadows engine was equally happy propelling cabin cruisers and light tanks and was a 10 year old design anyway, mounted in a very large chassis suitable for limousines. Thus the achievement of Hindmarsh and Fontes in successfully resisting all attacks by their half-dozen serious rivals, and setting such a pace that they all either fell behind or blew up, must rank with any of the wins in Le Mans history.

The galling thing was that no commercial advantage could be taken of it. No cars were being made and the skeleton staff were really only caretakers until the sale of the company was complete, so the rush of orders that should have followed such a win never happened. We will describe the restructuring of the company into LG Motors in a later chapter and now pursue the racing history of the Fox & Nicholl M45s. (Although they bear most of the Rapide characteristics, the cars are stamped as M45s and were regarded as such at Staines.)

BPK 201, Lewis's car in Ulster, had not appeared at Le Mans, but re-appeared for the 1935 TT, replacing BPK 203 which had been sold to Dr Benjafield. Naturally Fox had signed up Hindmarsh and Fontes to drive in Ulster in September, but in the interval between the races Fontes had lost his licence after killing a man in a road accident. Fox replaced him with Charlie Dodson. The new management at Staines were keen to keep the successful Fox & Nicholl connection going, since it generated useful publicity while new models were being prepared. It had probably helped Fox to buy BPK 201, which had rather languished throughout the year since the 1934 TT.

The factory testbed facilities were opened to Fox and fortunately the results have survived from his August 1935 tests. He had devised a new air inlet

Ulster, 1935. The Fox & Nicholl cars in practice, showing the revised, free-flowing exhaust system fitted for this race. Wilcockson is attending to car number 1.

pipe system that coupled the carburettors together, along with a new, freer-flowing exhaust system that came out of the side of the bonnet at cylinder head level and extended along the nearside of the car at that level. The first test performed by Charlie Gray was with the engine as received. This was M45/270, out of BPK 201, and clearly Fox had already been at it, since it now had a compression ratio of 7.75:1 and gave 135.75bhp at 3600rpm, 13.75bhp more than it had in 1934. He then tried reducing the tappet clearance from 0.008in. to 0.005in. This produced 4 to 6bhp more at all engine speeds except 3600rpm, where, oddly, it had no effect at all.

They then rigged up the Fox air-coupling pipe. This was beneficial right up the speed range and for the first time the power output at 3800rpm was higher than at 3600. Previously, the power had always dropped off a little after 3600. The new air inlet gave improvements to 139.5bhp at 3600rpm and 140.75bhp at 3800rpm. The second test was then repeated to see if the engine was freeing off. It was, to the extent of about 1bhp at each speed. Arthur Fox then produced another cylinder head, which was fitted, along with the air-coupler and the new exhaust system. This was a disappointment as it was actually less powerful at the lower engine speeds and only equal at 3800rpm. Brief tests on each magneto showed that the engine lost 5-8bhp when running on one set of sparks only. At this point supplies of Fox's secret fuel brew ran out and a 50/50 mixture of Esso Ethyl and benzole was substituted. For the eighth test the test shop exhaust system was tried and resulted in a 4-6bhp drop, showing that Fox's tubular system was well worth while. Finally the Vertex magneto was advanced 3 degrees with no perceptible result.

Apparently satisfied, Fox passed the engine as OK and it was returned to Tolworth for installation in the car. Standard SU HV5 carburettors had been used throughout, but fitted with WO needles, a great deal richer at full throttle than the standard KT ones. The camshaft was standard Meadows, but timed to open the inlet valves 9/16in BTDC, measured on the clutch cover plate. Both magnetos finished up timed at 7 degrees BTDC, plus 30 degrees automatic advance. So we see that Fox's very special racing engine with one-off inlet arrangements and six-pipe exhaust could just reach the power output claimed by the factory for the standard production Rapide.

Arthur Fox kept prying eyes off his air-coupling

pipe and to this day no one knows how it worked. It must have been quite large as an enormous cigar-shaped bulge was formed in the offside bonnet side panel to accommodate it. While this looked like a modern air-collecting box, there was no hole at the forward end to collect ram effect at speed. Both side panels were new, since on the nearside the new exhaust needed a slot to be cut nearly half the length of the panel, about four inches down from the hinge. From the photograph of the cars taken at scrutineering this was done first on 202, whose slot is roughly cut and ill-fitting, whereas the slot on 201 is neat and tidy. The new side panels were evidently produced by Fox & Nicholl as the ventilation louvres are punched outwards, in contrast to the normal Lagonda inward-punched louvres. In addition, a further row of smaller louvres was provided on each side of the bonnet top panel on each car. The new exhaust system was joined to a Brooklands silencer by a flexible section and, with Tim Birkin's fatal burn in everyone's mind, a little shield was provided for the passenger's left arm.

BPK 201 had acquired lamps at some point in its life, not fitted for the 1934 race, and the brackets were still on the car, although neither car carried lamps in Ulster. The supporting bracketry is seen to be a "Mark 2" version less obstructive to access than that used at Le Mans. BPK 202 still carried its extra crew ventilators, but these were not fitted to 201 as September in Belfast was less likely to fry the driver than June at Le Mans.

The Lagondas had the largest engines of the entry for the 1935 TT so, as in the previous year, they carried race numbers 1 and 2: number 1 on BPK 202 for Johnnie Hindmarsh, and number 2 on BPK 201 for Charlie Dodson. With last year's winning driver (Dodson) and the Le Mans winner both driving cars significantly more powerful than in 1934, there was no doubt that the Lagondas were the favourites for the race – except that it was a handicap and Eddie Hall was entered again, also in an updated version of last year's car, so a renewal of the Lagonda/Bentley duel was anticipated. Not that they were going to have it all their own way, for Brian Lewis and Lord Howe had entered unblown 3.3 Bugattis, with a local driver, Philip Dwyer, making up a team. In addition, there were four Rileys - for Freddy Dixon, Cyril Paul, Eddie McClure and A W K von der Becke - plus two teams of Aston Martins, a team of MG Magnettes and Tim Rose-Richards on a Railton. No less than nine manufacturers' teams would be competing for the SMMT Trophy.

The handicaps were published in August and the scratch group, containing the Bentley, the Lagondas, the Bugattis and the Railton, were set to average 79.06mph, just over 1mph faster than Hall's average in 1934. In the same way the 1.5-litre group were also required to go about 1mph faster, at 75.42mph. A third Lagonda, a blue Rapier, was entered by R Davies Millar, who had kept his engine at 1104cc and thus was the sole occupant of the 1200cc class. Since this guaranteed him a class win, provided he finished, the 1200cc class was abandoned and the Rapier had to compete in the 1500cc class. There was a scare when Hindmarsh went down with appendicitis, but he was confident he would be fit enough by September.

Practice produced no surprises and Lewis in the Bugatti turned in the fastest lap at 79.57mph, closely followed by Hindmarsh at 78.68mph and Dodson, learning to drive the heavy Lagonda, at 77.32mph. The weather was much better than the previous year. The complete absence of 750cc cars meant the organisation of the starting groups was altered so that the 1000cc cars started last, but with a credit lap, and the heavy metal next to last but without a credit lap. Alan Good, Lagonda's new owner, had offered the team a bonus for every lap in which they led the Bentley (up to a maximum of 15), so it is no surprise that they both outsprinted their rival at the 11am start. The Railton didn't start and the Rapier went out on lap seven with a broken oil pipe.

The outright lap record for the circuit was held by Birkin's blown Alfa Romeo at 83.20mph, set in 1932. This came under attack early on and Hindmarsh put in his ninth lap at 82.37mph. It became

Old racing cars make fast and exciting daily transport. This is the Le Mans winner competing in the 1937 London to Lands End Trial, driven by Christian Dietrichsen, who bought the car from Fox & Nicholl. He was not a finisher in the trial.

No peace for old racers. The late Denis Jenkinson in BPK 203 at a VSCC race meeting in the 1980s, when the car was owned by Mrs Robbie Hewitt.

clear, though, by noon, when the handicap positions were published, that Freddy Dixon's Riley was running away from everyone, the "works" Rileys included. Howe and Lewis were second and third and Hindmarsh fourth, 34 seconds "down" on Dixon. Dodson was 3 seconds behind Hindmarsh and Hall 9 seconds further back. As a complete reversal of the 1934 tactics, Fox was planning two stops for tyres and fuel, but Hall, perhaps sore at losing time at pit stops before, this year planned only one.

Hindmarsh's all-out driving got him past the Bugattis in the second hour and at 1pm he was in the lead by 17sec from Dixon, with Hall at 30sec and Dodson at 45sec. He then came in for his first stop, followed by Dodson on lap 12. The latter, irritated by a 130-second stop, drove off before the jack was removed, slowed down when the clatter made him think something had fallen off the car, then grinned when he realised what had happened and rushed off to make up the time. At 1.30 the first of what was to be a dismal series of Singer crashes occurred, caused by faulty steering arms, and Lewis set a faster lap than Hindmarsh's best, at 82.51mph. The Lagondas' stops had dropped them

down the field and at 2 o'clock Dixon was back in the lead with Hall at 28sec and Cyril Paul's Riley third. Hindmarsh was fourth, 3min 33sec behind but coming up fast. Hall had his one stop, which took 2min 12sec to Dixon's 1min 32sec, so Dixon gained 40 seconds for no effort.

By 3 o'clock, as the Lagondas drew near their second stop, Hindmarsh was again in second place to Dixon by 1min 19sec, with Hall third and Dodson fourth. Hall then passed the Lagonda while it was in the pits. At 4 o'clock the order was still Dixon, Hall, Hindmarsh when the hitherto trouble-free Lagonda ran into fuel feed problems, possibly a broken pipe, and was forced into a longish stop to rectify it. This allowed Lord Howe up into third, followed by the Aston Martins of Brackenbury and Penn-Hughes, with Dodson sixth. His fuel problem cured, Hindmarsh set off quicker than before and caught and passed Dodson, but worn brakes were hampering his speed and the race ran out just after 5pm with Dixon a clear winner at 76.90mph, just over a minute ahead of Hall, who had averaged 80.36mph (it was a handicap, remember). Hindmarsh came seventh at 78.87mph and Dodson eighth at 78.86mph. The race had been nowhere near as exciting as in 1934 and the Lagonda's appetite for tyres had been its undoing. Hindmarsh had led briefly, which he had not done the year before, and the long stop with fuel feed problems was the only mechanical derangement 202 ever suffered in a distinguished racing career, apart from other people's accidents. The Lewis Bugatti had gone out with clutch slip, but Lord Howe had made a late run up the field to finish third, having been sixth at 4 o'clock. There had been some excitements: McFerran in a Bugatti had hit the Town Hall a glancing blow at Newtownards, and Charlie Dodson had hit the bank at Glen Hill and dislodged a rock that shot the car sideways, but he had not been slowed by this. Of course, Freddy Dixon's driving had kept the spectators awake.

Lagonda, having booked advertising space in anticipation of something wonderful to say, were at a bit of a loss, but hit on the statement that both cars had made the fastest lap times ever recorded in the race by a British car and had finished in perfect order. Back at Tolworth the special Fox inlet and exhaust systems were removed and the cars were put up for sale, since the new Lagonda management had promised new cars for 1936. Both were advertised in October's *Motor Sport* "Reconditioned for ordinary touring". Christian Dietrichsen bought

202 for £600 and Frederick Benz acquired 201. Dietrichsen used his car for the Lands End Trial and covered 20,000 miles a year in it as it was perfectly tractable for road use; he even took part in a kind of motorised ice hockey on a frozen lake in Switzerland. He then bought 201, but found it rougher and slower than 202.

All three 1934 team cars survive: BPK 201 in California, 202 in a Dutch motor museum and 203 in New Zealand. In 1985, before they became so scattered and to celebrate the 50th anniversary of the Le Mans win, the Lagonda Club organised a reunion of all three at The Ship public house opposite the site of the Lagonda works (by then occupied by Petters). From there we progressed to the site of the Fox & Nicholl garage at Tolworth, now virtually cut off by an underpass on the A3. The event led to the exposure of acres of film and miles of videotape and was masterminded by the late Denis Jenkinson. As well as the three genuine cars there are today countless replicas, as Fox's simple body lines and the absence of complications like doors encourages "restorers" to cut up scruffy saloons, even nice saloons, and make cars for boy racers to pose in. The 10ft 3in 3½ Litre chassis is particularly vulnerable to this as it already has the Girling brakes and the correct axles.

"Jenks" and the Lagonda Club organised a reunion of the 1934/5 Team Cars in 1985 to celebrate the 50th anniversary of the Le Mans victory. Here the cars are seen on the forecourt of The Ship inn, opposite the old factory. From there they proceeded in convoy to Tolworth, where the old Fox & Nicholl premises still partly exist. The cars are now widely separated: one in the USA, one in The Netherlands and the third in New Zealand.

Chapter Four

The M45 Rapide

The M45 Rapide chassis, drawn in the autumn of 1934. The artist has correctly shown the new oil filler in the centre of the rocker cover, but has retained the old filler as well.

Lagonda's model range had become so complicated by the autumn of 1934 that the announcements in the motoring press ran to three pages of text covering the 13 models, plus nine pages of adverts from the dealers, including a triumphant one from Warwick Wright, now London and Home Counties Distributor, possibly as a thank you from Lagonda for the publicity following the TT. At the Olympia Motor Show in October two new models were introduced and one old one dropped. The Rapier was now in full production, chassis only of course, and from time to time the unsold ones tended to clutter the place up, being parked in all sorts of crannies. The bare chassis were ferried to Abbott's in Farnham by a team of drivers, each of whom had an ingenious little kit which held the canvas "wings" and nominal lights to make the chassis road-legal for the journey down and folded back into the wings for the return trip. Only very minor changes were proposed for 1935 for the Rapier. The M45 tourer body was altered from having one big door on the nearside and a small door at the rear on the offside (the T7) to two big front doors and no rear one (the T8). The pillarless saloon M45 was unchanged although semaphore indicators became an option.

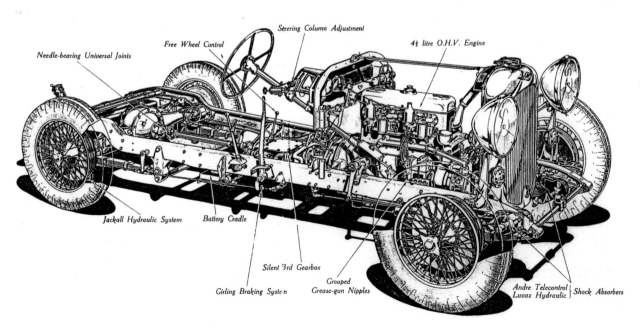

Needle-bearing Universal Joints

Free Wheel Control

Steering Column Adjustment

4½ litre O.H.V. Engine

Jackall Hydraulic System

Battery Cradle

Girling Braking System

Silent 3rd Gearbox

Grouped Grease-gun Nipples

Andre Telecontrol Luvax Hydraulic | Shock Absorbers

The M45 Rapide was new. It featured the 10ft3 in (3124mm) wheelbase chassis which had been on the Fox & Nicholl racing cars. This was a new design, since all the old converted 3 Litre chassis frames had been used up. This new one was designed from the outset to take the Meadows engine and gearbox, so the various makeshifts that had been needed with the original M45 frames were designed out and some judicious reshuffling of components enabled almost exactly the same amount of passenger space to be found, despite the six-inch shorter frame. In effect, the engine was further forward, as was the radiator, which was able to move into the space formerly occupied by the front brake perrot shafts. The elaborate free-standing "goalpost" framework which had hitherto supported the headlamps and front wings was replaced by aerofoil section alloy uprights cross-braced to the radiator and wings. All this reduced the wasted space at the front of the car. The M45's vacuum servo braking system was replaced by the new Girling rods-in-tension system, also found on the Fox & Nicholl cars, and although the M45 axles needed little change, extra stiffening ribs were added to keep the brake backplates perpendicular to the axles since the Girling system rods pulled transversely when applied and could distort the backplate under heavy braking. Just to be on the safe side, the halfshafts, crown wheels and pinions were all made stronger. These modifications added ¼in (6.3mm) to the track.

On the 3 Litre ZM chassis the earlier system of grouped grease nipples had been replaced with Silentbloc rubber bushes in some places and direct greasers in others. There had not been time to offer anything else when designing the M45, but for this new model, more upmarket and reflecting the increasing tendency for owners to resist grovel-

1935 M45 Rapide tourer, Car Number Z11213, owned by Peter Biggs.

M45 Rapide engine compartment. The owner has added the drip tray under the front carburettor to stop petrol dripping on to the magneto. A permanent solution to this was to move the sparks to the exhaust side, done by the factory with the Sanction 2 LG45 engine. On the Rapide the central boss on the inlet manifold was not needed for the brake servo offtake, but this car has a mysterious pipe fitted to it, possibly a reversion to the Ki-gass starting system for some reason, or possibly a vacuum gauge.

ling before their cars, the grouped nipples reappeared, connected by little copper pipes to the various chassis points that required lubrication. That made a second set of little copper pipes trailing round the chassis, for the Telecontrol damper system was retained. Then a third set appeared when the newly introduced Smith's Jackall system was added, which involved a built-in jack for each wheel, all connected to a master cylinder under the floor by the front passenger and operated by a detachable handle. As well as the Telecontrols, the Hartford dampers of the M45 were replaced by Luvax hydraulic lever arm ones.

One chassis change not greeted enthusiastically by everyone was the fitment of a freewheel, bolted to the back of the gearbox and controlled by a lever that looked exactly like a gearlever, causing the uninitiated to think the car had only two gears. The advantages of clutchless gearchanges were offset by lack of engine braking and not every owner agreed to have a freewheel fitted. Most have been removed since.

Many of the engine changes between the standard M45 and the Rapide have already been referred to when describing Fox & Nicholl's tuning of their cars. The new compression ratio was 6.98:1, although usually quoted as 7:1, and the stronger connecting rods ran on larger diameter crankshaft journals. Advantage was taken of the

stronger crankcase material to add another stud at the front. Fox's beloved Scintilla magneto became standardised on the inlet side and the primitive wire-gauze oil filter was supplemented by a Tecalemit full-flow one with a felt element. One of the problems with the Meadows engine had been that the oil filler was in direct line with the timing chain, and when the spring that held the oil filler lid closed weakened with age the offside of the engine began to get an oil bath. For the Rapide a modified rocker cover was devised with a filler cap in its centre, while the original oil filler was replaced with an aluminium tower-like device which held the fan base and also served as a crankcase breather. The drawings published in *The Motor* showed both fillers for good measure. The new rocker cover also had "Lagonda Rapide" cut into it instead of just the make.

Alfie Cranmer had originally wanted to build all the Meadows engines at Staines, but had been talked into letting Henry Meadows build them under the eye of a Lagonda inspector. However, with the increasing number of special Lagonda parts going in, the engines now began to arrive only part completed and the non-standard bits were added on site. Once complete, the assembled engine was run for four hours on the water brake and then tested for output. The foreman of the fitting shop then had to verify the output before

The Rapide pioneered the idea of placing the oil filler on the rocker cover thus solving the earlier engines' problems with oil spray from their low filler.

Instruction manual photograph of the Rapide engine. Note that a full-flow oil filter by Tecalemit has been added to supplement Meadows's rather primitive mesh filter.

accepting the engine. Once he had, it was stripped, inspected and re-assembled. There was then a re-test before the engine transferred to the finishing shop for installation. The power output was claimed to be 135bhp at 4000rpm, but this figure is pure fiction. The Rapide engine was undeniably more powerful than the M45's, since it propelled a heavier car faster, but the extra power probably only amounted to about 10bhp. You will recall that Fox's very special engines gave only

REV: COUNTER DRIVE

BREATHER

TAPPET COVERS

PUMP GLAND ADJUSTING SCREW

WATER PUMP GREASERS

OIL LEVEL DIPSTICK

WATER DRAIN TAP

CLUTCH WITHDRAWAL MULTIPLYING LINKAGE

OIL FILTER (PRESSURE)

MAGNETO VERNIER COUPLING

122bhp on the brake and the 1935 Monte Carlo Rally engine only 105, in both cases following much modification. About 102bhp for the unmodified engine would be the author's guess. Twin fuel pumps were standard on the Rapide as practically every M45 customer was specifying them.

The optional higher-ratio rear axle of the M45, 3.31:1, became standard on the Rapide and gave overall ratios of 10.3, 6.6, 4.2 and of course 3.31:1. Other chassis changes were minor, including higher-geared steering, a curved drag link to allow a better steering lock to the right, springs that were flat under static load, cadmium-plated brake drums and springs, the latter ungaitered since the plating was held to be rust-resistant.

At the outset only one body was to be offered on the Rapide, a tourer, designated T9. This was clearly a development of the earlier tourers, but featured Lagonda's first wheel arches to give extra elbow room for the rear seats. Hitherto, the bodies had fitted between the wheels with attached wings. Now the bodywork overlapped the wheels by about half the wheel width. The cutouts in the front doors were reduced to just token dips, as most of the doors were occupied by the sidescreens when not erected. In turn, this freed up space in the rear compartment and allowed the hood, when furled, to fold right down inside a double-skinned well and be covered by a hood bag which hid all the fabric. Several versions of the rear lamp mounting were devised, all omitting the Buick-style stalks, and eventually a combined lamp and number plate assembly was flush fitted at the foot of the tail panel, with internally illuminated numbers covered by a glass plate. Semaphore indicators were standard, mounted on either side of the scuttle. Probably the major recognition point was a new radiator, much the same as the M45's but wider at the top than at the bottom and fitted with a "streamlined" radiator filler, pear shaped in plan and swivelling sideways rather than opening vertically.

Inside the body, the dashboard was modified slightly from the M45's to fit instruments which were internally illuminated, instead of the external pull-out lamps used earlier. The ammeter and oil pressure gauges were combined into one instrument and the fuel and water gauges into another. With that done, the pull-out lamps were for some reason still fitted. The little central trapezoidal metal panel was turned upside down so that the lighting and ignition switches came to the bottom, where they would be more easily accessible in a hurry. This change meant that little grooves had to be formed in the main panel to allow their tails full

The T9 tourer body by Lagonda on Peter Biggs's car was the firm's first to feature wheelarches. All previous tourer bodies fitted between the wheels and did not overhang them.

travel. It is believed that the reason for these changes was the possibility, with the earlier layout, for the driver accidentally to press the starter button when groping for the lighting switch in the dark. The new control for the indicators came to live at twelve o'clock on the steering wheel boss, reducing the horn push to a small rectangle lower down.

The windscreen on this body was designed to fold flat, in contrast to the earlier practice with top hinges and stays. To enable this to happen the messy Klaxon wiper motor was repositioned inside the screen and was in due course replaced by a tidier design. A pair of aeroscreens were attached to the sides of the windscreen to act as wind deflectors when it was erected, and could be detached and used on their own when the screen was flat. The headlamps were Lucas P100s of course, but there was no room for the passlamp on the shortened front end of the Rapide, so it was abandoned and the "dip and switch" system installed, which allowed either one or both head-lamps to stay on in the dipped position, to the driver's choice.

It was clear that the Rapide was meant to be the flagship of the Lagonda fleet. It was more powerful than the M45, better equipped and more modern looking. The eager buyer found the sting in the tail, though, when he got to the bottom of the page, for the prices were well up on the M45 at £825 for the chassis (£150 more) and £1000 for the tourer (£175 up). This was an awfully big jump for the modest improvements offered, and the author feels it was really an admission that the M45 was underpriced, and that the time was wrong for a price increase. Also, the Rapide was now a direct competitor to the 3½ litre Bentley in everything but refinement and possibly handling. It was faster on top speed as well as more accelerative, just as well equipped and still a great deal cheaper. The Rapide buyer was spared the business of negotiating with a separate coachbuilder and the tedium of running the car in, since a proportion of the enhanced price went towards the firm's expenses in running the initial miles before delivery.

Lagonda at this point were getting very hard up, which showed in various little ways: sudden changes in fittings when supplies dried up and were not replaced until bills had been paid, and parts bought in when this proved cheaper than manufacture in-house. Another aspect of penury

The fold-flat windscreen is one of the distinguishing features of the Rapide tourer. The standard M45 tourer windscreen was top-hinged.

was a search for gaps in the market. The 3 Litre had been selling steadily, but slowly, since its introduction in 1928. It had acquired the T7 body and was now outwardly almost indistinguishable from the M45 in tourer form, although the saloons still had the earlier ST24 body. With the advent of the shorter wheelbase Rapide, a simplified version of it was utilised to make a new model, the 3½ Litre, which used a reworked version of the 75mm 3 Litre engine bored out to 80mm, bringing the capacity to 3619cc. For once, Lagonda quoted a power output of 88bhp at 3000rpm. Although the 3 Litre and 3½ Litre engines look alike, certain key dimensions are different enough to suggest that the block castings changed between the two models.

The Rapide chassis was stripped of its trimmings for this cheaper model: no Telecontrols, no built-in jacks and so on. Lagonda's own gearbox was used, mounted in a cradle-like subframe. Some of the crossmembers had to differ, but the body was a T9, just like the Rapide's and only different in details, like the radiator. The price was exactly the same as the earlier model, but the hated horsepower tax had just been reduced, so that the 3½, taxed as a 24hp, would from 1 January 1935 pay less than the 3 Litre, a 21hp, had previously. Unlike the Rapide, a saloon version was available from the outset. It was coded as ST44, and although a family resemblance to the ST34 was there the new body was noticeably more rounded. It was later to father a derivative, the ST54 , for the Rapide. On both these bodies a solution was found for the vexing problem of how to reconcile a raked hinge line with the pillarless construction, which necessitated trailing front doors. At this time most saloons had rear-hinged front doors and the shut edge could easily be a continuation of the windscreen line, making for doors much wider at the bottom than the top and hence easing access to the front seats. With trailing front doors, the earlier pillarless saloons had been forced to have near-vertical windscreens and a rather incongruous line on the elevation. The Lagonda bodyshop's answer to the problem was to reduce the number of hinges to two and to outrig the upper one so that it formed part of the waist moulding ahead of the windscreen when shut, thus preserving a vertical hinge line well in front of the screen. Shortening the fixed part of the scuttle and introducing a double curvature to the body sides so that the roof was no longer the widest part of the body all combined to modernise the appearance.

This is perhaps a suitable moment to remark on the process by which new body designs were arrived at in the Lagonda factory. Somewhere in late summer the first tentative designs by Mr Buckingham and his staff would be drawn as 1/12th scale profiles and these would be shown to the board in the person of Alf Cranmer, the Technical Director. If approved, the profile would be enlarged to full size with cross-sections established at 10in intervals and superimposed on each other. From this drawing a dummy body would be made up in plywood cross-sections and aluminium panels, hand-shaped by eye in the bodyshop, and this dummy shown to the management. Quite likely some changes would be called for, then that was it. A second proper body would be got ready for the Motor Show, usually in a frantic last-minute rush, with final modifications added on the lorry going to Olympia and on the stand after it got there. The panel beaters entrusted with this Show body were extremely proud of their skill and could boast - correctly - that when they shaped a panel it was truer to the line than the original drawing. They could demonstrate it, too, on occasions when the timber members, cut to the drawing, could be seen to not quite touch the panels, which were showing correct light lines and were therefore what the overall design required. It is not surprising that each succeeding body design, particularly the saloons, bears a clear family resemblance to its predecessor. The change from the ST34 to ST44 and ST54 is one of the more pronounced ones, but the line of descent is still obvious, and the drooping waistline to the rear that came in with these bodies survived and was indeed accentuated in the later LG series of bodies.

The catalogue that illustrated the 1935 range showed evidence of money shortage and was not printed in colour, confining itself to black and white with "Lagonda" in green on every page and printed on markedly inferior paper. Conforming to tradition, the illustrations relied heavily on the retoucher and one can deduce that a Rapide tourer had been built, but a 3½ Litre hadn't, since a Rapide photograph illustrated both, albeit from different angles. The 3½ saloon was illustrated by a profile drawing, doctored to show a false perspective, while the 3½ chassis photograph is of a Rapide with the top of the smaller engine drawn in but retaining the Meadows sump and showing a crossmember the 3½ did not have. The only indication of a saloon Rapide was a line drawing of a two-door body by Gurney Nutting. Even the catalogue compiler did not seem to know where the factory

was, since in inviting prospective customers to tour the works he said it was on the main Bath Road, at the southern end of Staines Bridge. Most people thought the A30 led to Exeter.

Lagonda had Stand 143 at Olympia, and with such a battery of models there must have been quite a wrangle about which to leave out. Naturally the new models predominated - there were two Rapides, a tourer and that Gurney Nutting, a brace of 3½s, an M45 pillarless saloon, a 16/80 tourer and a Rapier chassis. It was as well Lagonda had booked one of the larger stands, dominated by a large replica of the winged radiator badge on a pillar, from the tips of which were suspended two rather incongruous lamp fittings, rather as if the stylised bird was in fact a flying boat. To avoid wear and tear, all the bonnets had their side panels removed so that the engines were visible but the eye-catching looks were not spoiled by open bonnets. As well as Lagonda's own stand the place was crawling with Lagondas on coachbuilders' stands. Abbott's, as the official Rapier body builders, had nothing else, but one of their offerings was a road-equipped version of the Fox & Nicholl team cars on a Rapide chassis, though fitted with flowing wings and nominal doors. John

Charles had a close-coupled M45 saloon, built to Silent Travel principles but not pillarless. On this car the mid-1930s cliché of a letterbox-like windscreen was taken to extremes in the interests of presenting a continuous, smoothly curved profile from scuttle to tail light. Maltby's and Eagle (E J Newns) were full of Rapiers and Gurney Nutting, in addition to the Rapide saloon on the Lagonda stand, had an outlandish "Airflow" saloon on the Rapide chassis. This was so streamlined that the rear passengers would have had to be dwarfs had not the designer inserted a small gable in the rear roof with two tiny windows in it. The view through these must have resembled that through a reversed telescope, but at least it enabled two rear passengers to sit roughly upright. It has to be admitted that a body very similar had appeared on the still-born 1933 Pierce-Arrow Silver Arrow. Offords of Kensington were showing two drophead Lagondas, a 3½ and a 4½, both made for them by Carlton and both featuring a three-position hood which stowed flat when folded. Lastly, Vanden Plas showed what they called an "enclosed Continental tourer" which was really a four-door drophead coupé.

Thus there were 12 Lagondas on the coachbuilders' stands to add to the seven on the maker's

Lagonda made a point of designing hoods that did not spoil the lines of the car when erected.

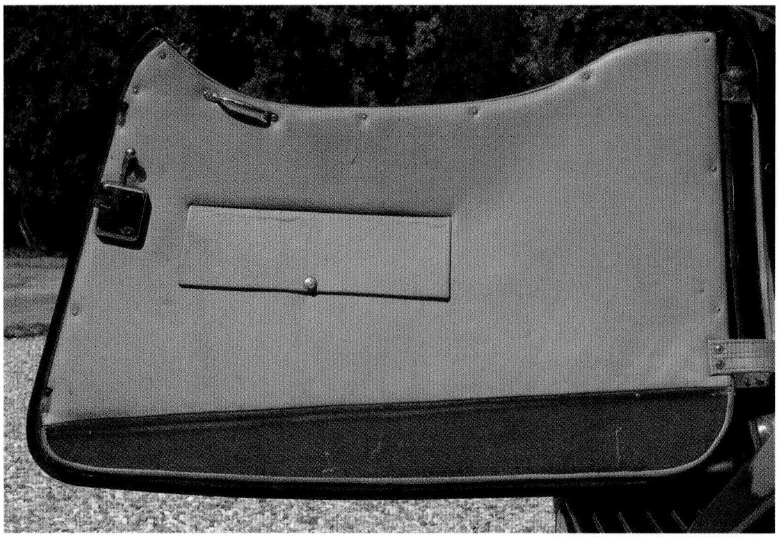

The T9 body features less pronounced cutouts on the door tops than were seen on the T7 body.

– the public was going to be hard put to it to avoid the things. Nevertheless there were mixed feelings at Staines, where a possibly buoyant market for new models had to exist side by side with hidden monetary crises. At Show time Frank King did an article for *Motor Trader* which really amounted to a cry for more agents. The firm operated a policy of only selling through their official distributors or direct from the factory, and the outside sales staff were at the disposal of the distributors. These outside sales staff involved practically any employee with a collar and tie, for both Bill Oates and Bert Hammond got conscripted into this work at times. In fact, Bill Oates became travelling troubleshooter and some of his remarks on surviving record cards are masterpieces of stiff upper lip. What do you say when you have been summoned from Surrey to Yorkshire to cure a 4½ Litre that won't start and all you discover is damp on the plugs? In his turn, Bert Hammond was once sent to demonstrate a Rapide to a prospective client in Malvern who was impressed by the car but insisted on having that one and no other. After a series of desperate 'phone calls to Staines, Bert returned by train with a cheque in his pocket, possibly his only experience of public transport.

The publicity set-up now became slightly confused. Woodwright continued to place advertisements but the firm also took on P G Tucker from Alexander Duckham to run publicity, leaving Frank King to hunt for sales. Woodwright's style became more insistent when they realised that the Rapide was the fastest unsupercharged standard production car made in Britain and they could say truthfully that it had been developed by racing experience. To drive this home a bit further, the next exploit was to select a standard Rapide tourer, BLA 903 (Z11212,) from the showroom and take it to Brooklands on the day before the winter shutdown to have a crack at putting 1000 miles into 12 hours. The car was actually Warwick Wright's demonstrator, and the attempt was under way within 36 hours of it first being mooted. The drivers chosen were Roland Hebeler from Fox & Nicholl and F J Stephenson from Lagonda. It was early November, so even with an eight o'clock start there were going to be four hours run in darkness. A V Ebblewhite was in charge if timekeeping.

Despite early rain the first hour was run at 91.69mph, the car being in full touring trim but with the screen flat. However, the rain got steadily heavier, and after the second hour the average had

A Gurney Nutting close-coupled saloon on the Rapide chassis. At least two of these were built. To give the rear passengers some headroom there is a sort of gable at the rear of the car with two tiny windows set in it. One hopes the three horizontal bonnet features are vents, otherwise things will get very hot under there.

dropped to 89.62mph as the puddles grew into lakes. The drivers soldiered on grimly, but by 3 o'clock it was beginning to get dark and there was a danger of falling behind the 83.3mph average needed to attain the target. Clearly the car would be slower in the dark, so after 561 miles the run was abandoned. They had completed 203 laps of which 164 had been at more than 90mph. To make sure nobody thought the attempt had been abandoned because the car had broken, it was arranged to keep it under lock and key at Brooklands overnight and then, on the following day, to hand it over to *The Autocar* for road test. Very creditable, except that something dreadful must then have happened, for the test was never published, and when the magazine finally drove a Rapide the following April it was a different car. The fastest lap during the attempt was 93.97mph, accomplished twice, and most of the motoring papers published a very dramatic picture of BLA up to her knees in water and leaving a wake that would not have disgraced a speedboat as she swished through the sizeable lake that had gathered near the Fork during the day.

The Scottish Motor Show was, as always, for dealers and Lagondas two Scottish distributors were there, Bass Rock Motor Co. from Edinburgh with an M45 saloon and a Rapier fixed-head, and Burton & Tweedy from Glasgow with that maroon Gurney Nutting Rapide from Olympia, a Rapide chassis and tourer, an M45 saloon, a 3½ saloon and no less than four Rapiers. It must have been a big stand.

The first road test of one of the new models came in *The Autocar* at the end of November. This was a 3½ Litre tourer which the testers regarded as a slower but cheaper Rapide; they certainly looked very similar. Analysing the results shows that the 3½ was little different in performance to the later 3 Litres, but the increasing luxury and hence weight had to be paid for in fuel consumption.

Just before Christmas the motoring magazines published their summaries of the year's road tests and here Lagonda really shone, with the 4½ litre collaring a lot of the bold print. To be specific, in *The Autocar*'s figures for British cars the M45 tourer

The 16-inch brake drums all but filled the wheels.

Twin Andre Hartford shock-absorbers are fitted each side at the front.

recorded the highest top speed (95.74mph), best acceleration 10-30mph and 30-50mph, best acceleration to 50mph and best figure for lb/cc. This latter figure was used in those days when manufacturers were shy about publishing power/weight ratios. It assumes all engines equally inefficient, of course, but it was some guide. The only 1934 cars which reached better than unity were the big Lagondas, the Bentley and the Siddeley Special. If we extend our view to American and Continental cars, only the V12 Hispano-Suiza had a higher top speed, but all the Americans could exceed unity for lb/cc, bearing out the editorial comment that all British cars were much too heavy.

The year 1934 had been one of Lagonda's best in sales terms, with about 200 M45s sold, along with approximately 250 Rapiers and some 50 3 Litres and 16/80s. A tentative toe had been dipped into an export market by exporting bare chassis to Tozer, Kemsley and Millbourn in Melbourne. Australian import regulations put stringent limits on the import of complete cars, but were less hard on chassis, presumably to encourage local bodyshops. The Metropolitan Police had bought APJ 367, which went to live at the Hendon police driving school, and after borrowing an M45 saloon for evaluation they had bought four special ones fitted with the earlier ST24 body, which had more legroom in the back. Non-standard requirements included a copper-covered floor to give a better earth for the radios, and reinforced running boards for heavyweight constables to ride on in an emergency. The "Mets" continued to buy a few Lagondas each year up to 1939.

It was by now axiomatic that a new numbering system would be started for the Rapide and the 3½. Both new models continued in the ongoing "car number" series, by now over 11000, and given the Z prefix, but Rapide engines were distinguished by an "R" suffix and started a new series at 100, stamped either M45R/xxx or sometimes just 45R/xxx. The 3½ started out being stamped 3.5, but soon turned to the thoroughly illogical M35R. Illogical because whether the M stood for Meadows or Maybach, the 3½ had neither, nor was it a Rapide.

There has been speculation where the name "Rapide" came from, particularly since de Havilland introduced their DH89 Dragon Rapide also in 1934. Research shows that the aeroplane was originally called the Dragon Six when first flown in early 1934 and that the Rapide name came later, around November, when Francis St Barbe of de Havilland's re-christened it. The French nationalised railway SNCF called their latest express trains Rapides, but so far the author has not found the date of introduction of these. This was probably the first use, however.

At the beginning of January 1935 the entry list for the Monte Carlo Rally showed 57 British entries out of 170, four of them Lagondas. Lord de Clifford in one of his special Rapiers was to start from Umea, P W Makinson in M45 AXA 645 (Z11110) would start from John o'Groats, while A E Dobell in Rapide BPK 743 (Z11134R) and Lt. Owen Cathcart-Jones in KY 8027 (Z11176R) would start from Stavanger. Cathcart-Jones had recently come fourth in the "Mac" Robertson air race from Britain to Australia and by returning at once had set up a round-trip record. He was thus a celebrity and there were many photographs published of him and his crew in matching Sidcot suits. His co-driver was Marsinah Neison, another celebrity pilot of the time and gorgeous enough to get her picture in every newspaper. Their car was a Rapide tourer with the springs set up to give increased ground clearance and twin side-mounted spare wheels, to which chains were already attached. As the Rapide was already nose-heavy, this combination must have given it a ferocious understeer. It also had the new Lucas "Long Range" headlamps instead of P100s. Dobell's car had had its engine specially prepared by the factory. Since it ran on a benzol/petrol mixture, likely to be hard to find abroad, he had a 38-gallon (173-litre) tank fitted, along with a 3.67:1 ratio axle in the interests of better acceleration.

The British competitors had marked out at Brooklands a replica of the "wiggle-woggle" tests that would be used at Monte Carlo, and had had a good number of rehearsals before they started. Lord de Clifford and Cathcart-Jones both got to Monaco unpenalised, despite adventures, as did Makinson, but Dobell crashed and although the car still ran he had to retire. As ever, nobody got through from Athens or Bucharest. The timed cold start on the front at Monte Carlo was no problem to Cathcart-Jones, but the Rapide's limited lock and sheer bulk were, and he came out 34th overall but ahead of Makinson (56th). Lord de Clifford was 24th. In the host of minor competitions, Lord de Clifford came ninth in the Riviera Cup and Cathcart-Jones fifth in the Coachwork Competition (open cars).

One of Frank King's ideas for drumming up sales in the notoriously difficult winter months was to set up a fleet of demonstrators to tour the dealer-

ships. The idea was to show the prospective customer the whole of the admittedly confusing range, rather than him only being able to see whatever his local dealer had in stock. This touring roadshow, for example, was in Leicester during the first week of February 1935 and in Grimsby for the second week.

Road tests of the M45 and Rapier had been appearing steadily all autumn and winter but no proper test of the Rapide had been published, only preliminary articles with no figures. This was rather odd, since most of the car was already well tried and one would not expect much in the way of teething troubles. The first road test to appear was in *Country Life*, where the Hon. Maynard Greville tested Gaffikin Wilkinson's T9 tourer. He didn't actually see 100mph but did achieve 3500rpm in top, which isn't all that far away (94 mph). He quoted Lagonda's make-believe figure of 135bhp for the power output and was fortunate in being able to compare directly an M45 tourer lent by a friend with the Rapide version. He was firmly in favour of the Rapide, saying that it in his opinion it was 10mph faster through any given corner and that the Telecontrols had a much more marked effect on the handling of the newer car. One has no idea of the mileage of his pal's car of course. This is a different view from that of present-day drivers, who tend to prefer the more predictable M45 to the Rapide, whose extra front-end weight bias can push it into understeer too soon. Greville did come up with a delightful remark: "It is not excessively noisy, but at the same time it sets about its work in no spirit of humility".

Bill Oates was in the chair for the Lagonda Car

The "streamlined" radiator filler was another innovation for the Rapide and continued for the succeeding models.

Club's second annual dinner at the Park Lane Hotel in February 1935. The club started a tradition, continued to this day, of not having long speeches, preferring several five-minuters to a bore droning on for an hour. Both Lord de Clifford and Owen Cathcart-Jones told of their Monte Carlo Rally experiences, the latter remarking that the rally was infinitely more strenuous and difficult than sitting still in an aeroplane, in danger of going to sleep from boredom. Sir Malcolm Campbell, who was shortly to add a special Rapier to his M45, was now a vice-president of the club. In the same issue of *The Autocar* as the report on the dinner there appeared one of the perennial paragraphs explaining that Lagonda was a British firm named, they said, after Wilbur Gunn's birthplace in South America.

At the end of February it was announced, somewhat prematurely as it turned out, that the future of the company had been secured by means of an agreement with a private syndicate of financiers, who would be represented on the board and take an active part in the firm. It is now believed that the mysterious syndicate was actually Alvis, who had substantially boosted their capital at the end of 1934 and afterwards made an offer of £35,000 for Lagonda. This was rejected as too low. Quite why Alvis would want to buy the firm isn't clear, unless it was merely to get rid of a competitor.

The 1935 RAC Rally attracted 308 entries, nine of them Lagondas, including Dobell, starting from London, as did W T Lanes (M45R Z11207) and D G Silcock (16/80). Eileen Ellison drove the works demonstrator Rapide CPC 743 (Z11266R), starting from Leamington along with T H Lewin (2 Litre).

Door tread plate on the Rapide tourer.

Denis Flather had a 2 Litre W 330 (OH 10020) from the Buxton start, while C Dodd (16/80), T C Mann (M45 AXD 56, Z10691) and Lord Walpole (Rapier) all chose Yarmouth. As was customary, practically the whole field arrived at Eastbourne unpenalised, the matter being sorted out in the driving tests and on a hillclimb. Dobell, Dodd, Silcock and Mann all got golds, Flather, Lord Walpole and Miss Ellison silvers. It was announced at this time that Eileen Ellison was entering a Rapide tourer in the Mille Miglia, with T P Cholmondeley-Tapper as co-driver and everyone wondered what the Italian public address announcer would make of the co-driver's name. It never arose, since the car she had entered was the works demonstrator and by Mille Miglia time the factory had sold it. Before then it earned its keep with road tests in weekly and daily newspapers. Tommy Wisdom, writing in the *Daily Herald* and *Sporting Life*, had achieved a 0-60mph time of 13.8 seconds, the best he had ever recorded in any car. He was not keen on the freewheel, though, and kept it locked out throughout his drive. He did see the magic 100mph on the speedo, at Brooklands with the screen flat.

One Rapide customer was Sir Dermot Hall-Caine, who drove it to take the Prime Minister, Ramsay Macdonald, to Doncaster in March. Naturally he demonstrated its amazing performance, to the dismay of the police escort whose duty it was to keep the premier in sight at all times.

The Motor printed the traditional buyers' guide in early March, adding two more versions of the Meadows power output to the growing collection: 110bhp at 4000rpm for the standard M45 and 125bhp at the same speed for the Rapide. They

went on to quote, in some cases for the first time, outputs for all the other models which sometimes differed from Lagonda's official figures, raising the question of where they got them from. Unfortunately there were a number of errors, which tend to undermine confidence. For example, the overall length of the M45 is quoted eight inches too short, the widths do not agree with the magazine's own test figures, and so on. *The Motor* also revealed an alternative rear axle ratio of 5.44:1 for the 16/80 - which must have been tedious - although one suspects it was only ever fitted to the giant seven-seater family saloons which Lagonda had been offering virtually unaltered since 1928.

Things were not going well at Staines. The traditional winter slack time had been abnormally extended by the advent of the 30mph speed limit in built-up areas, which came into effect on 18 March. Although in retrospect this was an inevitable and necessary law, bringing with it driving tests and pedestrian crossings, the instant reaction was the temporary collapse of the sporting car market. This market is an illogical one by definition and therefore one cannot complain if it behaves illogically. For some reason the Rapier was the worst hit and by the middle of April the factory was so clogged with unsold Rapier chassis that it became difficult to get about. They were parked in any workshop

not fully occupied and in every alleyway. On 18 April the bank acted, and as holders of the first debentures appointed a Receiver, Mr W Basil Holden, FCA. The next day was Good Friday and little was done except to extend the Easter holiday until the following Thursday, when Mr Holden posted a notice saying, "I cannot see, at this stage, as to what will be the future programme but conversations which are taking place lead me to believe that it is highly improbable that Lagonda will pass out of production".

Nevertheless, he then set off round the factory forbidding all movement of cars and parts until stock had been taken. At the same moment a very

Top left: Pressure gauges for the Telecontrol dampers

Above: The central metal panel on the Rapide dash was carried over from the M45 but its contents were put the other way up, necessitating little grooves for the tails of the lamp and ignition switches.

A late-1934 M45 Rapide T9 tourer. Silver was a popular colour for these in the Silver Jubilee year of 1935.

The later T10 tourer body on a 1935 Rapide. The spare wheel has gone into the enlarged boot and the wings are now valanced. The protruding petrol filler rather spoils the lines.

special Rapier chassis, which had been ordered by Roy Eccles, was being spirited out of the back door. The next act was to give notice to 125 employees, about a quarter of the workforce. Ironically, 26 April saw the long delayed road test of the Rapide in *The Autocar*, published in the same issue as reported the Receivership. Over the next few weeks the whole story began to emerge, Alvis put in their bid and had it rejected as too low, and Sir Edgar Holberton made a statement in which he exonerated the bank for being too hasty, explaining that they had shown forbearance for more than eight years. The impression was given to the newspapers that production was continuing, whereas in fact it had practically stopped, since no new parts were being made or bought and assembly consisted solely of making

up cars out of existing stock.

Lagonda was a company not noted for consistency in normal production ("they never made two cars alike"), but the cars turned out during the Receivership defy description. Strange cocktails of 3, 3½ and 4½ Litres were sold, some even with Maybach gearboxes found in the back of the stores. A J A Wallace Barr, the owner of Cellon Ltd, who supplied Lagonda's paint, was persuaded to accept a car in lieu of his bill and got a 10ft 9in chassis Rapide which was the first ST54 pillarless saloon, and very nearly the last. Only Gaffikin Wilkinson was advertising this design, since the Receiver had stopped all advertising after the great splash of colour in the special Silver Jubilee supplements of early May. The Rapide saloon was priced at £1125, compared with £1250 for the Gurney Nutting one shown at Olympia.

The Rapide tourer tested by *The Autocar* and other magazines was CPD 937 (Z11303) and carried the latest T10 body, only slightly different to the T9. The wings were all valanced and all aluminium and had different wearing strips, the fuel tank was moved forward and the spare wheel disappeared inside the boot. The testers revelled in the customary steam engine – like Meadows torque and the tourer was usefully quicker than the comparable M45, reducing the 0-60mph time from 15.8 seconds to 14.6, with a best top speed of 100.56mph. *Motor Sport* made it quicker still, at 13.5 seconds for the 10-60mph sprint, and drove it hard enough to record only 12.5 miles per gallon. *Motor Sport* were, as ever, more critical than the weeklies and felt that Lagonda had overdone the

Auctioneers' Announcements, Tenders, Etc.

Advertisements under this heading are charged at the rate of 22/6 per single column inch.

Preliminary Announcement re Lagonda Motors, Ltd
By Order of the Receiver, W. Basil Holden, Esq.,
F.C.A., Messrs.
FULLER HALL AND FOULSHAM

are instructed to offer for SALE by TENDER in lots the
BUSINESS AND ASSETS OF LAGONDA MOTORS LTD.
as a First Lot.
THE GOODWILL OF THE BUSINESS.
including Jigs, Tools, Stock, Stores and Spare Parts, the
FREEHOLD FACTORY AT STAINES,
together with the
FIXED PLANT AND MACHINERY
as a Second Lot. The Factory occupies a Ground Area of 4¼ acres, and the Buildings contain a
FLOOR SPACE OF 117,000 SQUARE FEET.
The FIXED PLANT and MACHINERY includes 400 ENGINEERS' MACHINE TOOLS by the best English and American Makers, and high-class WOODWORKING MACHINERY.
Full details will be contained in future announcements, or may be obtained forthwith from Messrs. Brooks, Williams and Co., Chartered Accountants, 37, Lombard St., E.C.3; of Messrs. Wilde, Sapte and Co., Solicitors, 21, College Hill, E.C.4; or of Messrs. Fuller Hall and Foulsham, 212, High Holborn, W.C.1.

Auctioneers' Announcements, Tenders, Etc.

Advertisements under this heading are charged at the rate of 22/6 per single column inch.

Re Lagonda, Limited.
By Order of the Receiver, W. Basil Holden, Esq.,
F.C.A.,
Messrs
FULLER HALL and FOULSHAM

are instructed to Offer for Sale by Tender in Four Lots the
BUSINESS AND ASSETS OF LAGONDA, LTD.,
Makers of the well-known
LAGONDA MOTOR CARS.
The Business has been carried on at Staines for the last 30 years, and it is estimated that at present there are some 2,500 cars on the road.
As a first Lot will be offered the
GOODWILL OF THE BUSINESS
to include the Jigs, Tools, Patterns, Drawings, Registered Trade Marks and Spare Parts.
As a second Lot
THE FREEHOLD FACTORY
and the
FIXED PLANT AND MACHINERY.
The Factory occupies a Ground Area of 4¼ acres, and the Buildings contain a floor space of 117,000 sq. ft. The Fixed Plant includes about 400 machine tools by the best English and American makers, and high class Woodworking Machinery.
LOTS 3 and 4 STOCK OF FINISHED CARS.

Tenders, which must be in the Form attached to the Sale Particulars, should be enclosed in a sealed envelope marked Tender re Lagonda, Ltd., and delivered at the Offices of W. Basil Holden, Esq., by 12 o'clock on Tuesday, 18th June.
Particulars with Plan and Conditions of Sale may be had of the Receiver, W. Basil Holden, Esq., F.C.A., Messrs. Brooks, Williams and Co., 37, Lombard St., E.C.3, of Messrs. Wilde, Sapte and Co., Solicitors, 21, College Hill, E.C.3, or of Messrs. Fuller Hall and Foulsham, 212, High Holborn, W.C.1.

The fateful advertisements that seemed to spell the end of Lagonda Ltd but were to lead on to greater things. They are not identical and represent a change of mind by the Receiver over a week in May 1935.

quick steering. With a heavy car like this, 1½ turns from lock to lock was too much hard work they thought, and if they were to use a Rapide in town a lot they would prefer the normal M45's 1¾ turns.

Steadily the staff drifted away as production ground to a halt, until there were only 25 left. Frank Feeley left at this time and went to Newns the coachbuilders in Thames Ditton, where his first job was to build a special Rapier two-seater for Sir Malcolm Campbell and where he went on to create the Railton Light Tourer. Finally, after a half-hearted sales campaign in May, the Receiver announced that the whole company would be put up for sale by tender in two lots, the first the goodwill with tools, stock and spare parts and the second the factory and plant. That week only four cars had left the factory, so his "full production" was something of an euphemism. Tenders were to be returned by 18 June, by which time the public image of Lagonda would have changed dramatically.

Before passing to the crowded events of June, this might be the place to try to analyse why the company crashed when it did. There were plenty of people, staff and customers alike, prepared to blame the Rapier, for the undoubted snobbery of a proportion of the clientele made them take a very dim view of the "cut-price Lagonda", not lessened when it proved nearly as fast as the bigger cars,

4½s excepted. There were many indignant letters on file at Staines about this. Unfortunately the Rapier never got anywhere near the output figures envisaged, with its best results barely 30 cars a week. It sold for about half the price of an M45 but must have cost much more than half to build, and since it was an assembly job rather than in-house manufacture, other firms' profits were concealed in the costs. Also, relying on other coachbuilders didn't help since delays that Lagonda had no control over were likely to occur. But we can't lump it all on to the Rapier. The incredible number of models didn't help, with the spares needed to service them all draining the very limited capital. A company whose products sold for about £1000 each needed a capital base far exceeding Lagonda's £50,000 to tide it over the slack period from November to March each year. The company might have staggered through 1935 as in previous years had the speed limit not been introduced which produced a dip in the sales graph at just the time when normally things would begin to pick up. It would have been temporary, like all over-reactions, but it was enough to frighten the bank.

M45 RAPIDE SUMMARY STATISTICS
All as M45 except:

Engine

compression ratio	6.98:1
brake horsepower	Arguable – see text
big end diameter	2⅛in
ignition system	Inlet-side magneto now Scintilla
carburettor needles	K
crankcase	RR56 instead of aluminium, larger diameter studs plus one extra, Tecalemit oil filter added

Chassis

wheelbase	10ft 3in (3124mm)
track, front	4ft 10in (1473mm)
track, rear	4ft 10½in (1486mm)
overall length (tourer)	15ft 7in (4750mm)
weight (tourer)	33.25 cwt (1689 kg)
weight (saloon)	Not published
turning circle	41ft left (12.5m), 43ft right (13.1m)
brakes	Girling. No servo
rear axle ratio	13 x 43 (3.31:1)
mph @ 1000rpm in top	26.9
dampers	Luvax hydraulic replace Hartfords
jacking	Inbuilt Smith's "Jackall" on both axles

Gearbox

freewheel added

Prices

Chassis	£825
Tourer	£1000
Saloon	£1125

Number built

52 (estimated)

Chapter Five

Renaissance – the LG45

A week or so passed after tenders for the company were received before any announcement was made. Four tenders had been submitted, and we know the sources of two. Rolls-Royce had shown an interest and were prepared to cough up to suppress a competitor, but the winning bid came from a 29 year old Lincoln's Inn solicitor, Alan Paul Good, heading a consortium funded largely by a merchant bank, Dawnay Day. Bored with the law, Good had taken to business dabblings and it is believed that he had a relative working at Dawnay Day in a position to assist. As Good had no motor industry experience he had signed up Dick Watney, then in the process of leaving Rootes, to act as managing director should his bid succeed, and Dick in turn had approached W O Bentley, whom he knew from the "Bentley Boys" era, to become Technical Director. Bentley had just completed the five-year contract at Rolls-Royce that was part of the settlement when Bentley Motors was wound up and was in no hurry to renew it, sensing that it was not a real job but a device to keep him under control.

The Receiver was well aware of the commercial value of the Le Mans victory and persuaded Good to offer more than his tender price for Lagonda as a going concern. The new company in the end paid £67,500 for the old one plus £4000 for the stores. Good's new company had a nominal share capital of £250,000 and within a fortnight had raised £175,000 of it, mostly from a nominee who later sold out to Dawnay Day. Good, Watney and Bentley were the only directors and the full capital

was in place by the end of 1936.

The first priority was to get back into production as soon as possible. Almost immediately after taking over, Good set off for Staines with Watney and Bentley and announced to the remaining 25 employees, "We are going to build the best car in the world and have just two years to do it in. That is your part of the job – mine is to find the money". It was a day of shocks for W O, as he recorded in his autobiography, when he first saw the tumble-

The new boss. Alan Paul Good in 1935, aged 29. A huge man, 6ft 5in and over 20 stone, he made sure Lagonda continued the tradition of bags of legroom. By the end of the Second World War he controlled the whole of the small diesel engine industry with the exception of Lister. He died not long after.

Dick Watney (left), the new Managing Director, had been one of the "Bentley Boys" in W O's Cricklewood days and was the link by which Good got to Bentley. He spent all his working life in the motor industry.

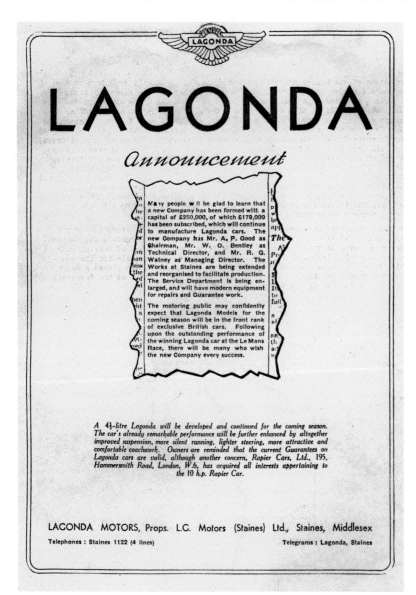

LAGONDA
Announcement

Many people will be glad to learn that a new Company has been formed with a capital of £250,000, of which £179,000 has been subscribed, which will continue to manufacture Lagonda cars. The new Company has Mr. A. P. Good as Chairman, Mr. W. O. Bentley as Technical Director, and Mr. R. G. Watney as Managing Director. The Works at Staines are being extended and reorganised to facilitate production. The Service Department is being enlarged, and will have modern equipment for repairs and Guarantee work.

The motoring public may confidently expect that Lagonda Models for the coming season will be in the front rank of exclusive British cars. Following upon the outstanding performance of the winning Lagonda car at the Le Mans Race, there will be many who wish the new Company every success.

A 4½-litre Lagonda will be developed and continued for the coming season. The car's already remarkable performance will be further enhanced by altogether improved suspension, more silent running, lighter steering, more attractive and comfortable coachwork. Owners are reminded that the current Guarantees on Lagonda cars are valid, although another concern, Rapier Cars, Ltd., 195, Hammersmith Road, London, W.6, has acquired all interests appertaining to the 10 h.p. Rapier Car.

LAGONDA MOTORS, Props. L.G. Motors (Staines) Ltd., Staines, Middlesex

Telephones : Staines 1122 (4 lines)   Telegrams : Lagonda, Staines

The first public announcement of the new company in August 1935.

down sheds that had served Lagondas since 1913 and realised that the roof of the drawing office was going to leak all over his drawing board. Nor was he too keen on Dick Watney as managing director, since the two men rarely saw eye to eye, whereas he liked Good and had thought he would be in charge. This animosity trickled down and eventually distinct factions of 'Watney-men' and 'Bentley-men' developed within the factory.

Very quickly, on Good's instructions, former staff were rounded up, but with some notable changes. There was no room for Alfie Cranmer with Bentley in his chair, and after some months helping to wind up the old company he took a job at Maybach. Ted Bolton, the works manager, was re-employed but resigned within the month. To

replace him Walter Buckingham stepped up to that post and the young Frank Feeley took over responsibility for body design. Bill Oates left to help found Rapier Cars and Bert Hammond went to work for Lammas Graham. Dozens of ex-Cricklewood Bentley employees had seen the announcements that W O was active again and he was able, usually very easily, to lure them away from their present employment and transfer to Staines. Stan Ivermee came back from Rolls-Royce and Percy Kemish from Squire, to form the new Experimental department, aided by Jack Sopp and Lionel Taylor, also ex-Cricklewood. By 1 August Charles ("Rex") Sewell had started as a draughtsman. Renowned as a gearbox "king", Sewell had worked for Bentley at Cricklewood and then at Napier on their abortive return to the car market. His first job was to add synchromesh to the Meadows gearbox, since its absence was seen as hindering sales when all the opposition offered it, Alvis on all forward gears. It only proved possible to offer smooth changes between third and top and even this was not without problems.

The next point to be considered was model policy. Within days of the takeover a decision was reached to concentrate solely on the 4½ Litre and drop all the others. This was undoubtedly right. The big cars sold at a comfortable price and made all the headlines; the smaller cars cost nearly as much to make, possibly more in the case of the 3½ Litre, where Lagonda did all the machining, but sold at a lower price. To reassure customers, though, an announcement was made that although from now on only the 4½ Litre would be sold, all past guarantees would be honoured. This meant a great deal to the customers and, what is more, the company actually did honour them.

Rapier devotees were unhappy with this decision. The car was a more modern design than any of the other models and only about 300 of the initial order of 500 had been sold, so there were loads of parts lying about. The new company could see the problem and agreed to the hiving off of the Rapier operation to a new company, Rapier Cars Ltd. It also transferred the London Service depot in Hammersmith to Rapier Cars, so that the building had a new lease of life as a car factory. The directors of Rapier Cars were Bill Oates, Tim Ashcroft and Nevil Brockelbank.

W O Bentley naturally tried out an M45 while deciding what improvements he could make to keep the car competitive. It was obvious that the company could not wait two years for Good's "best car in the world" to come to fruition and would have to soldier on with an improved M45 for the time being. Bentley later described the M45, in his autobiography, as " fundamentally sound, if rather coarse...and with a quite outrageous crankshaft roar". This last remark, published in 1969, puzzled the Lagonda Club, none of whose members had ever experienced such a roar. The truth emerged in the 1990s when the club's then chairman had the flywheel work loose on his M45. Thanks to thoughtful design, it cannot fall off and still transmits drive while roaring in protest. One imagines W O drove a frazzled old works hack, since the Receiver had sold off all the good cars.

But both Bentley and Good wanted to make something much more modern than a facelifted M45. Bentley's aim was to produce a saloon which would propel its four occupants and their luggage at 100mph in complete silence. He had had the same aim for his 8 Litre, but design had progressed rapidly in the intervening years and he would not now have to use such an enormous engine to get the same result. By going to a higher rev. rate he could get the performance out of a short-stroke V12. Designers with V12 experience were not exactly numerous, but fortuitously one of them, Stuart Tresilian, had just had a blazing row at Rolls-Royce and stalked out. It is a truism that all engineers are either spacemen or dodos. "Triss" was definitely a spaceman, always embracing the very latest technology. Going straight to Rolls-Royce from Cambridge in 1927, he had played a

key part in developing the "R" racing engine for the Schneider Trophy seaplanes, had devised an ohc head for the Bentley 3½ Litre that wasn't used and had designed a V12 for the Phantom III using these heads that wasn't used either. This led to the row with Hives and his exit, just when Bentley was looking for a designer. He started at Staines in February 1936.

Tresilian quickly produced a very advanced design which owed a lot to the Phantom III, all alloy with wet liners and two oil pressure systems supplying different pressures. Some of this was too much for Bentley and cast iron was ordered. The compromises continued. W O contributed a cruciform-based chassis with the cross as far forward as

Other key players. This 1945 picture, taken to celebrate the first running of the LB6 engine, shows, left to right, Stan Ivermee (Head of Experimental), Percy Kemish (his deputy), W O Bentley (Technical Director), Charles Sewell (Chief Draughtsman) and Donald Bastow (Chassis designer).

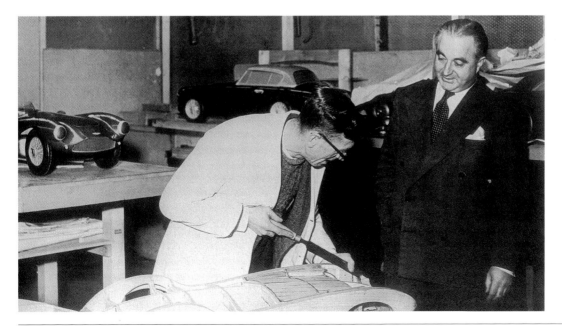

Frank Feeley (right), taken in later days at Feltham in the 1950s. Born in 1912, he assumed design control for Lagonda's coachwork at the ripe old age of 25

The first product of the new company, the M45A. This would have been the 1936 model year car had the old company survived. Only about 10 were completed, all saloons, before the LG45 was ready.

The LG45 drophead coupé offered better weather protection than the tourer. Wind-up glass windows instead of sidescreens and a padded hood gave a lot of the feel of a saloon, but back seat passengers had better not be claustrophobic.

possible, which gave excellent weight distribution but meant that the by-now antiquated arrangement of a separate gearbox was perpetuated. Tresilian contributed independent front suspension by unequal wishbones with springing by very long torsion bars anchored to the cross of the frame. He then went on to seek a de Dion rear axle, suspended on coil springs and controlled by a Watt linkage. That was vetoed by Bentley, who could see enough trouble getting the engine and gearbox right without all these added complications. Tresilian also gathered round himself some associates from his previous career, notably Leslie Stark,

who had designed the Amherst Villiers supercharger, Reg Ingham, later to be Lagonda's works mamager, Eric Easter and Jim Bowering from Rolls-Royce and Frank Ayto, another old Cricklewood hand, later to head the drawing office.

The extra money which the new company could deploy meant that at long last the projected expansion of the factory could take place. Not only that, but professional architects could be employed instead of the Gunn DIY approach. As Surrey County Council also had plans to widen The Causeway, for which they needed land from Lagonda, a big rebuilding programme was set in motion that had not been finished by the outbreak of the Second World War and continued during it. As part of this, The Ship public house was relocated to the opposite side of the road, revealing the various holes in Lagonda's workshops that gave machine shop denizens access to the pub without the formality of clocking off.

The first new building to go up was a long-needed proper office block and reception area, opened in August 1936. More immediate was the problem of what to make. By the first week of July 1935 the new management revealed to the press a revised M45 which would have been the 1936 model year car had the old company survived. In fact two of them had been built before the Receiver arrived. It was a kind of merger between the M45 and M45 Rapide, called the M45A. Only a few, perhaps ten, were ever made, as Bentley was determined to get his newer model out in time for the

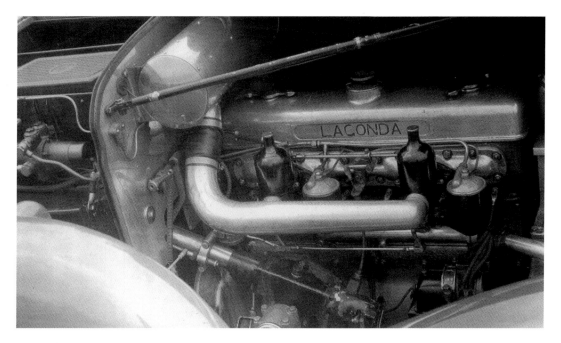

Underbonnet view of an early Sanction 1 LG45. At the Receivership there was a load of surplus rocker covers with "Lagonda Rapide" engraved on them. Lagonda never threw anything away, so they were ground out and re-engraved with a plain "Lagonda". The double SU fuel pump (left of the picture) had just been introduced. M45s used two ordinary ones, mounted back to back.

Motor Show. The M45A used the 10ft 9in wheelbase chassis, but had its engine in the more forward position of the Rapide. It used the Girling brakes but a standard M45 engine and small Lucas "Long Range" headlamps. All were saloons, using a longer version of the Rapide saloon's ST54 body, designated ST64. In practice, the ST44, ST54 and ST64 bodies are remarkably alike and you have to stand them side by side to see the subtle differences.

There was an unexpected battle with Companies House, which refused the new company the name Lagonda anywhere except on radiators, solved by calling the new company L.G. Motors (Staines) Ltd until such time as the old company had been wound up.

In the last week of September Lagonda were able to reveal the revised 4½ Litre to the press. In the time available since taking over in June, Bentley and his staff had not been able to do more than a face-lift, but it was a very considerable one, even bearing in mind that the starting point had been the M45A and not the M45 or Rapide. Bentley's aim was refinement and, unable to achieve this with the Meadows engine without substantial and time-consuming redesign (which was to come later), he concentrated on wrapping

A very early LG45 Sanction 1 saloon, showing the likeness to the M45A. This is chassis 12006 (LG45s begin at 12000) and was used by W O as his personal car for a year or so. It later had the first G10 gearbox installed `for testing.

This 1937 LG45 tourer, Car Number 12262/G10/S, is owned by Peter Blenk and again carries Lagonda's own coachwork. The front wings now curve further forward over the wheels than on earlier tourers.

The frontal treatment is typically unfussy, although there is now a bumper, fitted to control front-wheel tramp.

Only the offside wheelcase has a wheel in it. The matching nearside one holds the tools and jack. In this shot the windscreen is folded flat.

There is a suggestion of a pointed tail in the rear end treatment.

There was a decent luggage boot on this model.

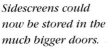

Sidescreens could now be stored in the much bigger doors.

the steering column if the driver thought fit. Chassis lubrication was fully automatic, consisting of a Tecalemit pump operated by the clutch pedal which distributed lubricant from the sump by the traditional little copper pipes to all the important chassis points. It was an admirable idea, but suffered from the Meadows engine's enormous output of sludge, which finds its way into the little pipes. Modern owners are advised to use a separate supply of clean oil and not rely on the stuff in the sump. A front bumper was fitted, another Lagonda first. It was supposed to ensure that the springs and chassis frame could not vibrate at the same frequency, causing tramp.

The engine was of course still the Meadows in roughly Rapide form, with a fractionally lower compression ratio of 6.68:1 and two magnetos instead of one and a coil. The new magneto was a Scintilla Vertex and both magnetos now had automatic advance systems, although a manual control was still fitted for extreme circumstances. The SU carburettors now had adjustable jets and the Kigass starting aid was dropped. Bentley was determined to quieten the car and far more elaborate silencers were fitted, along with a large cylindrical air cleaner/silencer on the inlet side, mounted on the bulkhead and connected to the carburettors by an expensive looking tapered branched pipe. Engine mountings were more complicated than before and markedly softer.

its head in a blanket to isolate the occupants from noise and vibration. The forward engine position was retained but the cast aluminium bulkhead, unchanged since 1929, disappeared and was replaced by two plain ones, the forward one full height and the other lining up with the rear bonnet edge. Between the two, diaphragms formed five little compartments for fuel pumps, batteries and the radio (a Lagonda first). The radiator was the Rapide one but the front of the chassis was further cleaned up by repositioning chassis crossmembers and headlamp support tubes out of sight. The Meadows clutch was replaced by one from Borg & Beck which was considerably less bulky, so that the rather Heath Robinson cut out and replate operation needed on the M45 was abandoned. Dampers were hydraulic by Luvax but were now linked together with a self-energising pump contained in one which could increase damping effect on a rough road. It could be overridden from

The gearbox was still the Meadows, but now a special Lagonda one with a longer case. Previously the constant-mesh and third-gear sets had been double-helicals, with first and second plain. Now second was also a double-helical and synchromesh was provided between third and top. Unfortunately, cutting synchromesh cones on gears not designed for it weakened the second gear cluster,

not a problem when new but high mileage cars would show it up. This new gearbox was designated the G9. Its internal ratios were changed, with second now 1.67 instead of 2.01 on the T8, putting second gear slightly closer to third. With synchromesh fitted there was no need for the clutch stop and it was dropped. The rear axle ratio remained at 3.67:1 but overall gearing dropped slightly following a change of tyre size to 6.00 x 18, one inch smaller overall and running 4psi softer. In keeping with the new softer image the steering lock-to-lock was now reached in 2.5 turns. The Jackall system was retained, but while the first cars had the operating gear below the floor as on the Rapide, for production it was installed, along with all the other tools, in a dummy wheelcase on the nearside wing, matching the real spare wheel on the offside one.

The Girling braking system was kept and with it the central throttle pedal, which gave it a much simpler layout. There was some cost-cutting where it would not show. The earlier cars had aluminium brake shoes with a small roller interposed between them and the operating wedge. Now everything was iron or steel and there were no rollers.

The new model was to be called the LG45 and three body styles were offered from the factory: a saloon, a tourer and a drophead coupé. This last was a new departure for Lagonda, brought on by customer demand which Frank Feeley was happy to fulfil even if his predecessor would not. It took some time to come and was not illustrated in the catalogue, even though described and priced. Buckingham's aversion to dropheads stemmed from the weight of the huge doors they had to have to allow dignified access to the rear seats. Tourer doors did not carry any glass, so were much lighter. Feeley hoped to overcome this problem with stiff bracing of the doorpost, concealed under the trim.

Once Frank Feeley began to design the hoods they became noticeably better in shape. The LG45 tourer had no cutouts in the door tops.

The aeroscreens, when not in use, attach to the sides of the windscreen to make wind deflectors.

The ride control to the Luvax hydraulic shock absorbers is mounted on the steering column. On the other side is the mixture control.

Sanction 1 LG45 saloon, pillarless like its predecessors. Removing the spare wheel from the bootlid to the offside wheelcase enabled the lid to open flat for additional luggage.

The saloon continued to be a pillarless design and was visibly descended from the M45A one, but with wings which came much further round the wheels at the front, almost touching the bumper. The tourer, equally, was a descendant of the T10, but had lost the cutouts in the doors and had a larger boot. All three bodies were more sober in some indefinable way. Inside the cars the same refining operations had gone on. The instruments were set into the walnut dash with no visible bezels and all were lit from behind Their number was reduced by combining instruments in one casing. The ignition switch no longer read "Off, Coil, Mag, Both' but simply "Off, 1, 2, 1 and 2'. The windscreen wiper, hitherto rather an afterthought, now vanished under the bonnet and drove the blades through a cable rack.

All in all, the LG45 models were more sober than

their predecessors. One has a mental picture of the typical M45 owner in blinding tweeds at a racecourse, while the typical LG owner was more likely to be in the Law Courts in black coat and striped trousers. Nevertheless, the performance was much the same, the comfort and silence much improved. The bare chassis was priced at £795, the tourer cost £1000, the saloon £1085 and the drophead £1125.

In keeping with the new one-model policy, the whole confusing mass of type numbers was swept away, and while the new company used a similar system of identity plates as before, types were confined to TB (tourer body), SB (saloon body) and DHC. The "car number" system was retained but started at 12000. The old company had got as far as Z11450, the last Rapide, but the system had got confused when the Rapier company had carried on issuing numbers in the same series, including some overlaps where two cars had the same number, one from each company. As Bentley had in his mind several later improvements to the LG45, he brought in a Sanction code, the first Sanction, usually abbreviated to S1, being stamped on the engine in the form LG45/145/S1. It is believed the first sanction was for 100 cars.

Another long overdue reform was to the owner's instruction manual. The proliferation of models made by the old company had led to a loose-leaf instruction manual system, whereby each model had the relevant pages added or subtracted from a master set. This led to anomalies in page numbering that had to be explained to every owner who asked where the missing pages were. Also, a tendency had grown up of merely including an engineering drawing of, say, a rear axle, with no explanation of how it came apart or went together again. As these drawings had originally been 40 x 30 inches and were reproduced at 9 x 6 inches, they weren't a lot of help. So the opportunity was taken to rewrite the whole book, since it now only had to cover one model, and to use a higher quality paper that would take photographs better as well.

With the new company not formed until June 1935 it was believed it would not be possible to get a stand at Olympia, but Delage cancelled at the last minute and after several reshuffles Lagonda got Stand 110. On to it they moved the exhibition they had been planning to hold at the Berkeley Street premises of Kevill-Davies and March, the newly appointed Distributor for London and the Home Counties. A new dealer network was being

formed, with some old faces and some new ones. Hugh Kevill-Davies had, of course, been sales manager for Bentley Motors. Warwick Wright and Gaffikin Wilkinson both started with the new company but did not stay long. But Central Garage, Bradford, stayed on, even after their star salesman "Mac" McCalman had been made Lagonda's sales manager.

A series of advertisements started, featuring splendid drawings by Harold Connolly of the cars superimposed on suitable backgrounds. The saloon drawing, easily the best, omits the wheel-cases, perhaps because the early car he was commissioned to draw didn't have them or perhaps because at that early date it was not established that they were to be standard. The drophead coupe did not figure at this time, nor was there one on the Show stand, but it was available by the end of the year and soon became more popular than the tourer, despite the price difference, as the weather gear was so much more civilised.

Despite the appearance at Olympia, no LG45s were delivered before the end of 1935 and only a handful then. To some extent production was

LG45 tourer cockpit with the windscreen flat and aeroscreens in place.

This car has the G10 gearbox, normally fitted with a centre change, but here with the optional right-hand one. This was the first Lagonda gearbox to have synchromesh.

The factory about 1936. Wyndham Hewitt are installed (see the left-hand gate) but the line of the buildings has not yet been set back to allow the widening of The Causeway. The Lagonda lettering up the factory chimney was lit by neon tubes at night.

LG45s had the Car Number stamped on the engine too, so for the first time it can be checked for originality.

hampered by the game of "musical shops" being played at Staines as the factory was rebuilt one shop at a time, with the more mobile operations shunted around as the builders set about adding strength to the creaking old factory. By 1935 Wilbur Gunn's corrugated iron palace was in an appalling state, not helped by the ceaseless cutting about and rebuilding that had gone on. Gunn had installed conventional, for the time, overhead line shafting powered by a gas engine (he made his own gas; you might have guessed). This drove all the machinery, via forests of flapping belts. The engine failed regularly and if a belt broke when it stopped with a bang, the dust of centuries would be dislodged and turn the shops into fog for half an hour, giving everyone an unwanted (unpaid) half holiday while it was repaired.

In 1929 the gas engine had been replaced by six giant 42hp electric motors to power the shafting, but continual expansion meant these were so overloaded that the electricians, who looked after the factory electrics as well as wiring the cars, had to nurse the motors and the switchgear, which ran red hot at busy times and had to be switched off at lunchtime to allow it to cool. The main switch, operated by a metal pole 3ft long, finally exploded one day, landing one electrician in hospital. By 1936 the structure was in such a state that when starting up in the morning it was necessary to start the main motors simultaneously in opposite directions to avoid pulling the whole roof in. Having got the shafting going without disaster, when the whole machine shop was working the roof and walls of the building vibrated and swayed in unison and appeared to be in imminent danger of collapse, so that there was a great need to get rid of the overhead shafts.

In the Meadows era, the machine shop was a touch too large for Lagonda's requirements, since the only engines being made were the 3 and 3½

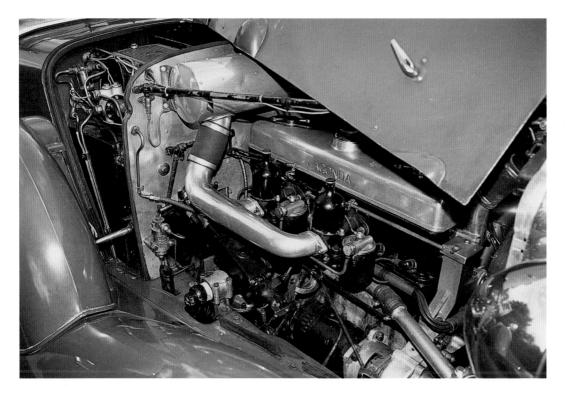

The engine compartment of Peter Blenk's LG45. Note the spark plug leads coming round the front of the block from one of the magnetos on the other side.

Litre, plus of course axles, gearboxes and Lagonda-sourced extra parts for proprietary components. However, W O Bentley could see a future need for all the facilities when his V12 was ready. Alan Good came to the rescue by forming a further company called Wyndham Hewitt Ltd. Hewitt had been Chief Operations Engineer for Imperial Airways and was keen to set up a company to profit from the re-armament drive in the aircraft industry, just getting under way. He had secured a contract with the Bristol Aeroplane Co. to make

the adjustable gill-rings that control the cooling of air-cooled radial engines, but had nowhere to make them. Good arranged that Wyndham Hewitt would buy out Lagonda's machine shop and take over the machining operations for Lagonda, while using the otherwise surplus capacity for his aircraft components. Good was chairman, Hewitt managing director and both Watney and Bentley were directors.

Hewitt thus inherited the problem of replacing the shafting. He wanted to do away with it and

Identity plate (far left) shows body type TB1, unchanged throughout LG45 production. Twin Scintilla Vertex magnetos (left), a feature of all Lagonda Meadows engines from Sanction 2 on.

Glamorous from any angle, this is Roger Firth's 1937 LG45 Rapide, Car Number 12235R. The Autocar achieved 108mph in a road test of a Rapide.

install individual electric motors for each machine but the best delivery he was offered was 18 months, so he looked for secondhand motors and was able to buy some from the disused Minerva plant in Brussels, just as old as Lagonda's but in better condition. Then there were problems with Charlier, the Belgian machine shop superintendent, who wasn't keen on the aircraft job and took refuge in not understanding English when it suited him, despite Hewitt's fluent French. In the 1970s, when interviewed, Hewitt said that in retrospect he was amazed at his temerity in attempting to make a top-quality car on the equipment available.

Wyndham Hewitt had also taken over the installation of synchromesh on the G9 gearboxes. Charles Sewell recalled that there was a terrible spate of trouble with the first G9 double helicals, which all snapped teeth off like carrots. As the gears were cut by Sykes from blanks supplied by Derrington, then hardened by Lagonda and sent to the Gear Grinding Co. for grinding, there were a lot of different people and processes to examine to find the cause of the dental trouble. After much research it was discovered that the Sykes machine

was not keeping the correct helix angle, and although the error was less than one degree it resulted in all the load being at one point instead of spread along the gear. Sykes were then duty-bound to replace all the suspect batch. Later, when Lagonda/Wyndham Hewitt were making their own G10 gearboxes, the gears were all copper flashed to check mating before being test-run.

These problems with synchromesh and the impossibility of a synchronised second gear on the Meadows gearbox led Bentley to start design on a replacement 'box intended for the V12 which could be fitted to LG45s so that the bugs could be out of it before the V12 went into production. (It was a Lagonda tradition that the first customers did the development testing.) The new 'box was quite different in concept to the Meadows. Bentley was concerned that aluminium casings expanded too much when hot and upset the spacing between the mainshaft and layshaft, with consequent noise. An iron casing overcame this and was quiet, though heavy. The compromise, called the G10, was based on three vertical circular malleable iron plates carrying the bearings, separated by cylinders of

The rear wing treatment harked back to the Speed Model of 10 years before.

The twin fuel fillers are set very low and can give trouble when the tank is nearing being full. There being no wing-mounted wheelcases, the spare occupies the boot and just about fills it.

The rear seat of the Rapide is practical, more so than one might expect from a car so sporting

aluminium that acted as the casing. Synchromesh was provided by very large cones – drums would be a better word – on second, third and top, with the second-gear drums on the layshaft. This was a rare, but not unique, arrangement which gave a lighter gearchange. The gearbox had its own oil pump, driven by an eccentric off the input shaft and feeding oil to the plain bearings used for the constant-mesh gears and the spigot bearing in the centre. All the other bearings were ball or roller and included a special double-row affair.

The whole gearbox, which was designed to take a great deal more power than Mr Meadows was providing, was very massive and was supported in the LG45 by four legs bolted to two longitudinal tubes joining the main chassis crossmembers. By 1936 the stigma of a centre gearchange was disappearing and the G10 was designed for this form of control, with three remote-control rods going forwards from the main box to a turret bridging the forward drive shaft and fixed to the front chassis main crossmember. This arrangement gave very nearly a clear floor in the front, at the expense of a long gearlever which looks as if it might be willowy but isn't.

The new gearbox was undeniably stronger than the G9 and trouble-free in service, but unfortunately it was a devil to make and very difficult to get quiet. Throughout its production life the gearbox assemblers were plagued by complaints from the testers that the gearboxes were too noisy and the author has a 14-page memo from Reg Ingham to Mr Bentley outlining all the troubles and what was being done about them.

The first G10 was installed in Bentley's personal LG saloon, (chassis 12006, DPD 28). The first problem was to get it in, since the long lever travel fouled the dashboard in first and third. This was remedied by cutting an inverted V-shaped notch and moving the switches elsewhere. In later production, a little bridge piece carried these between the two half dashboards that resulted.

In February 1936 *The Motor* was the first magazine to get its hands on an LG45, borrowing Kevill-Davies & March's demonstrator, a tourer registered CLO 549. February wasn't ideal for testing a tourer and all tests were made with the hood up. The testers covered 400 miles in two days and took the car to Brooklands on a particularly nasty one for high-speed motoring, made worse by the perennial repairs at The Fork. They were delighted with the car and got an indicated 100mph (actually timed at 97.7) on the Railway Straight. *The Motor* were, as always, a little cavalier about rev limits and took the car up to 4100rpm in third to get 80mph. This was a hundred revs over the red line, now set at 4000 after the Rapide-type bottom end modifications had become standard. When compared with the same magazine's figures for the M45 we find, more or less as expected, that the later car was 3cwt (152kg) heavier and only produced a little more power, so that the acceleration figures were all a little slower, but the extra revs in each gear permitted better maxima. Fuel

Businesslike controls and dash of the LG45 Rapide.

The rear tonneau cover is stretched over the backs of the front seats. The driver's seat is cut away to facilitate gear changes.

consumption was identical. The new softer springing and more scientific damping were judged a great success. Braking was excellent and the handbrake was already working on all four wheels, as it does when the plunger sticks. In fact the only faint criticism in the whole test was the limited view through the rear window of the hood. This was the letterbox-like slit conventional at the time and its usefulness had been further diminished by adopting a convex mirror mounted on the scuttle rail.

By May 1936 the first Sanction of LG45s had all been delivered, and without any public announcement the Sanction 2 arrived. It only differed in ignition layout, but the changes were quite substantial. The horizontal magneto on the inlet side of the engine was replaced by the dynamo, and a second Scintilla Vertex appeared on the exhaust side, with its plug leads led across to the inlet-side plugs. Sanction 2 was something of a stopgap and few cars were made since the third sanction, with much greater changes, was imminent.

Bentley had been much impressed by the work of Harry Weslake, who had recently set up on his own in Kingston, specialising in gas flow in engines and in cylinder head design. An LG45 engine was sent to him to see if he could prevent the standard unit's marked drop in power above 3400rpm. As Arthur Fox had discovered, this was easier said than done, and although a small benefit was found by reducing the exhaust valve size to speed up gas flow, the real problem was on the inlet side. Bentley eventually allowed Weslake to design a totally new head. The new head, which was to become the Sanction 3, had the inlet manifold cast within it, in the form of a tube running the whole length apart from a diaphragm in the centre, pierced by a small hole for balancing purposes. Tubular ports led off this to the valves and to the carburettors, which bolted directly to the outer surface of the head. At the rear a new water-transfer passage was added linking head to block to aid cooling in this region (except when brand new all these Meadows engines tend to run hot as the successive enlargements of engine capacity left the water circulation areas smaller). There was a problem with the location of the head studs, solved by passing them through the manifold and sealing round each stud with a special fitted copper washer. The inlet valves, by now a special Lagonda item, were very slightly enlarged. Some minor chassis changes accompanied the Sanction 3 engine. Lengths of Bowden cable replaced rods in the parts of the braking system that had tended to rub on the axles with the softer springing; this change also removed the reaction at the brake pedal sometimes felt when travelling on rough roads. At the rear, a spring steel "stabiliser bar" - what we would now call an anti-roll bar - was added, linking the inner ends of the damper levers. Engine mountings were also changed and made adjustable

When the first Sanction 3 engines came back to Staines from Weslake they were naturally tested on the brake, and test house staff were worried when they couldn't get within 20bhp of Weslake's claimed figures. A row ensued, settled when Weslake came to inspect Lagonda's test shop and found that the exhaust silencer, which discharged into a concrete-lined pit full of coke, was badly blocked with 20 years of soot and oil. This discovery rendered all the readings suspect. Bentley was very cross and said that if he had known this, he would never have hired Weslake in the first place. This knowledge casts doubt on all the power outputs quoted hitherto from the Staines testbed, and shines a more favourable light on the outputs claimed where they differ greatly from testbed figures.

Nevertheless, and despite W O's pique, the new head did produce more power and by July the Sanction 3 was in production. Four of the early engines were earmarked for four special lightweight chassis to be supplied to Fox & Nicholl. Fox had an entry for Le Mans, but had not previously committed himself to a make. We will cover the LG45 competition cars in the next chapter.

Meanwhile, a note in the technical press that A H Cranmer, MIAE, had been appointed technical director of Maybach Gears Ltd was a reminder that the sad business of winding up the old company was still going on. It was to take a further year.

Lagonda announced their 1937 model programme unusually early, on 28 August and in the middle of practice for the TT. The two events were not entirely unconnected, for it would not have escaped the notice of the scrutineer on the Friday that the three Lagondas entered by Fox & Nicholl, supposedly production models, only vaguely resembled the tourer in the catalogue. Mind you, the TT Bentley of Eddie Hall even less resembled the production tourers and the Derby firm never did make an out-and-out sports car. Lagonda, however, proposed to do so and introduced the LG45 Rapide, which was quite like the Fox & Nicholl cars in concept, although its

Sanction 3 LG45 engine, showing the carburettors bolted straight to the cylinder head with no visible inlet manifold, which is contained inside the head. Petrol pipe runs had to be altered. This engine has one of the early rocker covers, presumably a replacement.

ancestry was in fact totally different.

The new Rapide was Dick Watney's idea in the first place. He felt that the Lagonda range had become too sober and that although the performance was enough for anyone, the process of refinement had taken the sporting edge off the cars. He therefore charged Frank Feeley with the pleasant task of creating an eye-catching sports car on the LG45 chassis. It was not intended to have a shortened wheelbase or many special components, but there was huge scope for weight saving while at the same time providing seats for four people. The sort of car Watney had in mind was the rather outrageous kind of sporting carriage personified by the 500K Mercedes, with huge chromed outside exhausts and a vast bonnet. Feeley was in his element. He had the once in a lifetime chance to be extravagant, and produced exactly what Watney wanted. Watney was delighted. He didn't alter a single line – a rare thing for him – and ordered the building of a prototype at once. Bentley's reception was at best lukewarm, but he and his staff were preoccupied with problems on the V12 and he let Watney get on with it.

Very few changes were made to the engine,

Sanction 3 of course. The compression ratio was raised to 7:1 simply by fitting different pistons. A ratio of 7.5:1 was also available to any owner prepared to mix his own fuel brew, as this was too high for the pump petrol of the day. An output of 150bhp was claimed, and as the engines were externally identical to standard the stamped engine number had an "R" suffix. The G9 gearbox was retained as it was felt that sporting owners would prefer it and also because the narrow body didn't leave much room for a centre change. The high first gear used on the team cars was incorporated, together with the 3.31:1 rear axle ratio the M45 Rapide had pioneered, giving about 27mph per 1000rpm in top gear.

The bodywork was dramatic. For this sports model, where heat and noise were of little consequence, Frank Feeley returned to the cast aluminium bulkhead used since 1929 and even shaved a little off the width. The car was a comfortable four-seater with ample head and legroom but only 42in (1067mm) wide across the back seat. Helmet wings were developed into a luscious new shape to go with vestigial running boards, and the rear wings were curtailed into a

The highly finished engine compartment of Roger Firth's Rapide. Note the steering drop arm, which lay outside the bodywork.

Right-hand change version of the G10 gearbox, necessary with such a narrow body. This car was at one time fitted with hand controls for a disabled driver, but they have since been removed.

modern rendering of the Speed Model's. On the nearside a pair of huge chromium-plated external exhaust pipes merged into one at the rear edge of the front wing, the single pipe disappearing under the bodywork near the running board. These pipes, which were in fact chromed flexible tubing, slid over a normal steel pipe with spacing ribs in between, so as to avoid the blueing to be expected if the actual pipe were chromed. The design was based on Fox & Nicholl's racing exhausts and to get the pipes in, the nearside bonnet panel had to be cut in half, with only the upper portion lifting with the bonnet. The whole body formed a set of graceful curves, with a dipping waist moulding concealing the supports for the fold-flat windscreen, two cutaway doors and a tail which came to a blunt point, hinging up to reveal the spare wheel, the fuel tank and not much room for anything else. The built-in jacks were abandoned, along with the wheelcases, and a specially designed hood meant that the car looked just as good with it erected. Making the front edge of the hood, which was curved to match the windscreen top, stay watertight at 100-plus mph was a considerable development problem, but it was overcome.

The appearance of the car was flamboyant and extrovert, so much so that there was some muttering about it being a car for "Promenade Percy", to quote a phrase of the time. This was dispelled for ever when the top speed achieved on road test was published in the autumn and it was realised that the car's performance was as outstanding as its looks.

The introduction of the Sanction 3 engine was

closely followed by several changes to the established models in late August. The G10 gearbox was available as an option, except on the Rapide. Its internal ratios were close to those of the G9. First was 3.25:1 instead of 3.14, second 1.67:1 (1.68), third 1.25:1 (1.30). What was not obvious was that chassis crossmembers differed if the G10 was fitted, so it would be expensive to have a last-minute change of mind. Later on, after the G9 was stopped, the factory devised a right-hand change version of the G10 that could be fitted even in the Rapide. This was used in the other models if the customer wanted a right-hand change. Along with the G10, the rear axle ratio was revised slightly to 3.58:1 (12 x 43), which gave quieter cruising at the expense of acceleration.

Drophead and tourer bodies continued unchanged but the saloon body was altered quite noticeably. It had occurred to Feeley that moving the batteries to the scuttle had created space alongside the rear axle that was now being wasted when it could be occupied, in part, by the passengers' bottoms. A revised rear seat was devised, based on a series of 2in rubber straps which would sag down into this space when the seat was occupied. Feeley could then lower the rear roof and boot line. The result was a body whose highest point was just behind the windscreen instead of halfway back. To accentuate this, the waist moulding, which had previously swept up and over the boot lid, now drooped to meet the rear wing. There were a whole series of small changes, all calculated to make the body look more modern, both inside and out. The body code SB on the car's

Free-flowing exhaust gives an appreciable amount of extra power at the expense of accessibility.

identity plate now changed to SB3 (nobody knows what happened to SB2) and since not every buyer liked the new design, later versions of the earlier body shape were denoted as SB1. In keeping with Lagonda tradition, the introduction of Sanction 3 bodies does not coincide with the introduction of Sanction 3 engines.

The potential performance of the Rapide must have frightened someone at the factory, for the guarantee was altered for this model alone to a mere twelve months, renewable twice. Furthermore, the company would not sell a Rapide bare chassis until they had examined the design of the body that the purchaser proposed. In fact, no Rapide bare chassis were ever sold, but whether this is because this clause was strictly interpreted or whether nobody ever wanted one, we shall never know. Much to the surprise of the motor trade, but a good selling ploy, the Rapide was priced at £1050, exactly the same as the tourer.

For once we have an unambiguous record of power outputs from Sanction 3 engines as test results from April 1937 survive - and this is after Weslake's revelations about the Lagonda test house exhaust system. One presumes something had been done to rectify it. Engines 381/S3 and 383/S3 were tested to check proposed alternative exhaust systems. Apart from the Rapide compression ratio, both were standard S3 engines and were later installed in ordinary cars. Connected to the standard car exhaust system, 381 peaked at 119.5bhp at 3200rpm, falling to 117 at 3600. So despite all that work and the new head, power still fell off over 3200rpm, although not by much. The alternative silencers supplied by Burgess gave 128.25bhp at 3600rpm, so it is no surprise to learn that they became standard. For interest, it was recorded that the same engine gave 131.25bhp at 3600rpm running with no manifold, 124bhp at 3400rpm with the standard iron manifold and 133.5bhp with a Fox & Nicholl system. Thus something like 14bhp was being lost in the standard exhaust system. The catalogue still claimed 150bhp. The trouble with fictitious power output claims is that you debase the coinage, as it were. Having quoted 140 for the Sanction 1, you can hardly admit to 130-odd for the sports version.

After the September announcement everyone thought they knew what Lagonda's 1937 programme would be, so it was something of a bombshell when the V12 was revealed on the eve of the Motor Show. To produce a car of this calibre in only 15 months, starting from the proverbial blank sheet of paper, was quite fantastic, especially when the six-cylinder car had been extensively redesigned too, in the same period. Old sweats at the Staines factory were accustomed to the pre-Show rush but the 1936 one was a prize example. In fact the deadline proved impossible to meet, and the car so proudly displayed with locked glass bonnet side panels had an engine that couldn't run, while the glittering "aluminium" sump was actually a product of the carpenters' shop. The stand staff claimed that their first duty every morning was to sweep up the woodlice.

The saloon body shown was very much a prototype and bore only a passing family resemblance to what would eventually go into production, having a lower version of the SB3 rear end grafted on to a standard-looking front – except for a raked radiator – no wheelcases and a much more steeply raked windscreen. This concealed a considerable struggle at Staines between the Watney and Bentley factions. Frank Feeley, egged on by Watney, felt that this crucial new model should have an eye-catching and if possible ultra-modern appearance. Everyone could see that cars were gradually changing to full-width fronts, so Feeley designed and made a whole series of alternative versions and the mock-ups were all laid out in the bodyshop for Bentley to approve. W O's tastes were more conservative ("We want to sell this car to his lordship, Feeley, not the milkman") and he went to elaborate lengths to avoid having to make a decision, even on occasion going outside the building, round the shop and back in again at the other end, rather than be drawn into the full-front battle. In the end conservatism won and the V12 kept its separate wings and radiator. Feeley was to get his revenge, but only after the war.

We will defer the description of the prototype V12 until the appropriate chapter, where all the changes that crept in before production started can be examined. There is no doubt that Alan Good bounced Bentley into showing the V12 in 1936 years before it was ready and to some extent wrecked the impact it should have had when it did appear.

Rather overshadowed on the stand were an LG45 pillarless SB3 saloon with the G10 gearbox and a radio, the first public showing of this model, a grey LG45 drophead with a G9, and a dark green Rapide. Although delivery dates were vague, to say the least, prices for the various V12 models were quoted and, at £1450 for the saloon, were a huge increase on the LG45. It was clear that Good was serious in his aim of challenging Rolls-Royce.

The financial problems of 1935 seem to have scared off customers of the bespoke bodywork builders, and only Freestone & Webb and the Mayfair Carriage Co. showed bodies on Lagondas in 1936. On the opening day of the Show the Lagonda company gave a lunch at the Royal Palace Hotel in Kensington at which every speaker sung the praises of the V12. First Alan Good, then the Duke of Richmond, representing Kevill-Davies & March, and then Dick Watney added his piece. Bentley, who hadn't wanted to come in the first place because he felt it was all very premature (the car had yet to turn a wheel) sat there going redder and redder. Finally to chants of "Speech, speech" he was forced to his feet to respond. "Thank you very much" he said, and sat down again.

In November *The Motor* got a chance to test the new Rapide. This test put paid to any notion that the Rapide was all image and no performance. The top speed reached was 108.2mph, sustained over a half-mile with the screen flat. On the way to its top speed the car had accelerated from rest to 50mph in 9.4 seconds and achieved 0-60mph in 13.2 seconds. These figures were substantially better than those of the M45R, as one would hope, given more power in a lighter car, but it was not achieved at the expense of fuel consumption, which remained at the 16mpg the Meadows engine seems to give under any conditions. The testers found the car so "right" that they put 50 miles into

the first hour, in monsoon weather, and earlier criticism of flattering speedometers had been answered so well that the Rapide's one actually read slow – unheard of in 1936. Generally it was a eulogistic test, for this was no unmanageable racer but a tractable road car that could trickle through towns and then accelerate to three-figure speeds without a hiccup. While it wasn't as roomy as the slower models, there was space for four adults even if it was better if they were good friends. One of the features of all Lagondas has been generous legroom, which follows from the happy chance that all the bosses have been tall people, Alan Good topping the list at 6ft 5in and over 20 stone.

The test Rapide, EPF 242 (12140), led the usual hard life that Lagonda demonstrators had, and when in the hands of *The Autocar* got caught in a sudden blizzard on Salisbury Plain, being abandoned in a snowdrift. A month later the Technical Editor of *The Motor* reported on 16,000 miles with CLO 549, which he had bought after the road test. He was still delighted with it but did remark that the G9 gears had begun to whine.

In March 1937 an unexpected new model was introduced. This was a long wheelbase LG45 saloon called, rather confusingly, the De Ville. This term is normally applied to a limousine whose front compartment can be opened, leaving the rear roof closed. The Lagonda version was just a more dignified saloon with an optional winding division.

The LG45 de Ville had a nine-inch longer wheelbase but looked very similar to the Sanction 3 saloon. However, as a division was an option, it could not be pillarless.

Comparison between the tails of Sanction 1 and Sanction 3 (the nearer car) saloons at a Lagonda Club AGM.

The buyer had an option about the siting of the rear seat, which could vary by five inches according to whether legroom or luggage space was the priority. The new wheelbase was nine inches longer at 11ft 6in and only the G10 gearbox was available, although all the right-hand chassis members had the oval hole needed for the G9 but not required for the G10. Although very similar in appearance to the SB3 body, it was not pillarless, since that would not be possible with a division. The rear-hinged front doors made access to the

front seats noticeably easier. The De Ville was priced at £1195 with the division £30 extra.

In early April the first road test of a Sanction 3 saloon appeared in *The Autocar*. The test car, EPF 243, also had the G10 gearbox, its first appearance in print. The testers felt that the revisions made the car silkier than ever. Although they were not really very keen on a central change, the synchromesh on second was welcomed, even if judicious use of the spark control made the car virtually a top gear only vehicle. They felt that the mirror was inadequate and that the front seat backrest angle was wrong, although they didn't say whether it should have been steeper or flatter. The Sanction 3 engine gave the extra performance promised, so that the saloon now tested was quicker than the Sanction 1 tourer, 0-50mph taking 11.7 seconds instead of the earlier car's 12.6 seconds. The top speed of 93.75mph was a touch slower than the tourer's 96.77, but this was probably just a question of frontal area. It is illuminating, though, that this figure was the only aspect of performance where the LG45 saloon improved on the M45 saloon of 1934 which, helped by being 4cwt lighter, was consistently faster on all the acceleration figures but ran out of puff at 90mph.

The same car, EPF 243, was tested by *Practical Motorist* in May. It was rather out of their line of country, and they were probably the only magazine that would think of trying to start the engine on the handle. (It fired after a quarter of a turn). They were not too happy with the central throttle

A row of genuine original LG45 Rapides at the 1975 Lagonda Club AGM. All four have subtle differences. In the old-car boom of the 1980s, scores of replicas were built but only rarely did the builders get the front wing shape right.

pedal and criticised the access for the driver when the handbrake was on, although this was less of a problem with the G10 gearbox fitted, the G9 having been far worse. In fact EPF 243 was getting a bit care-worn by this date and many of the complaints can be attributed simply to wear.

The last week of April saw the special Coronation issues of the motoring magazines, nearly an inch thick and crammed with coloured art supplements. The versions of Lagonda's history were as inaccurate as usual, but in the advertisements accompanying them we see the first dilution of Lagonda's warranty system. The economics of the used car trade at the time, where precipitous depreciation meant that the possible bill for refurbishment if you returned your car to Staines after three years would probably be greater than the car was worth, did not encourage lengthy ownership, but some owners did persevere and the firm honoured their guarantee to the letter. From April 1937, however, the chassis was only guaranteed for three years, with no renewals, and the bodywork for just one year.

In the course of their June road test of the Rapide *The Autocar* had lapped Brooklands at over 100mph. The earlier snowstorm episode must have had some awful effect on the car involved, for the photos within the test were of a different car, FPC 452, first registered in March 1937 and fitted with a right-hand change G10 gearbox. As usual, their figures were slower than those of *The Motor* and the best top speed was 104.65mph with the screen flat. The artist who drew the plan view for the test imagined it to be more glamorous than it was and endowed it with a second set of outside exhausts on the offside as well.

As part of the Coronation celebrations in Staines a parade around the town was organised and Lagonda was persuaded to lend an LG45 De Ville. They also borrowed an 11.9hp for the occasion and to emphasise the firm's long history they also fielded Alan Good's Tricar, which he had bought from Gaffikin Wilkinson. Derek Rutherford, one of the firm's testers, drove the latter and had great difficulty with overheating since the pace of the procession was set by marching primary school children.

In August Earl Howe, who was still recuperating from his May crash at Brooklands, opened the Monaco GP circuit in LG45 tourer EPL 736, which was in France as part of a selling expedition seeking Continental dealers. The trip also produced a five-page touring article for *The Autocar* and a win in the concours at Cabourg.

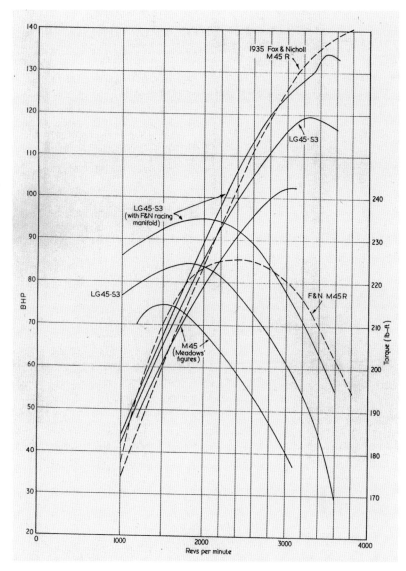

September 1937 saw the advent of Sanction 4 engines, although the only difference was a minor change to the timing, but the wiring layout was also altered to make use of an improved control box, and the dashboard layout was changed to group together more switches together, previously scattered about. LG45 production petered out in the autumn of 1937 as the V12 design was finished, along with its six-cylinder brother, and the last cars were delivered in December, plus a late order for a Rapide in 1938. In all, 278 were built, 25 of them Rapides and the rest split between tourers, which became rarer as time went on, dropheads, the various saloons and bare chassis supplied to outside coachbuilders. These last were never very numerous as Lagonda's in-house bodies were the equal of anyone else's and were delivered far more quickly.

Power and torque curves for all the Lagonda versions of the Meadows engine. The Sanction 4 version, found in late LG45s and all LG6s, developed the same power as the Sanction 3 and only differed in timing.

LG45 SUMMARY STATISTICS

Engine

As M45 except:

compression ratio		6.68:1, Rapide 7:1
valve timing	S1	io 5° btdc, ic 55° abdc, eo 55° bbdc, ec 20° atdc. Inlet opens for 240°, exhaust for 255°
	S3	io 5° btdc, ic 57° abdc, eo 52° bbdc, ec 19° atdc. Inlet opens for 242°, exhaust for 251°
	S4	io 7° btdc, ic 53° abdc, eo 51° bbdc, ec 12° atdc. Inlet opens for 240°, exhaust for 243°
brake horsepower	*(claimed)*	140 at 3800rpm (standard), 150 at 3800rpm (Rapide),
	(actual)	128 at 3600rpm (S3)
big end bearing		2.125in (54 mm) diameter
ignition system	S1	Horizontal Scintilla magneto plus Scintilla Vertex
	S2-4	Twin Scintilla Vertex
tappet clearances (hot)		Inlet 0.005in (0.127mm), exhaust 0.008in (0.203mm)
oil capacity		2.5 galls (11.4 litres)
clutch		Single dry plate Borg & Beck, no clutch stop
carburettors		SU HV5, needle KT (standard), K (Rapide)

Chassis

wheelbase	10ft 9in (3277mm) standard, 11ft 6in (3505mm) De Ville
track	4ft 9¾in (1467mm)
overall length, tourer	15ft 4in (4674mm)
overall width, tourer	5ft 7½in (1714mm)
kerb weight	Tourer 35cwt (1778kg), Saloon 37cwt (1880kg), Rapide 29cwt (1473kg)
turning circle	44ft (13.41m)
wheels and tyres	6.00 x 18in on 3.62in rims
tyre pressure	30psi
brakes	Girling, rods in tension, no servo
steering box	Cam Gears, 18:1 ratio
rear axle	Lagonda spiral bevel, semi-floating
ratios	Tourer 3.67:1 (with G9 gearbox), 3.58:1 (with G10 gearbox), Rapide 3.31:1

mph per 1000rpm in top	23.72 (3.67:1), 26.23 (3.31:1), 24.25 (3.58:1)
oil capacity	3.5 pints (2 litres)
shock absorbers	Luvax hydraulic
fuel tank capacity	20 galls (91 litres)

Gearbox

type (standard)	Meadows/Lagonda G9 four speed, synchromesh on third and top
internal ratios (standard)	Top direct, third 1.3:1, second 1.67:1. first 3.14:1
internal ratios (Rapide)	Top direct, third 1.3:1, second 1.67:1. first 2.62:1
type	Lagonda G10 four speed, synchromesh on second, third and top
internal ratios	Top direct, third 1.25:1, second 1.67:1. first 3.25

Prices

	1936	1937
Chassis	£795	£875
Tourer	£1000	£1050
Saloon	£1085	£1195
Drophead	£1125	£1220
Rapide	£1000	£1050
De Ville		£1195

Number built 278

Chapter Six

The LG45 in Competition

Freed from the restraining influence of the bank's man peering over their shoulder, the new company could indulge in competition more openly and not just pretend to assist private owners and dealers. The first inkling of this policy came early in 1936 when a pair of special LG45 tourers were entered for the Monte Carlo Rally, in those days a very severe test of a car and its crew. It was felt that the rather close-fitting LG standard front wings were liable to fill up with snow and be

difficult to clear, so ordinary M45 long wings were fitted and two spare wheels were carried in high-set sidemounts but without the cases. Both spares were fitted with knobbly-treaded winter tyres. DPE 121 (car number 12028) was scheduled for Alan Good and W O Bentley, but the latter had to cry off when he developed appendicitis and his place was taken by Good's wife Doreen, an experienced rally navigator in her own right. The second car, DPE 120 (12061) was loaned to T G Moore, the

The "works" LG45s for the 1936 Monte Carlo Rally. Alan Good (left) drove DPE 121, but DPE 120 was lent to T G Moore, the proprietor of Motor Sport *(it is not him in the picture). Good crashed at Riga and withdrew but Moore finished. The cars were fitted with M45 wings, less likely to get blocked with compacted snow.*

Moore's car at the finish of the 1936 Monte Carlo Rally. He is the man wearing a helmet. They came 41st overall. The crew member on the left obviously considered his university scarf sufficient warm clothing.

proprietor of *Motor Sport*. Both cars were to start from Tallinn in Estonia and, anticipating really foul weather, Good's car was fitted with an electrically heated clear-vision panel on the windscreen, which unfortunately had such a heavy frame that it probably obscured as much as it made clear. Good's rally didn't last long, for he crashed at Riga and although the car was extracted, it wasn't driveable. Moore got through to Monte Carlo successfully and came 41st overall.

There were two other Lagondas on the rally. Conrad Mann came 60th overall in AXD 56 (Z10691), a car still being rallied by the Mann family, and A E Dobell competed again in BPK 743 (Z11134), coming 29th overall and winning his class in the confort competition. As a sidelight to the earlier confusion about the Meadows' capacity, Mann's car was listed as 4429cc, Dobell's at 4467cc and the LG45s at 4453cc, reflecting the various figures quoted by the firm from time to time. The correct figure is 4453cc.

In March 1936 the RAC Rally followed tradition in that virtually the whole entry got to the finish unpenalised on the road section, so that the elimination tests determined all the results. Of the 316

entrants, five were Lagondas. Doreen Good in a works LG45, probably one of the Monte Carlo cars, gained a second class award. One of the problems besetting the historian writing of this period is that the term 4½ Litre was used for all such cars and it is difficult to be sure which were M45s, M45 Rapides or LG45s. Largely this is because the factory itself didn't specify and the terms we use today were factory codes that didn't appear in publicity or in catalogues at the time.

With the 1935 Le Mans win so important it was obvious that the new management would try to capitalise on it, and Fox & Nicholl were equally keen. Four early S3 engines were sent to Tolworth for Fox's experts to turn into racing units, and the factory produced four special lightweight chassis, without unnecessary bits like running board brackets, to put the engines into. Ever since the beginning of the year it had been known that Arthur Fox had a Le Mans entry, although he had not committed himself to a make. By March he had taken a second entry, this one definitely a Lagonda and in the name of Lord Howe. The M45 team cars had been sold after the 1935 TT, and clearly if two Lagondas were to be entered they would have to be LG45s. A slight problem arose in that the LG only came on a 10ft 9in wheelbase, so there was no way legally to enter shorter cars. As the extra length meant extra weight, more power needed to be found, so it was lucky that the Sanction 3 would safely go to 4000rpm in the gears and be usefully faster in top speed if geared the same.

The four special cars comprised two four-seaters, aimed at Le Mans (whose regulations demanded this), and two two-seaters for other, shorter, events. The four-seaters were built first, but Le Mans in 1936 was first doubtful, then postponed and finally cancelled amid industrial unrest in France. The French GP that year was for sports cars, to stop Mercedes or Auto-Union winning it, and it was arranged that Fox would control the two two-seaters, one to be driven by Marcel Lehoux and the other by the Léoz brothers. The race was timed to be two weeks after the original Le Mans date and was held at Montlhéry on 28 June.

Arthur Fox had clearly had a hand in the designs and the two-seaters and four-seaters were almost indistinguishable in appearance, the four-seaters having a small slot in their slightly longer tails where the token rear seats were. The bodies were a fraction wider in the cockpit than the 1934 cars, but tapered rapidly to the pointed tail. This contained the spare wheel, which under Le Mans regulations had to go on the car first at a tyre change. No figures survive of the power output, but as Fox had found an extra 36bhp for his 1934 cars it would not be unreasonable to suggest that he extracted about 150bhp from these Sanction 3 engines. The G9 gearbox was retained, but with a closer-ratio first gear (2.618:1 instead of 3.14) driving a 3.14:1 rear axle. According to circuit needs both 18in and 19in wheels were available and both 6.00 and 6.50 section tyres.

When finished, all four cars were lined up outside the Fox & Nicholl premises and photographed, the four-seaters painted Fox's favourite bright red and the others some lighter colour, probably blue. The Le Mans cars had full lighting equipment, as you would expect, but the others had the smallest lamps that would comply with sports car racing rules. The former were road registered as EPB 101 and 102, but the others were not registered for the time being.

The French GP took on a kind on mini-Le Mans atmosphere in 1936, with a run and jump-in start, officially supplied 80 Octane fuel and even a trophy from *The Motor* for the best placed British entry. There were three capacity classes, with the Lagondas in the largest, over 4 litres, which only

The 1936 Fox & Nicholl Team cars, photographed outside the Tolworth garage. The four-seaters have high set headlamps and the two-seaters the low ones. The only other visible difference is the tonneau cover over the rear "seats" of the four-seaters, where the two-seaters are plain metal.

held three other cars, all Hudsons. It looked as if the class prize ought to be a walkover, even if the Bugattis, Delahayes and Alfa-Romeos in Class 2 might well be quicker overall. The race length was 1000km, 80 laps of the track, with no chicanes. The crowd was disappointing, as a result of a clash with an important horse race at Auteuil, and so was the entry, at only 37 cars. There were, in effect, three separate battles for the class prizes and the main battle, in Class 2, lay between the Bugattis of Wimille and Benoist and a flock of Delahayes, the Alfas having withdrawn.

There had been a rash of pirate programme sellers on practice day, so all cars were re-numbered on race day. (More confusion for the historian.) As for the Lagondas, Lehoux had a co-driver called Roccati in number 98 and the Léoz brothers had number 90. After ten laps Lehoux led the large car class by six miles, but he was driving the car far beyond the capacity of its brakes and when they all disappeared there followed a 35-minute stop for replacement shoes, which dropped him to five laps behind the Hudson of Trintignant. Once on the move again, he drove even more ferociously, so that although he got the class lead back, the second set of linings lasted no longer than the first and he was forced to retire at about 750km. The Léoz brothers took up the struggle with the Hudsons and slowly picked up places as the opposition ran into trouble, finally winning the class at 64.4mph. This was fine, but a bit embarrassing when you realise that the winning Riley in the 2 litre class averaged nearly 69mph and the Wimille/Sommer Bugatti achieved 77.85mph to win Class 2.

It was said that the Léoz brothers were lucky to win their class, since they were only marginally less fierce than Lehoux and at several pit stops had great difficulty stopping within the length of the pitlane. Lagonda's French distributor was present and Fox had to call him in to dissuade the Léoz pair from retiring with "no brakes" when they were lying second in the class and the leading car was obviously sick.

The cancellation of Le Mans led to a rush of enthusiasm for the Belgian Grand Prix, a 24-hour race at Spa-Francorchamps on 11 and 12 July. Fox & Nicholl joined the rush but could only get an entry for one Lagonda, one of the four-seaters, to be driven by Dick Seaman and Freddie Clifford and starting number 18. Before the Belgian race Lehoux had entered his Lagonda for the Marne GP, held only a week after the French GP on the

Rheims circuit, which attracted only 22 entrants and gave another win to Wimille's Bugatti. Lehoux finished this time, probably because on this fast circuit the brakes had an easier time, especially as it rained for the second half of the race, curbing his driving so that he ended in twelfth place at 79mph, four laps behind the winner. This was his last outing in the car as the fiery little Algerian was killed in an ERA at Deauville in July when he collided with Farina's Alfa. The Léoz brothers had entered here as well, but withdrew after what they regarded as the farce of the French GP.

There were 34 starters in the Belgian GP facing the traditionally dubious Spa weather. There were six classes this time, with the Lagonda in the over 4 litre class, and once again the likely winner would be in class 4, where the Bugattis and Delahayes lurked. It was dry for the first quarter of the distance, and the lead was contested by two blown Alfas, a Bugatti and a Delahaye. Then rain started and continued for the rest of the race, getting very heavy at times. Both Seaman and Clifford, newcomers to a racing Lagonda, drove a magnificently steady race and contrived to average 78mph overall despite the rain. As ever, the Lagonda's weak point was its appetite for tyres, forcing too many pit stops, where, under the race rules, the drivers had to do the changing. At the end of it the Lagonda won its class and was 4th overall at 72.33mph to the winning Alfa's 77mph. Everyone remarked how standard the Lagonda was compared with the opposition, and from this time on the versions of sports cars encountered on the racing scene began to look and behave less and less like road cars.

Lagonda dragged out the big print to celebrate the class win, rather excitedly claiming (and having to retract) that the Fox & Nicholl cars had recorded the fastest lap in the 1935 TT and that the Belgian GP car had averaged 72.9mph (actually 72.33). The drivers weren't named, but a fortnight later the Kevill-Davies and March advertisement put this right, with a testimonial letter from Dick Seaman and a photograph of the car in action before it rained.

The Tourist Trophy race was shortened to 410 miles for 1936, to be run on the unchanged Ards course. Whereas the entry for the 1935 race had been almost exclusively British, the 1936 one was much more mixed. BMW had entered a team of three 2-litre cars for Aldington, Fane and Bira, and there were seven Delahayes, some works-supported and some private. Eddie Hall was back

in the Bentley, now a 4¼ Litre with a new body. He must have felt he was due for a win, having come third in 1932, fourth in 1933 and second in both 1934 and 1935. Arthur Fox entered three Lagondas, as promised, two of them four-seaters for Earl Howe and Pat Fairfield and a two-seater for Brian Lewis. Freddie Clifford was the nominated reserve driver. Everyone looked forward to Round 3 of the Bentley/Lagonda duel.

Practice was supposed to be on both the Wednesday and the Thursday, but the last minute discovery of a fair due to be held in a village on the course resulted in the extension of Wednesday practice to three hours and a curtailment of Thursday's. The best Wednesday time was that of Tom Clarke (Delahaye) at 81.55mph. Fairfield was the fastest of the Lagondas, since he needed to learn both the car and the course. In contrast, Eddie Hall and Earl Howe had both driven in every Ulster TT.

The two-seater Lagonda was the newly registered EPE 97 (12111), Lehoux's car from the French GP. The other GP car had come back from France and was languishing in Jack Lemon Burton's dealership, up for sale. EPE carried race number 1, Fairfield's

car was number 2 and Howe's number 3.

As forecast, 5 September was wet and squally and the cars set off in pouring rain, except for a number of the Delahayes, whose ignition had got drowned waiting for the start. The Lagondas had no such trouble and at the end of the first lap Lord Howe led Lewis and Hall through the spray. Within five laps it became clear that Freddie Dixon (Riley) looked set to repeat last year's victory, leading on handicap from Dick Seaman (Aston Martin). Lewis and Hall were having their annual battle and by coincidence both were driving their first race of the season. Lewis was, in fact, to retire at the end of 1936. The Delahayes were proving very fast when running but a mite fragile for the rough and bumpy course, with prolonged pit stops for repairs. At the end of the second hour Dixon still led but Lewis was second, until he spoilt it by hitting the bank at Newtownards and had to come in to replace a wheel. Up to that point his average had been 79.36mph. For this shortened race Fox reckoned on only one pit stop, but Hall startled everyone by not stopping at all, having fitted a 40-gallon (182-litre) fuel tank in order to run through non-stop. This was not really surprising given the

Start of the big-car class, Ulster Tourist Trophy 1936. Earl Howe in number 3 is fractionally ahead of Pat Fairfield in number 2 and Brian Lewis in number 1.

1936 Ulster TT. Brian Lewis in Lagonda number 1 chases Hall's Bentley in round 3 of the Bentley/Lagonda duel.

general opinion that his pit stops in the previous races had cost him a victory.

For the second half of the race Dodson took over from Dixon without losing the lead, Hall was second and Lewis had fought back to third. The roads were drying and consequently speeds increased; in response to a lap by Hall at 81.07mph, Lewis produced first 82.51mph and then 82.79. The Delahayes, robbed of possible victory by unreliability, went all out for the lap record, which ultimately fell to René Lebegue at 85.52mph.

Just before the fourth hour Lewis suddenly called in to the pits for more oil. The engine compartment was a shocking mess, for a stud had broken in the timing case and had fallen out, allowing the timing chain to pump all the oil out through the hole. Not only was the sump empty but also the supplementary tank that Fox had fitted since the 1935 Le Mans race. Less visibly, much of the bearing metal had gone too, and Lewis was reduced to limping round to a finish, although he had been travelling so rapidly before that he still lay third at the fourth hour. His fastest lap, at 83.20mph, had been exactly equalled by Hall. Behind all these fireworks, Fairfield and Howe had been running unspectacularly, most of the time in fourth and fifth places.

Thus the race ran out with Dixon/Dodson winners by one minute from Hall, eternally second, even when non-stop. Fane (BMW) was third, leading his team to the team prize, and Fairfield and Howe were fourth and fifth at 78.49 and 78.40mph respectively. Lewis eventually finished 14th at 76.12mph but made up the team, the only other one to finish complete. Right at the end, Fairfield threw all caution to the winds and did one searing lap at 83.91mph that was (and remains) the fastest ever recorded by a British car at Ards.

Once the race was over the news was released that a local Riley driver, Jack Chambers, had skidded into a lamp column in Newtownards, knocked it down and careered into the crowd. There had been eight fatalities and more injured. To avoid a panic nobody had been told about this while the race was on, so that ambulances could get to the spot without having to battle with leaving spectators. Yet the total lack of any crowd control, with spectators standing in suicidal positions to get a good view, meant that the Ards circuit was never to be used again.

It had been an interesting race, for with hindsight the omens were apparent that the traditional hard-sprung, weighty English sports car was about to be ousted by the light, independently-sprung

Continentals. The Delahayes had been very fast, but temperamental. Just as soon as they managed to stay screwed together for the duration of a race, the Lagondas and other big cars were going to have to fight very hard indeed. In the smaller class the BMWs had been an equal revelation. It looked as if Le Mans, with its long straights and smooth surface, was going to be the last stamping ground of the English heavyweights.

Fox & Nicholl had now hastily to rebuild the engine of EPE 97 as the car was entered for the BRDC 500-Mile race at Brooklands only a fortnight away. Fortunately little was required beyond new bearings. One of the charateristics of the alloy crankcase on a Meadows engine was a tendency for it to "run away" from the crankshaft when hot, as the crankcase expands more than the steel shaft. The oil pressure drops in proportion, but the actual throughput of oil is unchanged as the powerful oil pump pushes more oil (but at a lower pressure) through the enlarged annular spaces. This was borne out after the 1935 Le Mans win, when , on dismantling the winning engine it was found to be undamaged, despite running for the last few laps with barely a pint of oil in the sump.

For the 500-mile blind on the Outer Circuit EPE was stripped of its front brakes, wings and lamps,

the second seat was cowled over, the radiator slats were removed and a streamlined cover was fitted to the front of the chassis. A special straight-cut 3:1 rear axle ratio was coupled with 7.00 x 21 tyres (the largest Dunlop could provide) to give 36.17mph per 1000rpm in top gear, enabling the Lagonda to lap at 120mph consistently, without exceeding 3500rpm.

The 500 was a handicap race and there is a wonderful photo of the start in the Fox archives. Only three cars are left on the line. Jack Duller in

1936 Ulster TT. Lewis chases Earl Howe at Quarry corner. Crowd control was pretty sketchy, since watching the TT was free. It is difficult to credit the angle of roll that Lewis has achieved in the hard-sprung Lagonda.

There were any number of unforgiving hard objects on the Ulster course. A dab of white paint was deemed enough to draw drivers' attention to this bridge abutment.

The start of the big-car class in the BRDC 500 Mile race at Brooklands on 19 September 1936. Brian Lewis leads off for Lagonda, flanked by the Pacey-Hassan (No. 22) and Jack Duller in Whitney Straight's Duesenberg.

Whitney Straight's Duesenberg hasn't moved, but the Lewis Lagonda is within inches of the Pacey-Hassan as they get away. All round the cars cluster a group of men, perhaps 40 of them, some in plus fours, others in overalls. One of them is Earl Howe, Lewis's co-driver, but dressed as for Ascot. All have their backs to the track where, out of the mist on the Byfleet banking, the limit cars are rapidly approaching. In the middle distance a lone flag marshal stands in the centre of the vast width of The Fork, uncertain which way to look and holding out a warning flag horizontally at arm's length. No massacre of racing notables is on record, so we must suppose they all got out of the way in time.

Arthur Fox was by now well aware of his car's appetite for tyres and his drivers were instructed to drive very high up on the banking as it was believed this was the best way to preserve them. This the drivers did and engaged in a spirited duel with the Hamilton/Belleroche Alfa, both cars lapping at 120mph. It was traditional that this race, the last major one of the season, should be conducted with the right foot pressed to the floor, since the whole winter would be available for any

rebuild needed. Hence the retirement rate was expected to be high. Only 17 cars started and three went out in the first hour. At this point Freddie Dixon (Riley) was leading at about 122mph with two more Rileys of Paul and McLure second and third. At the first refuelling stop Dixon lost his lead to Bertram in the Barnato-Hassan, but Charlie Martin got it back again when the big car stopped in its turn. After the Lagonda's pit stop it began to misfire, leading to other stops to change plugs, although eventually it was thought the problem was fuel feed and it did rectify itself later. Eventually Dixon's car, boiling merrily, won at an average of 116.86mph, followed by the Pacey-Hassan and the Lagonda in third place at 113.02mph, having shaken off the Alfa in the end. For this result, Fox & Nicholl won a green marble clock on tubular legs, very Art Deco, called the Walton Trophy, which was bequeathed to the Lagonda Club by Mrs Fox and is now the VSCC's Fox & Nicholl Trophy, competed for annually at Silverstone by road-equipped sports cars.

The 500 was the end of the racing season and the two four-seaters disappeared for ever, either broken up or, more likely, cannibalised and trans-

formed into slightly lighter than usual dropheads. EPE 97 was retained by Fox & Nicholl, however, for the 1937 season while the other two-seater was still up for sale, at steadily reducing prices.

Alan Good had his own Rapide available for the Monte Carlo Rally in 1937. He took Charles Brackenbury as navigator in CAR 733 (12142). They started from Tallinn again, as number 124, and A E Dobell again drove his M45 Rapide as number 131 from the Stavanger start. It was a tough winter and only 81 cars got to Monte Carlo; of them only 63 were unpenalised. On the way south the Tallinn competitors had a lot of trouble with deep frozen ruts and Alan Good hit his sump on one of them, starting a leak that wasn't bad enough to make them retire, but meant the crew had to give up eating and sleeping to keep to schedule. Good's driving style was definitely on the courageous side, and "Brack", who was a superb raconteur, kept the Staines canteen rocking as he described adventures such as crossing a Polish river on parallel tree trunks after the bridge had been swept away in a blizzard. Good's method was to approach the trunks at full speed to get it over with, while Charles cowered in the back with a blanket over

his head to avoid seeing his coming doom.

Both Lagondas got through to Monaco, although well down the list. For the driving tests Brackenbury was to drive since he was several stones lighter than Good, and the Rapide was the fastest British car in 23.6 seconds. The fastest cars were the Delahayes, the actual French GP cars, but fitted with lamps and wings, of a kind. One of these came out the overall winner, driven by Lebegue and Quinlin. Good/Brackenbury came 40th and Dobell 74th, but the latter won, for the second year running, the Open Car class, over 1500cc, of the confort competition

The 1937 RAC Rally fell foul of harsh Spring weather and there was a lot of snow and ice about to sort out the entry on the road. The Bwlch-y-Groes was completely impassable, for example. The finish this year was at Hastings and the SS Jaguars had a field day, finishing first, second and fourth. Bicknell and Cade in the works demonstrator LG45 Rapide were 15th in class from the Stirling start.

The Inter-Varsity Speed Trials at Syston Park attracted the usual high-quality entry, including Christian Dietrichsen, who had bought the Le Mans

Pit stop for EPE 97 in the 500 Mile race. Donald Wilcockson attends to fuel while his colleagues deal with the huge tyres. The front brakes were removed as not needed on the Outer Circuit at Brooklands.

Alan Good at the wheel of his mount for the 1937 Monte Carlo Rally (Car Number 12142). Charles Brackenbury stands in the doorway. Note the shovel storage, a problem with the Rapide's small boot, and the electrically heated panel in the windscreen.

winning Lagonda and demonstrated her versatility by entering the Lands End Trial too. At Syston, BPK 202 could not match the speed of J G Fry's 4½ Litre Bentley, which won the class.

By June, when Le Mans came around, Arthur Fox was reduced to one car, the faithful EPE 97. Following the cancellation of the 1936 race, all the 1935 results had been carried over as if 1936 had not happened. Luis Fontes had lost his licence in the interval, so Charles Brackenbury was recruited to partner John Hindmarsh. Fox himself had less time to devote to racing as the rearmament drive had led him to take on sub-contract work for Hawkers, which involved extending the Tolworth premises. Streamlining came to Le Mans in 1937 and the Type 57S Bugattis, one of which won, the Peugeots and an ultra-modern Adler saloon all contrived to make the Lagonda look a trifle Early English. It is possible that Fox was forced to paint EPE green for this race - contemporary accounts are vague - but when the car arrived with its number 3 painted on both front wings, a method accepted at Ards, he was made to blot one out since it could be construed as number 33.

Brackenbury took the first stint, which was marred by a nasty crash at the White House that killed Rene Kippeurt (Bugatti) instantly and Pat Fairfield the following day. Brackenbury had been following team orders and had refrained from the customary first-hour mad blind, but his restraint was not rewarded and the car began to give trouble, leading to eventual retirement by 10pm. Brackenbury, pressed for the reason, said it was "loss of breath", tactful but unhelpful. Anthony Blight suggests that Lagonda themselves had tuned the engine and had mistakenly planed the head instead of the block to raise the compression ratio. This operation had left insufficient metal between the lower face and the plug holes, leading to cracking. Fox was using an 8:1 compression ratio, which would mean 2.87mm had to come off somewhere, starting from a Rapide head, so this theory is perfectly plausible. At the time, *The Motor* said a valve had stretched. This retirement in 1937 was the only one in the Meadows/Lagonda era not fully explained. It was John Hindmarsh's last race too, for he was killed shortly afterwards at Weybridge in a Hawker Hurricane he was testing. It was a shame his last race was not more distinguished. The race was won by Benoist and Wimille in the "Tank" Bugatti and, as the first French win since 1926, resulted in huge celebrations. The only consolation for the British contingent was Aston Martin's win in the Rudge-Whitworth Cup competition.

The Eastbourne Concours d'Elegance had by now grown into a showbiz type event to encourage visitors to the resort in July. There were pages of prizes and one feels practically everyone won something. Mrs Good entered a black LG45 saloon, coming second in the "Closed Cars over £1000" class and winning the "Smartest Ladies' Car over £600" class. Viscount Curzon entered a green LG45 Rapide and won the "Open Sports Cars over £1000" class. Other class winners included Tommy Farr, the boxer, in a Lammas Graham, and Mabel Constanduros, a comedienne, in a Mercedes.

In the absence of Ards, the new venue for the TT had been settled as Donington Park, not without mixed feelings, for the three-and-a-bit mile circuit, even with its new extension, was a complete change from all the previous circuits with their very long laps and possibilities for sustained high speed. When issued, the regulations called for doors to be fitted on the cars and at least three teams, Lagonda included, had to perform hasty hacksaw work. The doors on EPE 97 were constructed at this time and while complying with the regulations, are not actually any use for entering the vehicle. Following from this, the exhaust pipe had to have another three bends put in it to avoid conflicting with the new doors.

The Lagonda was the largest car in the TT,

towering over the other entries. Hall had entered his Bentley and, when it failed to appear, broke his record of competing in each race since 1928. Strong teams from Talbot-Darracq and BMW, and a works Delahaye, showed that Brackenbury and Charles Martin in the Lagonda were in for a considerable fight. The plot was for Charles B. to drive the first half and Charles M. the second, changing over at the only pit stop. The weather was dry but threatening, and 21 starters embarked on the 312-mile race. The Lagonda was quite unsuited to this short circuit racing and although both drivers performed valiantly, even the long Donington straight wasn't enough to get the Lagonda really flying. At the quarter distance there was a dramatic moment when Brackenbury overtook Bira's BMW just as Bira was overtaking Dodson immediately before the Melbourne corner, the new downhill hairpin. There was a big tangle but no crash, much to everyone's surprise.

By 1.15 the race lay between the Talbots of Comotti and Lebegue, the BMWs going out with axle trouble. The rate of retirements was very high, reflecting the number of gear changes and the hard acceleration called for. With only three laps to go the Lagonda, which had had no trouble up to then but just wasn't quick enough, leapt into the headlines when a stub axle broke as Charles Martin braked for Melbourne. It was at this exact second that the photographer from *Speed* pressed the

After the war EPE was still competitive in sports car racing and was shortened and lowered and fitted with an ENV epicyclic gearbox. Bill Michael (in jumper) prepares it for a race at Brands Hatch.

The engine compartment of EPE 97 showing the Fox & Nicholl free-flowing exhaust with a heat shield to protect the magnetos. The filler on the scuttle connects to the sump for speedy pit stops. Only two fuel pumps are now fitted but for Le Mans a second pair would be installed, though not wired, so that they were available as spares.

shutter release, getting a remarkable shot of the car sitting down on its offside front corner. Martin held the car under some sort of control in the ensuing excitements and escaped unhurt, but was of course out of the race, which was won by Comotti at 68.7mph from Lebegue and Bira. No team finished complete.

This was EPE's last big race, but there was one last exploit before the six-cylinders were put out to grass. *Speed's* editor Alan Hess was keen to have a crack at the "Sports Car Hour" record, a fashionable if unofficial record, and persuaded Dick Watney to let him have EPE for an attempt. This

was agreed, and after a short stay at Fox & Nicholl for tuning and fitment of lamps, Hess got under way on the afternoon of 7 October 7 in drizzle and gloom. A passenger was carried, Jesse Heitner, editor of *The Sphere*, who wrote up the attempt for the pages of *Speed*. Thirty-eight laps of Brooklands were put into the hour, resulting in an average of 104.44mph which handsomely beat the current record held by Sammy Davis.

The lap times were remarkably consistent, only varying by a second or so, with 1 minute 34.4 seconds (105.52mph) the fastest and 1 minute 35.6 seconds the slowest, apart from the opening lap, of course. There followed a notable party at Tolworth to celebrate. The only sour note came when Hess sent Fox & Nicholl's bill of £25 to Watney for payment and Watney refused to honour it, despite a "gentleman's agreement" beforehand that he would. This rankled with Hess for the rest of his life, for Lagonda gained a lot of publicity from the record. The same issue of *Speed* that carried the account also featured an advertisement from Jack Lemon Burton, who was continuing to try to dispose of the other two-seater, still unregistered and now available for £499, having covered less than 1000 miles.

The final works competition outing for the LG45 was the Monte Carlo Rally of 1938. The rules of the event stopped Lagonda using a V12 as it had not

Still racing. Bill Michael in EPE (cut and shut) leads Lord Dunleath in the other two-seater, HLL 534, (unchanged) at a VSCC race meeting in the 1960s.

been in production long enough, so Good took Brackenbury as navigator in FPG 56 (12214), a drophead, starting from Athens as number 114. Brackenbury must have been either a masochist or had a very short memory after his "never again" accounts of the previous year's rally. The factory devised and fitted a magic de-ditching gear and Brackenbury took Derek Rutherford, now Chief Tester, on a run to try it out. The trip involved visits to numerous pubs, in all of which Brack was well known. Eventually, Derek reminded him of the purpose of the trip, whereupon Brack immediately applied full lock and they landed in the ditch. Amid much laughter and falling about they rigged the magic de-ditching gear and fortunately it worked.

For once the Athens starters did get through to Monte Carlo, and at the finish of the road section Brackenbury said it had been uneventful, but he also said he was too tired to get out of the car, which rather belies that statement. The Good/Brackenbury LG45 came 29th overall and second in the over 1500cc confort competition. The winners were Schut and Ton in a Ford V8, narrowly beating Lebegue by inches in the final driving test.

There was a possible entry for EPE 97 in the South African GP, but it fell through when Charles Brackenbury fell ill, and the car was put up for sale

in April 1938 for £595. It wasn't an easy sale for the big heavyweights were now definitely outclassed in racing. The other two-seater eventually found a buyer at £300, appearing at Brooklands in 1939 driven by P N Nuttall and owned by Captain Millar. EPE, however, has never stopped competing somewhere and after the War made appearances in the 9 Hour Race at Goodwood, where it was 14th out of 18 finishers. After several lightening and shortening modifications had made the car almost unrecognisable, it was eventually restored to its original appearance in the 1980s and still competes to this day in Vintage events.

Brooklands Reunion, 1980. Alan Hess (left) reunited with EPE 97 after it had been restored to original by David Dunn (in glasses).

Nearside of the restored EPE. The silencer now prevents the useless door opening anyway.

Chapter Seven

The V12 and LG6

Catalogue illustration from 1939 of the V12 chassis. You can see how long the front suspension torsion bars are, as there is a cutaway by the silencer to show the rear mounting at the centre of the chassis

Left to his own devices, W O Bentley would have liked to take as long to develop the V12 as Rolls-Royce habitually spent on their new models, but Alan Good was in a hurry and the 1936 Motor Show announcement of the V12, made at his insistence, was wildly premature, as the car was nothing like ready and the proposed delivery dates absurd. By the following year's Show a very different car was shown, the result of twelve months of frenzied work and still not entirely developed, so that changes continued throughout 1938 and 1939, some of them announced and some not, including surreptitious modifications to customers' cars when they came in for service.

Most of the second half of 1935 had been occu-

pied with the LG45, but after Tresilian arrived in February 1936 the V12 engine and chassis design pushed on apace, with Frank Stark joining in April to do the carburation and lubrication system. The cylinder block drawing was signed off on 10 July by Eric Easter. As an example of Rolls-Royce brainwashing it is amusing to record that all the 1936 and 1937 V12 drawings were given drawing numbers prefixed by LeC, standing for Le Canadel, Royce's house in France, which had nothing whatsoever to do with Lagondas or Staines. Just force of habit, one assumes.

Once the decision to have independent front suspension had been made, and despite W O's public assertions that there was no need for it (he was after all, trying to sell LG45s at the time), it was possible to lower the engine into the space hitherto occupied by the front axle. This led to a lower propeller shaft line and eventually to a hypoid rear axle, although the 1936 car had Lagonda's vintage "heavy" axle. Thus the whole car could be built much lower than any previous Lagonda and still retain the flat floor in the front which was a traditional feature.

The front springing was to be by long torsion bars, attached to the inner end of the lower wishbone at one end and to the chassis frame cross brace at the other. This was an excellent arrangement which took the twisting load off the front extremities of the chassis. However, problems arose with getting precision manufacture and led to the prototype having a complicated adjustable anchorage at the chassis end. Once production

started this was simplified, but even so a tuning process became part of chassis assembly and dire warnings had to be printed in the instruction book not to meddle with the factory settings.

The frame itself was basically a deep channel section swept up over the rear axle, but with substantial parts boxed in. There were numerous holes in places to allow cables and pipes through, and at the extreme front, to mount the wishbones. The 1936 car had a Girling braking system, just as the LG45, but by 1937 a hydraulic system by Lockheed had been substituted, it being realised that the independent front suspension led to a track change from full bump to full rebound and short of fitting a sliding splined joint to the transverse rods the Girling design could not cope with this. Similarly, a conventional draglink and track rod steering system would not work with ifs, and instead the drag link operated a three-armed bracket connected to the offside track rod, a transverse link to a slave bracket on the nearside, and the nearside track rod. It was clearly designed for easy conversion to left hand drive, should the need arise. Much the same benefit was attached to the G10 gearbox with its centre change, although this did come under some attack from owners who expected to change gear with their right hand in a quality car and regarded the centre change with an element of derision.

After the 1936 Motor Show was over, *The Automobile Engineer* published its annual appraisal of the exhibits and naturally devoted a lot of space to W O's latest creation. Their man had spotted that

substantial bits of the engine were made of wood (perhaps the knots were a clue) and he made the telling remark: "It is still largely experimental, it having been put on exhibition more as an indication of future policy than as a finished car". How true. He must have spoken to Tresilian, for there was a further remark that although the block/crankcase casting was in chrome alloy cast iron, "It is the intention to experiment with an alloy cylinder block and liners". Not if W O could do anything about it, it wasn't.

Carburation was proving to be one of the biggest headaches. As a start Starke had fitted a twin-choke 1¼-inch downdraught Stromberg from

This 1938 V12 Short Saloon, Car Number 14053, is owned by Peter Blenk.

Running the first V12 engine on the test bed. Left to right: W O Bentley, Stan Ivermee, Stuart Tresilian and Charles Sewell. The timing case later grew stiffening ribs.

FPK 550, the first prototype saloon, had more exaggerated front wings and "bosoms" than the eventual product. This photograph shows (on the original) how the chromed horn grilles had been painted black to avoid exciting elderly politicians.

FPK 550 in 1980 after being rebuilt. It was re-registered by the factory after the War. For the 1938 attack on the 100 miles in the hour record the wheelcases and running boards had been removed and every conceivable part peppered with holes. Unfortunately this car has now been converted into yet another Le Mans replica.

America that Rolls-Royce had tried for the Phantom III. To a present day eye it looks woefully small for a high-revving sporting engine like the Lagonda, although it might suit a dignified high-torque unit like the Rolls-Royce. This carburettor was shown on the Motor Show car and also in the photograph taken to celebrate the first running of a V12 engine on the test bed. However, at about this time Stromberg decided to drop this model, leading Rolls-Royce to develop their own design and Lagonda to look elsewhere. A Solex carburettor was tried, for which test bed results survive, but it produced nothing like enough power, 125bhp at 5500rpm, less than the Meadows could achieve; torque was down too, at 200lb ft at 2000rpm. SU came to Lagonda's rescue at exactly the right moment by announcing a downdraught

version of their normal horizontal unit, with a spring replacing gravity to operate the dashpot, and at the same time they brought out a thermostatically-operated starting carburettor which removed the need for a jet-lowering device and its control complications. This was not the end of the story, for the torque curve produced by two of these SUs had a strange double hump, with a peak at 2000rpm and another at 4000rpm. Most of this experimental work fell to Stan Ivermee and Percy Kemish, both brilliant practical engineers, even if self-taught. They soon found that four SUs answered most of the problems, but W O would not hear of this, partly because of the complicated control runs they needed and partly - most likely - the cost. Eventually Percy Kemish made up a special inlet manifold with Pyrex windows in it in an attempt to see what was going on, and was duly horrified. Vee engines always have rather congested inlet arrangements and Tresilian had made this worse by designing exhaust ports that crossed to the inside of the vee to give an exhaust-heated hotspot.

Even so, there was still a problem with a lack of low-speed torque, and efforts to increase this without losing the top-end power carried on up to and into the War period after 1939. And since the war too: in recent years attention has been focused on camshaft profiles. Lagonda tried several different ones, each with different aims, since the silence and refinement W O was seeking were to some extent at odds with the free-breathing, high-revving nature of the engine, which was going to have to cruise at 5000rpm to give the 100mph

performance required. In the opinion of the present Lagonda Club, W O erred far too much towards the refinement criterion. When members have made up camshafts to one of the earlier, discarded designs from 1936/7 the transformation in torque has been magical, also giving something like 35bhp more at top speed. The principal problem seems to be that the top faces of the tappets are radiused and the original cam design had hollow flanks to match. This would follow Rolls-Royce practice. But at some point this design was replaced with one featuring tangential (straight-sided) cam profiles, perhaps because it had worked well elsewhere. This mismatch caused most of the trouble. There is also the issue of whether the inlet valves were too big, a subject we will return to when looking at the 1939 Le Mans cars in the next chapter.

By the 1937 Motor Show enough of the problems had been resolved for there to be five cars on the stand, all of them runners, and for delivery dates to be realistic. W O Bentley had got his hypoid rear axle by buying it whole from Salisbury's in the USA, and discovered to his surprise that it was lighter than Lagonda's part-alloy one, despite being all-steel. It was also cheaper than he could have made it in-house, bearing in mind that

Wyndham Hewitt would have had to buy special machinery to cut the hypoid gears and were not keen to do so.

There were some surprises, principally that the six-cylinder Meadows engine was to remain available in a new model, now known as the LG6, using a longer version of the V12 chassis. The 1936 announcement had set out 11ft (3.35m) and 11ft 6in (3.5m) wheelbases for the V12. In 1937 these were joined by a shorter one of 10ft 4in (3.15m) which was to prove by far the most popular, outselling the others by 2 to 1. The range of bodies offered was also now wider, comprising saloon, drophead and tourer bodies on the short wheelbase, saloon de ville and sedanca de ville on the medium wheelbase, and a 7-seater limousine by Thrupp & Maberly on the long one. The LG6 wheelbases were slightly longer, to accommodate the longer engine, so that a 10ft 7½in (3.24m) short version mirrored the 10ft 4in short V12 and an 11ft 3½in (3.44m) the 11ft medium V12.

The LG6 bodies were nearly identical to the V12 versions, the sole recognisable feature being a flat front panel next to the radiator, with the horns poking out of it, in place of the voluptuous curves of the V12 which concealed the horns. The extra length is not noticeable. Rather oddly, the LG6,

The V12 had Frank Feeley's first Lagonda saloon body that didn't use the Silent Travel pillarless patents. It is lower and wider than the LG45 that preceded it.

which had higher gearing to reflect the Meadows engine's limited rev-range, retained Lagonda's spiral bevel rear axle. Thus the propeller shaft line must be higher and the tunnel in the rear compartment deeper, but it doesn't look it.

The new splendours of Earls Court had no effect on the last-minute rush at Staines and when the cars were announced, a week before the show, only one drophead was far enough advanced to be photographed. The magazines and catalogues had to make do with profile drawings. W O and tradition had won the day over the front end styling and the cars were recognisably descendants of the LG45. A new radiator design was wider and taller than before but set 2 inches nearer the ground, so actually looked smaller, with the aperture for the starting handle some way up the slats. The longer versions had a taller design, purely for aesthetic reasons, since it held no more water. All the radiators were slightly raked.

The front wings were considerably more bulbous than the LG45's, rising nearly to the level of the top of the bonnet and extending a long way ahead of the front wheels. Between them and the radiator all the chassis parts including the trumpet horns were faired in by a pair of protruding "bosoms" which in the first cars even had chromed grilles for the horns in the "nipple" position. The coarse allusions that these provoked came to the ears of the Minister of Transport when he toured the show, and his evident disapproval and veiled threats led to a redesign, less likely to excite elderly politicians, for the production cars. Before the show opened the offending grilles were painted black.

Each of the bodies was a clear development of its predecessor and in each case was noticeably lower and wider, particularly in the front, where the wide V12 engine led to a wider bulkhead and an extra 4½ inches (114mm) across the dashboard. A noted change was the departure of the pillarless saloon body, as the new design had all its doors hinged on the centre pillar. The doors were of two-piece construction, full thickness up to the lower edge of the glass and then a thin channel only above that. Dick Watney had wanted a totally clear opening above the waist, but sealing problems between the glass and the wood-framed body led to this idea being dropped and a compromise sought.

The De Ville was a more upright and sober design, with six lights and fully framed doors. It was 6 inches taller, all of it available as headroom. On all these saloon designs Frank Feeley solved the tricky re-entrant angle between the rear quarter and the boot lid by continuing the waist belt round the junction as a quarter-round section, giving the area a strong and rigid look.

A tourer body was illustrated for the V12 - rather oddly the LG6 version was called the Rapide but the V12 wasn't. Neither was popular, only about three of each being sold, since the design looked gawky beside the very modern dropheads. While the V12 tourer had an identical mechanical specification to the other V12s, the LG6 Rapide had a higher compression ratio of 7.5:1 (standard was 6.68:1) and a "taller" rear axle at 3.31:1 instead of 3.58:1.

Lagonda proposed to offer the 11ft 6in wheelbase in chassis form only but quoted a Thrupp & Maberly limousine of truly regal proportions and an exotic Sedanca de Ville by the same firm as standard productions, although the catalogue contradicted itself about wheelbases here. In practice, of course, as a result of the special requirements of the upper-bracket customers Lagonda was now trading with, all the artificial divisions of the catalogue got blurred and we find bodies of all kinds on each of the wheelbases and by all the famous coachbuilders, although it is true to say that Lagonda themselves never built a body on the long-wheelbase V12.

The interiors followed the family look, but the lower-built V12 could have a shorter gear lever that didn't conflict with the lower edge of the dash. The two large instruments continued to work in opposing arcs, but now with the zeros at the top. All the minor ones were combined into a single circular instrument with four quadrant dials within it. They were of the recently-introduced electrical type, with sender units operating at a lower voltage

By using a taller radiator and bodywork, the de Ville on the 11ft chassis doesn't look any longer than a short saloon. A division was an option, but was rarely ordered. (Photo Michael Bolger)

From the front, too, the 1938 V12 is notably lower. The radiator, for instance, appears to be shorter by setting it nearer to the road.

The foglamp had to be folded out of the way if the starting handle was to be used. By 1938 this would probably only be when being serviced.

Twin fuel fillers were standard.

rather than through capillary tubes or whatever. Only short-chassis cars had a rev-counter as standard, and when it was absent all the dials moved one to the right. In front of the passenger was a matching circular panel with six switches in it controlling lamps, ignition, wipers and starter. This panel continued after the War, following the hallowed Lagonda tradition of using up the boxfull, and is found on Lagondas and Aston Martins up to the end of the David Brown 3 Litre.

Changes to the chassis had been less drastic, but the new hydraulic braking system included a tandem master cylinder so that failure of a wheel cylinder did not leave the car totally brakeless. Adoption of hydraulics freed the designer from the layout restrictions that mechanical systems dictated, and for the first time a Lagonda had a right-hand throttle pedal. Rubber-covered pedals

were another first, while the adoption of a hand-brake lever that lay nearly horizontal, coupled with a central gear lever, meant that for the first time since the 12/24 the driver could get into the car as easily as the passengers.

Nothing much had changed in the suspension, although the method of adjusting the torsion bars had been simplified. Armstrong hydraulic dampers were fitted all round, the rear ones controllable from the steering column. The front ones were adjustable too, but not remotely. In fact, acting as they do on the inner pivots of the upper wishbone, they are not very effective. The Marles-pattern steering box needed 3¾ turns from lock to lock, a far cry from the M45 and its 1¾ turns and more likely to appeal to women drivers not possessed of Popeye-like biceps. The rear springs continued to be semi-elliptic, but a Bentley innovation was screwed shackle pins which take out side-thrust. The maze of little oil pipes to lubricate the chassis grew more complex still to lubricate the independent front suspension. The Tecalemit pump which charged the system was initially fitted to the clutch pedal, but experiences early on with owners who scarcely ever moved out of top gear led to it being coupled to the brake pedal instead.

To go with the five possible wheelbases the complete range now featured no less than six rear axle ratios: 4.273:1 (11 x 47) for short V12s, 4.455:1 (11 x 49) for mediums, and 4.727:1 (11 x52) for the 11ft 6in wheelbase. The equivalent LG6 ratios were 3.308:1 (13 x 43) for Rapides, 3.58:1 (12 x 43) on short cars and 3.8188:1 (11 x 42) on long ones. All used the G10 gearbox with the same internal

As on the LG45, only the offside wheelcase had a wheel in it. "Ace" wheel discs were a common extra and saved a lot of work keeping wire wheels clean.

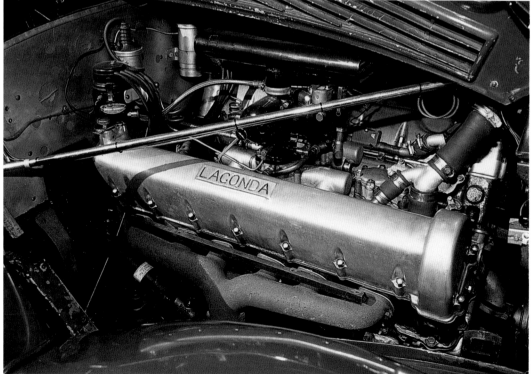

The V12 had a long central gear lever

Near side of the Sanction I V12, clearly showing one of the pair of distributors and the two SU carburettors mounted in the vee.

ratios. But of course owners could specify otherwise and many short V12s had the 4.45:1 axle to give better acceleration - at the cost of only 20.24mph/1000 revs in top. Tyres were 6.00 x 18 for LG6s and short V12s, 6.50 x 18 for the longer models of V12.

It is now necessary to describe the V12 engine, W O Bentley's masterpiece and for its day a unit of formidable complexity. The two cylinder blocks and the upper half of the crankcase formed one "Chromidium" nickel-iron casting, and the cylinder heads, which are not identical to each other, were made of the same material. The upper crankcase ended at the crankshaft centre line, the lower half being an alloy casting, closed by a detachable bottom plate to form a shallow sump. The cylinders, each 75 x 84.5mm, giving 4479.7cc, were bored in the two blocks, set at 60 degrees, with the offside cylinder in each pair just over one inch (25mm) further forward than the nearside. The crankshaft had four main bearings, with two intermediate crankcase webs to support the middle ones. At the rear intermediate position a cast-in one-inch pipe carried water from one block to the other to reduce external plumbing.

The crankshaft had bolt-on balance weights, and as an example of Tresilian's Rolls-Royce born attention to detail (the unofficial R-R designers' motto was "It's never too late to complicate"), the

Bare V12 chassis in the process of restoration. The big tubular crossmember at the front can be detached for access, a modification introduced after problems with the prototype, where a rectangular section box was welded in. This car is to have telescopic dampers added to improve front wheel adhesion.

balance weights had their centre of gravity at 30 degrees to the plane of the crankpin. The reasoning being that since the crank only revolved in one direction, this offset would distribute the wear more evenly than if centrally placed. All crankshaft bearing surfaces were nitride hardened and the Duralumin connecting rods ran directly on the crankpins with no bearing metal in between. Main bearings were 2½in (63.5mm) diameter and the big ends 2¼in (57 mm).

To lighten the reciprocating masses, all the bearings were drilled as far as possible and then filled with aluminium plugs, themselves drilled for the oilways. The rear main plug in particular was drilled in the most labyrinthine way to carry out several different functions. Each crankpin had a little ridge to separate the two big ends it carried, and those big ends were drilled for oil grooves on the side as well as in the conventional places for lubrication. The different thermal expansion rates of Duralumin and steel led to rather large annular spaces when hot, but a vice-like grip when cold, so an extra hole was provided in the caps to allow excess oil back to the sump when the annular space was at a minimum in cold start conditions, and thus avoid excessive oil pressure building up. The pistons were of anodised aluminium by Specialloid, with tapered oval skirts and four rings, all above the gudgeon pin.

Each cylinder bank had a single overhead camshaft, driven by chain from a fibre half-time wheel, itself driven by a smaller steel gear fixed to the nose of the crankshaft. The camshafts ran in aluminium galleries with seven bearings, and operated in-line valves via mushroom tappets running in phosphor-bronze guides, with adjustment by screws and locknuts. At the rear end of each bank was a Delco-Remy distributor serving the plugs in its bank; one revolves clockwise, the other anti-clockwise. Both distributors have to be removed if the cam covers are to be lifted. Each distributor had its own coil, for even a six-cylinder engine at 5500rpm was nearing the limits of a standard coil ignition system's capacity.

The 14 mm plugs were installed on the upper side of the heads, although the centre ones are still rather difficult to reach. The valves were laid out along the head in the order E-I-I-E-E-I-I-E-E etc., a slightly unexpected layout, which has been known to lead to trouble with cracking caused by uneven temperature distribution. The firing order was 1-2-9-10-5-6-11-12-3-4-7-8, using Lagonda's notation which has number 1 the nearest to the radiator on the offside bank and number 2 its companion on the nearside bank. This is equivalent to a six-cylinder engine firing 1-5-3-6-2-4, and another firing 60 degrees after it. Although Ferrari, notably, has used this firing order, it is basically smoother if the two camshafts are timed to fire at a 420-degree interval, and this is what Lagonda eventually came to use when the Sanction 2 engine arrived.

In addition to the duplex timing chain, the near-side timing drive had another chain to an auxiliaries shaft driving the water pump on the front, the dynamo at the back and a skew gear to the oil pumps in the middle. The twin oil pumps were set to give 70psi from one, to lubricate the crankshaft, and 15psi from the other for all the other lubrication functions. Each system was quite separate and had its own rather crude filter, its own relief valve and bypass. Oil pickup was from the centre of the wide, flat sump, and to stop oil rushing about too quickly under cornering or due to gradient, a series of gravity-operated trap doors slowed all this activity down. The oil level was shown by an indicator needle, operated by levers from a cork float. It may be that nobody could work out a sensible route for a dipstick, but luckily the floats rarely sink. The question of accessibility

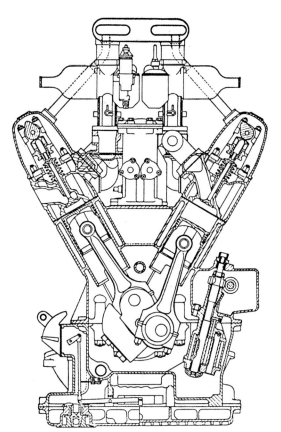

is one of the V12's less endearing features, especially in Sanction 1 form. The oil filler, for example, nestles cosily next to the left-hand exhaust manifold and guarantees burns to anyone rashly attempting to add oil to a hot engine. It is rumoured that some of the servicing operations were made deliberately difficult to put off amateur mechanics and generate service revenue for the factory. It is certainly true that anyone specialising in V12 maintenance generates a rack of special tools for the purpose.

As on all vee engines, the two SU carburettors were in the centre of the vee and both exhausts were on the outside, but two of the exhaust ports on each bank were linked by an external pipe on the inside to create an exhaust-heated hotspot. In production form the two exhaust systems were completely separate, although the prototype car, whose chassis formed the subject of a much-reproduced F Gordon Crosby drawing, had the two systems joining near the gearbox and there-

V12 engine partly dismantled. The cylinder heads can be lifted without disturbing the timing, which is as well considering the labour needed to reset it once lost. The largest timing wheel was made of "Fabricoid" in the interests of silence.

Cross-section of the stillborn Sanction 3 engine with only one oil filter and offside oil level float.

Underside of a V12 engine. The Lanchester-type torsional damper right at the front of the crankshaft is concealed within the timing case when the engine is assembled.

after a single tailpipe.

A Lanchester-type torsional damper was fitted to the nose of the crankshaft, but concealed within the timing case, which had grown stiffening ribs since the prototype. The rubber engine mountings were supplemented by special spring-loaded torque-reaction dampers to control the sideways rocking motion of the engine. Drive was via a Borg & Beck clutch to the G10 gearbox, and thence to the Salisbury rear axle through a Hardy-Spicer needle-roller propeller shaft.

The power output claimed for the V12 at introduction was 180bhp at 5500rpm, using a 7:1

compression ratio. This seemed reasonable if one accepted the 140bhp quoted for the LG45. However, test bed figures are less optimistic, and in 1937 the best figure yet attained was 156.5bhp at 5000rpm. It took a great deal of development before the 180bhp was reached in production, although it was eventually, perhaps as a result of the work done to produce the engines for Le Mans in 1939. The torque curve of the standard V12 is rather odd, as noted before, and is more or less flat between 2500 and 3000rpm. Thus the slowing of the engine as a result of starting on a hill, say, does not result in an increase of torque as the owner might expect, and this leads to the notion that the V12 lacks "lugging power", an accusation often levelled at it in the 1930s and since.

All the foregoing adds up to a complicated engine taking a great deal of time and care to set up properly, and difficult to get at when in place. However, if installed correctly and not disturbed unnecessarily, practice has shown that it will run for countless thousands of miles with no more than routine servicing. It is not uncommon for a new owner to take three days to get the sump off, only to discover that he still can't see anything because of its two-piece construction and that two of the bolts that hold it on are 10 inches long and go right to the top of the block. Percy Kemish, who had dismantled more V12s than he had had hot dinners, reckoned it took 18 hours, even if he knew exactly what to do next and had a rack of special tools.

With the complicated model range proposed

Sanction 1 V12 engine. Each bank has its own distributor. The air cleaner had to be extremely shallow to clear Feeley's low bonnet line. The cowling over the exhaust manifold was an attempt to keep under-bonnet temperatures reasonable and it lined up with the grille in the bonnet side

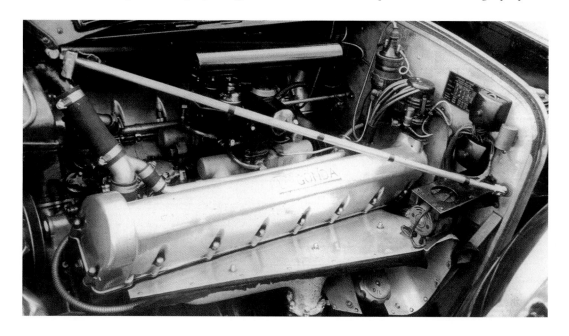

after the 1937 Motor Show, it is probably easiest to explain with a table:

	V12			LG6	
Wheelbase	10ft 4in	11ft 0in	11ft 6in	10ft 7½in	11ft 3¼in
Chassis	£1200	£1225	£1250	£875	£895
Drophead	£1575	-------	-------	£1220	------
Saloon	£1550	£1625 (De Ville)	-------	£1195	£1295 (De Ville)
Tourer	£1285	-------	-------	£1150 (Rapide)	-------
Sedanca	-------	£1870	-------	--------	£1540
Limousine	-------	--------	£1850	--------	--------

Naturally enough, a new system of Car Numbers was evolved. LG45 numbers had reached about car number 12270 by Show time, and the last one delivered was to be 12277 the following spring. It was more than likely that the LG6 would be available much earlier than the V12 and the first one delivered was given car number 12310 in December 1937. But instead of a single series, as always used hitherto, it was decided to issue car numbers in different series, according to wheelbase, with short V12s starting at 14010, delivered in February 1938, mediums at 16010 and longs at 18010. Following this new philosophy the long wheelbase LG6s started at 12510 in March 1938. Clearly there might have been a problem with overlapping had there been a long production run, but this never arose.

Lagonda had Stand 107 at Earls Court and crammed on to it a short saloon, de Ville and seven-seater V12s, and drophead and tourer LG6s.

In the rush to get them there the short saloon was fitted with the one foot longer de Ville gearlever, upon which a jokey Guards officer hung his bowler hat on opening day, causing fury from Dick Watney and feverish work after closing time to change it. The Duke of Kent, opening the Show, unexpectedly approached the stand as some last-minute work was being done on the tourer body and, there being no time to get the trimmer out of the body, the tonneau cover was battened down on top of him, accompanied by hissed instructions to pull his feet in.

The V12 wasn't the sensation it had been the previous year, of course. You can't do the rabbit-out-of-a-hat trick twice. But Bentley was relieved enough at the work they had done since 1936 to

By opting for the low radiator on the 11ft chassis, James Young gave their Sedanca Coupé a really exotic look. Four were built.

A V12 drophead on the short chassis. Only tiny changes were made to this body in the two years of production. For example, the 1940 model year cars do not have the small radius at the back of the wheelcases where they join the running boards.

In contrast with the James Young Sedanca Coupé, Thrupp & Maberly built this extremely formal limousine on the 11ft 6in chassis.

permit himself a 20-word speech at the Lagonda lunch at the Royal Palace Hotel. He meant it too, for the works demonstrator LG45s were put up for sale at the same time.

To get magazine and newspaper publicity, one of the prototype V12 saloons became the Press car. This was FPK 550, whose bodywork was closer to the production design than the 1936 LG45/V12 hybrid car had been, but still had a number of differences. *The Autocar* took FPK for a tour of Devon, followed by a full road test in March 1938. This was the first of what eventually became almost embarrassingly frequent road tests of V12s and LG6s by the magazine, whose staff had clearly fallen in love with the cars and used all the permutations of wheelbase and body type as reasons for testing every version the works would let them have. The series even extended into wartime, with 1940 tests conducted on Pool petrol and in the blackout.

Concerning the character, behaviour and performance, the road test was pure eulogy. The car was expensive but worth it, and the performance had not been achieved by producing a rorty sports car. On the contrary, the V12 was docile and quiet, it handled well and it was extremely comfortable and well equipped. The acceleration (0-60mph in 12.9 seconds) was better than anything in its class by miles, and the braking inspired perfect confidence. The best timed speed was 103.45mph and Brooklands was lapped at 97.95mph. At top speed the engine was turning at

5200rpm, so the gearing was exactly right for an engine red-lined at 5500rpm. There were a few small criticisms: at least four sparking plugs were difficult to reach, the dipstick (this was a prototype, production cars did not have one) was extremely difficult to reach, and the boot was none too large. The engine started at once, as V12s always should, and ran rather cold, as no other V12 in history ever has. One suspects the radiator had been filled with that special Staines water that boils at 80° on the gauge. Considering the weight (39.5cwt/2007kg, empty), the fuel consumption of 12-15mpg was reasonable.

From the spring of 1938 the first V12s were finding their way into customers' hands - and frequently coming back again to cure overheating. A lot of it was simply friction as the engine bedded in. A total of 48 piston rings generates quite a lot of this, as do 12 tight-fitting big ends. The first modification was to cut a grille in each bonnet side, and fit an aluminium cowling that mated with it, in order to exclude the heat from the under-bonnet area. This made the oil filler even harder to get to and the long-term answer was to redesign the offside cam cover to incorporate the oil filler, which became a distinguishing feature of the Sanction 2 engine.

The Motor had given quick impressions of a run in a V12 de Ville back in December, but their first proper road test of the new chassis was an LG6 short saloon and appeared at the beginning of

May, followed a fortnight later by the full test of the V12 de Ville. They liked both cars a great deal and were most impressed by the ride and handling, although it raises a smile nowadays to discover that the "really colonial going" over which they tested the suspension was really the infield at Brooklands from the paddock to the railway straight. Not many termite mounds there, or flash floods. The performance figures were good – 0-50mph in 10.4 seconds and a top speed of 94mph - but so they ought to be compared with M45 and LG45 saloons. There are no comparable saloon tests by *The Motor*.

Their rival magazine, testing GPE 624 in June, found that the LG6 was lighter than the LG45 and slightly faster, but both the Bentley designs were less accelerative than the M45, probably because they were heavier. On the other hand, they had higher top speeds as a result of the higher permitted revs.

The table shows the progress from 1933, the cars getting lower, wider and faster but with worse acceleration. The otherwise steady gain in weight was offset by Bentley's new chassis which, for all its apparent massiveness, was surprisingly light when bare.

	M45	LG45/S3	LG6
	saloon	saloon	short saloon
0-50mph	10.4sec	11.7sec	11.3sec
0-60mph	15.8sec	17.3sec	16.4sec
Top speed	90.00mph	93.75mph	95.74mph
Weight (empty)	35.5cwt	39.4cwt	38.75cwt
Consumption	17mpg	14.5-16mpg	12-14mpg
Length	15ft 6in	15ft 4in	15ft 6.25in
Width overall	5ft 8in	5ft 10in	6ft 0in
Height	5ft 3in	5ft 5in	5ft 0in

The summer of 1938 was enlivened by a visit from *The Automobile Engineer*, resulting in most of one issue and a host of photographs showing rows of V12s and LG6s being built on a good imitation of a production line, hampered by the lack of space, which caused some of the bodies to be at right angles to the others to fit them in. We learn that production was averaging 12 cars a week, evenly divided between the two models. Despite the lack of space, the bodyshop was also engaged in making utility bodies on Ford and Commer commercial chassis. It is of interest to add the running-in procedure which old test bed hands recall. Each V12 engine was run light (unloaded) for 10 hours at 800-1000rpm, followed by a run-up

More V12s went to outside coachbuilders than any previous model and the factory found it necessary to issue this drawing giving all the key dimensions and vital access points. It has proved invaluable to later restorers.

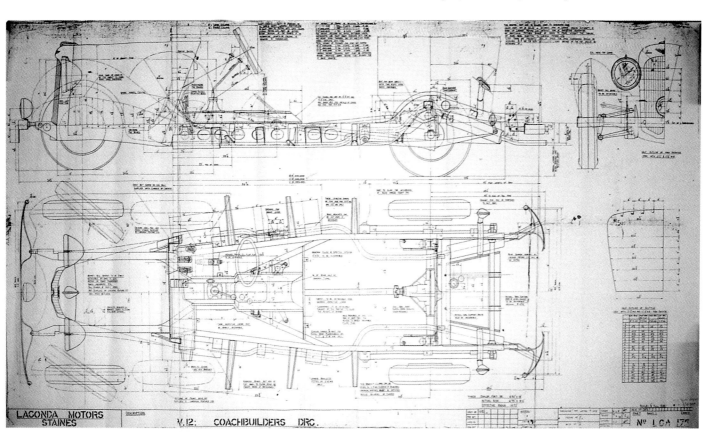

LACONDA MOTORS STAINES   V.12: COACHBUILDERS DRG.   No LCA 175

to 4500rpm to test power (3600rpm for a Meadows). The engine was then stripped and the valves ground in. It was reassembled and run on the bench for 5 hours and then tested for maximum power. If pronounced fit, it was then released to the assembly shop and eventually went out on road test for at least 300 miles.

The rest of the summer of 1938 was busy but uneventful at Staines and was punctuated by V12 road tests. *The Motor* tested an experimental de Ville, GPC 895 (Chassis E 3037), getting this tall and dignified saloon up to 101.12mph at Brooklands and, downhill, 109mph on the "con-rod straight" of the A11 near Newmarket. Even on the 4.455:1 axle this represented only 5390rpm and, as the tester remarked, this sort of engine speed from a 4½ litre unit sounded absurd, but the proportions of the cylinders were those of a 1500cc four, and the V12 had to be considered in those terms. As is not uncommon, this experimental car was rather quicker than production ones, and its standing quarter-mile time of 18.7 seconds could not be matched by the ordinary short saloon tested in September, the latter being 50-odd pounds lighter and lower but taking 19.1 seconds. On the other hand, the shorter car was using the 4.27:1 axle, which would not help initial acceleration.

The false impressions of performance brought on by lending experimental cars to magazines are confirmed by *The Autocar*'s results. They tested a prototype saloon, FPK 550, which returned the best acceleration figures of all the six published V12 tests, taking 12.9 seconds for the 0-60 dash, only 0.1 of a second slower than the LG45 Rapide,

an out-and-out sports car half a ton lighter. Subsequent tests on production saloons and dropheads were nowhere near as exciting, the best drophead result being 13.1 seconds on Pool petrol in 1940.

The 109mph figure reached by the de Ville in *The Motor*'s hands stirred up an obscure politician called Sorensen, who raised it as an issue in the House of Commons in July, calling on the Minister of Transport to ban the sale of cars capable of over 100mph. Mr Burgin, the Minister, replied that Section 10 of the Road Traffic Act forbade him from doing any such thing, while *The Motor* was suitably outraged and devoted an editorial to an attack on Mr Sorensen for trying to cripple the industry.

Comparing the merits of the two models, for his extra £300 or so the V12 customer got a reduction in the 0-60mph time of about 3 seconds and silky smoothness at all speeds. He also got hot feet and the indefinable cachet of owning the "in" car of the period for, no doubt about it, W O Bentley's new creation was stealing customers from Rolls-Royce. The car offered a dashing sportiness that the Phantom III did not, with more refinement than the 4¼ Litre Bentley and more performance than either. The customer list at Staines didn't start to read like Debrett, but it did start to resemble Who's Who in Show Business. Quite a number of sales were helped by Lagonda's ability to deliver virtually "over the counter", since the coachbuilding was in-house and not subject to other people's priorities. The ready availability certainly counted in Briggs Cunningham's case. For this visiting American millionaire, the irksome process of

A headache for the Registrar. FPJ 553 was W O Bentley's own transport. As a prototype LG6 it was perceptibly lower than the final product and had different body details - no wheelcases, for example.

ordering a chassis and a body separately, involving two different sets of delays, was overcome at Staines by lending him a demonstrator V12 for his holiday. In the meantime the factory built him a special car which was ready for him to take back to the USA at the end of his stay.

The export market was beginning to be important and the centre change of the G10 gearbox meant that left-hand drive cars were easily possible, although none was actually built. Film stars seemed to be particularly attracted to the V12 and some showy bodies were built on the 11ft wheelbase, which lent itself better to coachbuilders' excesses, frequently with the shorter radiator specified to enhance lowness. It was said earlier that the typical LG45 customer wore a black jacket and striped trousers. To continue the idiom, the typical V12 customer was as likely to have a mink coat and dark glasses.

At the same time this type of customer could be extremely demanding, and Dick Watney set about raising the Lagonda standard of quality control. Dick had worked at Thrupp & Maberly and knew the sorts of results he wanted. He instituted a policy of picking a car at random on a Friday evening from those awaiting delivery and taking it home for the weekend. There he would go over it with the proverbial toothcomb, and on Monday morning all the department heads would be seen converging on his office for the post mortem. He had sat in all the seats and measured the headroom. Why was it an inch more on the left than on the right? The bumper was nearer the ground on one side. Why? He wasn't sure all 12 plugs were firing. See to it. It could go on for ages in the same vein. After a bit the heads gave up arguing and the quality did improve. Not that things were skimped before, but under the Watney regime there was no room for "that'll do" - it had to be right.

The same standards were applied to the chassis, and axles and gearboxes were swapped wholesale to get quiet ones. The record for one single chassis, presumably for some very important customer, was 23 axles and 17 gearboxes. Watney made the works construct a detachable truck-like cabin to go on the rolling chassis, which would magnify the noises and make them easier to identify. The constant rejection of gearboxes led to friction with Wyndham Hewitt Ltd and the eventual resignation as managing director of Hewitt himself, although he stayed on the board as the technical contact with Bristol Aircraft. Watney took his place and thus inherited the gearbox problems, which

were to some extent brought on by the design of the G10, whose dissimilar metals tended to distort in the manufacturing process and particularly if left part assembled over a weekend. There is no room here for Reg Ingham's 14-page memo on the problem and possible solutions, but it grew to be such a talking point that Percy Kemish and Fred Shattock built up a gearbox out of scrapped parts and tweaked it until it was totally silent, resulting in a lot of red faces and the threat to transfer them to assembly since they were so good at it. At one stage a magic axle-quietening machine was bought from Detroit, but it proved to be useless, not as good as Bill Amiss with his stone and piece of chalk.

Dick Watney, like many a boss, felt it incumbent upon him to amend anything put before him, to show he had thought about it. Each year, Frank Feeley would produce the one-tenth scale profile drawings of next year's body designs for the MD's approval. Each year Watney would produce a pencil and make a trifling alteration, sometimes less than the thickness of a pencil line, and get Frank to agree this was an improvement. Unbeknown to him (Watney), the whole drawing would have to be redrawn anyway to translate the scale drawing to full size for the bodyshop to use. But it kept the management happy.

When the Motor Show arrived in October the message was that production would continue unchanged, apart from the introduction of a slightly more sporting Rapide coupé model. There had proved to be no market for the V12 tourer, probably because sidescreens and aeroscreens were of no appeal to the new market, but there was a market for a more sporting open car. The Rapide was mechanically identical, apart from a

The same car as it emerged from the factory after W O had done with it. It now sported a production drophead body.

The very short-lived 1938 LG6 Rapide tourer. It was not popular and only two are thought to have been built. There was a near identical V12 body called the tourer and illustrated in the 1938 catalogue. Even more unpopular, only one was built.

The controversial bonnet swaging mentioned in the text. The sales people were generally able to talk customers out of ordering this, which was not only ruinously expensive to do but also delayed delivery and hence payment. On this restored V12 the owner has used the swages to divide the two-tone colour scheme.

noisier exhaust, but had a shorter body with no wheelcases and only vestigial running boards. In theory it seated four: three abreast in the front and a single seat, set sideways, in the rear. But in practice it is better for the front seat passengers to be very close friends if three are to be accommodated. The hood was more like the drophead's but lacking the landau irons, and the frameless glass windows ensured a clean body line when they and the hood were lowered. The windscreen folded flat. As the spare wheel had been driven into the boot by the removal of the wheelcases, there wasn't much room for anything else in it, and the jacking system had returned to the underfloor position it had used in the M45 Rapide. There was to be an LG6 version too, almost identical in appearance.

Despite the assurance that there would be no changes to the other models, the mouldings on the drophead were altered because of the horribly costly trouble the bodyshop had had with the 1937/8 ones. The drophead shown in the catalogue illustration, which was a drawing, not a photograph, featured a swage line which ran from the radiator cap diagonally across the top of the bonnet to reach the door edge by the handle, and which then continued down in a long sweep to the front of the rear wing. There were matching swages in all four wings. This proved extremely difficult and expensive to do. All the panels had to be made up with extra metal all round, and assembled. Then Frank would have to mark out the swages and all the panels were taken off again to form the swages with a "jenny", after which they were trimmed to size and re-assembled. Fortunately, most customers could be persuaded to delete these swages on the grounds that next year's car would not have them, but a few persisted and Lagonda made no profit on these cars. The 1939 cars were to have only a simple waist moulding, and no arguments.

There was an additional model, which was slipped into the catalogue with no other announcement. It was called simply the saloon, and was in essence an 11ft version of the short saloon, using the low radiator and a rev-counter. It was there to answer criticism of lack of leg room in the back of the short saloon, and the extra eight inches were devoted to this. Again, there was an LG6 version on the longer wheelbase. The sedanca no longer appeared in the catalogue, although this

did not prevent customers ordering a few. All the established models saw no change to their prices, and the two new ones were:

V12 Rapide £1575   LG6 Rapide £1250
V12 Saloon £1600 (11ft)   LG6 Saloon £1270 (11ft 3⅜in)

As was normal then, the Motor Show produced a brief flurry of orders. Then these tailed off and the slack period lasted until the following spring. By then the Sanction 2 V12 engines were arriving, although there was never any public mention of the alteration, and even the owners' instruction book only had the changes inked in by hand. There were a number of modifications, the most visible being the oil filler, which now was placed at the front of the offside cam cover, a far more accessible position, ending the burnt finger problems of the earlier

version. Inside the engine, the little rib separating the pairs of connecting rods on each crankpin disappeared and the rods were made wider and slightly offset as a result. This was part of a more fundamental review of the lubrication system, brought on by the fact that the two-pressure system just didn't work. In brief, the high-pressure side wasn't enough and the low-pressure side was too much. So as cars came in for service a small hole was drilled linking the two, coupled with a pressure-reducing valve on the auxiliary side. Both pumps then produced high-pressure oil. The two separate oil filter chambers remained, even on the S2, but were linked internally.

A more noticeable change was to the firing order, which had probably been a Tresilian idea originally. With Sanction 2, Lagonda reverted to the

A 1939 V12 Rapide drophead coupé, Car Number 14073, owned by Mark Walker. At one time it was registered AT 1.

Lagonda claimed this Rapide dhc body was a four-seater, three in the front and one sideways in the rear. With no wheelcases, the spare wheel has been banished to the boot

more conventional V12 order of 1-12-9-4-5-8-11-2-3-10-7-6, which results in much better distribution of explosions along the crank. In fact, all that changed was the timing, so that the nearside bank fired 420° after the other, not 60° as before; the camshafts themselves were the same. Valve stem length was altered and there were a few other minor changes. A more puzzling change had the full-flow oil filter on the bulkhead deleted but not replaced by anything. Thus this advanced engine had worse oil filtration than its LG45 predecessor. One theory is that the filter was regarded as obstructing the oil flow too much and hindering the already marginal lubrication under some circumstances. A further clue that suggests lubrication problems was the change to a higher-viscosity oil recommendation.

Another problem that was never publicly acknowledged came to light when engines assembled on hot summer days came to be faced with a really cold winter start. The differential expansion rates of duralumin connecting rods and a steel crank resulted in one seizing the other in a quite immovable grip. Fortunately the special Bosch starter motor had a slipping clutch and didn't burn out, but many engines came back for the "1½ thou" treatment, which was works jargon for increasing the big-end clearance to that figure.

This V12 Rapide has a Sanction 2 engine fitted with the rare Le Mans four-carburettor cylinder head, with great benefit to bottom-end torque.

The cutout in the bottom of the dash makes room for the gearlever.

On the rest of the car, 6.50 x 18 tyres were now standardised, with increased pressures. The reserve petrol tap and its second fuel line vanished and were replaced by a green warning light on the dash, a change not always welcomed, and the G10 gearbox was replaced by the G11, externally similar but with different bearing arrangements and different, wider-spaced, intermediate ratios, so that the 1.25, 1.67 and 3.25:1 ratios of the G10 became, respectively, 1.33, 2.0 and 3.47:11. Coupled with this, the 4.27:1 axle ratio for the short-wheelbase cars was dropped and the 4.45 ratio replaced it, with 4.73 standardised for both 11ft and 11ft 6in cars. All these changes point to more emphasis on acceleration and less on high-speed cruising. The LG6 also acquired the G11 'box, but with no other changes.

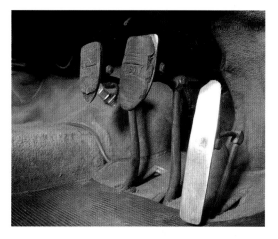

For the V12 and LG6, having fitted hydraulic brakes, Lagonda fell into line with other makes and put the throttle pedal on the right.

A closer view of the four-carburettor set-up.

Lagonda had stand 157 at Earls Court and squeezed five cars on to it: a V12 Rapide in mushroom, a metallic grey 11ft saloon, a black Thrupp & Maberly limousine, a grey and blue LG6 drophead, and a burgundy and buff LG6 de Ville. Customers were scarce, however, as the Munich crisis had frightened the rich, and the sales graph took a nasty dive. By Christmas there were no orders at all, and none appeared in the first four months of 1939, although a few V12s were delivered in this period, an indication of the long time some outside coachbuilders took to finish their orders. Fortunately Wyndham Hewitt Ltd had plenty of work and were steadily taking over more and more of the Lagonda factory as the rearmament programme got into top gear. The two

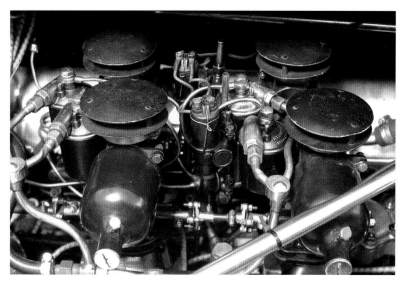

The Long Saloon reproduced the short saloon on the 11ft chassis with all the extra eight inches devoted to legroom in the rear. This is a 1940 model year car with the revised radiator, featuring a shallower top tank and fixed, not thermostatically opened, slats.

companies grew more and more integrated, and during the war Hewitt was definitely the major partner, the identity cards issued to staff reading "Wyndham Hewitt/Lagonda Ltd".

Alan Good, meanwhile, had set about cornering the small diesel engine market for himself, and by the end of 1938 was chairman of Lagonda, of course, but also of Heenan & Froude, Petters, Associated British Engineering (itself an amalgamation of several of his firms), Darwins, Fielding and Platt, and Mirrlees, Bickerton & Day. To those one should the deputy chairmanship of Brush Electrical, and directorships of Guardian Assurance and two other engineering firms. All at the age of 32. Another of his acquisitions was Bryce Berger Ltd,

who made fuel injection equipment for big diesel engines, and to accommodate them Good bought the site of "Ironbarks", a large house on the opposite side of Thorpe Road from the Lagonda factory. The War prevented the demolition of the house, but its substantial outbuildings and paddocks were soon incorporated into the Lagonda empire.

In 1935 W O Bentley had taken out a patent with George Constantinesco for an electrically-controlled gearchanging mechanism which interposed itself between the driver selecting another gear and the cogs actually engaging. Accepting the Lagonda job had then sent this project on to the back burner until 1938, when he returned to it in the form of what would have become the G12 gearbox, with only three speeds and intended for the limousine end of the Lagonda market. The actual gearchanging was done by solenoids, but before it got very far Bentley installed a Cotal epicyclic gearbox in a V12 and was very impressed with it, causing him to drop the G12. The postwar LB6 was designed to have the Cotal as standard, and substituting a conventional gearbox was one of David Brown's first changes after he took over in 1947.

At Christmas time in 1938 Alan Good dropped another of his bombshells by announcing a works team to be entered at Le Mans in 1939. We will cover this in the next chapter. The project took up far more of Bentley's time than he wanted to spare, since he was still hunting for more bottom-end torque for the standard V12 and making alter-

The same Long Saloon from the rear. The junction of the rear window and the boot is a tricky one for the stylist. Frank Feeley solved it with a quarter-round section belt which looks good and is also mechanically strong.

ations, admitted ly minor, to the chassis at the same time. Tresilian had left by now and Sewell was doing more of the design work. Rolls-Royce were taking their rival seriously and had introduced an overdrive version of the Bentley 4¼ Litre at the 1938 Show, while articles in February 1939 publicising the Embiricos Bentley, with its 142bhp engine and 110mph cruising speed, led Good to instruct W O to prepare a rival on the V12 chassis. With the Le Mans team to preoccupy him, this took ages and the car was not ready until 1940.

The propaganda war between the two firms was continual. Lagonda published fortnightly advertisements with notable owners, always famous and frequently titled, photographed beside their cars. They also contrived to get into the technical pages with illustrations of the latest radio installation or revised jacking system. In March a brochure recounted a trip to Germany where 97.24 miles were put into the first hour and 83.33 into the second, including a fuel stop. Lagonda's publicity machine became very good at lending a car to a celebrity if there were likely to be cameras about, so that the Duke of Kent opened 1938 Donington Park GP in a saloon V12 and at Brooklands John Cobb drove a Lagonda as the pace car for the rolling start to the International Trophy race in 1939. When Goldie Gardner was attacking international records on the autobahn in his MG, Alan Bicknell, Lagonda's Press Officer, managed to get a V12 saloon, GPL 691 (16030), into nearly every shot published in the motoring magazines.

A late change which was never publicised was that 1939 cars, or most of them at any rate, were fitted with two-leading-shoe brakes, Lockheed's latest model, which gave more even wear on the front shoes but had the minor disadvantage of removing practically all braking effort when travelling in reverse.

Production of the second Sanction of V12s finally got under way in May 1939, and as the 1939 production records have survived it is interesting to examine them. May's production was six V12s and three LG6s, comprising, for the V12s, two short saloons, a drophead, a long saloon and two chassis. The LG6s were a drophead and two Rapides. June saw 16 cars, July 18 and August 12.

The opposite way round to the factory, Barker, who built this two-door saloon, used the tall radiator on the short chassis.

The special "Bentley Chaser" saloon (Car Number 14117) with lightweight body by Lancefield. It had flush door handles and perspex side windows, since curved safety glass had yet to be invented. The car is shown here on completion in 1940 with wartime headlamp mask and compulsory white paint markings. It had one of the spare Le Mans engines.

In September, despite the outbreak of war, six cars were finished, with production ceasing, probably on government instructions, on 26 September. A lone LG6 Rapide was finished in November. In all, 62 cars were produced, 41 of them V12s. All the unfinished cars and parts were cleared from the factory and stored in a disused chapel in Flood St, Chelsea, while servicing was taken out of the factory, now under strict security as an armaments establishment, and installed in Bridge Garage and Bones Garage, firms the company owned in Staines. But the "phoney war" period ensued, and by the beginning of 1940 the company had persuaded the authorities that they should be allowed to complete all the Chelsea cars and sell them. This was agreed, with the stipulation that they should be exported to America in return for much-needed dollars. The cars were finished and sold but very few went across the Atlantic. The final production chassis were numbers 14120 on the short version, 16069 on the medium and 18021 on the long V12. LG6s ended at 12373 and 12527.

It was in this period that Good's "Bentley chaser" got finished. It was based on a V12 Rapide chassis but fitted with one of the spare Le Mans engines. On this, Lancefield built a very streamlined saloon body with a vee windscreen, curved perspex windows and a long sloping tail. It looked rather French, with faired-in headlamps and a concealed radiator. A quick trip to Brooklands just before it

closed in 1939 showed it had a 120mph top speed, and Good's plans were for it to sell at about £400 more than a standard V12, with a 120mph guarantee. It went to Chelsea unfinished but was completed and sold in 1940 to Lord Lovat, who had to be dissuaded from breaking a bottle of champagne over the fragile aluminium body as a launching ceremony.

In March 1940 *The Autocar*, still in love with the V12, managed to road test a drophead, although it wasn't one of the latest series. Running on Pool petrol and with no Brooklands testing it isn't surprising that top speed was down to 94.74mph. This was the only published test of an open V12, which was 1.75cwt (89kg) lighter than the 11ft saloon. No figures seem to have been published pre-war for the Rapide.

Work did not stop on the V12, as the firm had every intention of reintroducing it as soon as the War was over, and engine V12/110 was the "mule" on which a whole series of experiments were carried out in 1940 before the Experimental Dept turned their hands to more lethal products. It was fitted with an 8.4:1 alloy cylinder head to go with the four carburettors and gave 210bhp at 5000rpm when running on a 50/50 Discol/benzole mixture. There were also a series of tests to determine optimum settings for Pool petrol, which eventually produced, rather surprisingly, a power drop of only 5bhp. Important people, able to get a petrol

The Rapide drophead coupé's lines are equally effective with the hood up. Running boards are now a thing of the past.

ration, were still using their Lagondas and servicing continued throughout the War.

Then there was the "Boom Defence Boat" engine project, which was a code name for a high-speed manned torpedo. The idea was pinched from the Italians, who attacked our fleet using Alfa Romeo engined boats with a propeller that could be retracted out of the water to skip over a defence boom. The craft was then aimed at the target, and the crew baled out and did their best to evade capture. The Lagonda V12 engine was initially picked to power our version of this weapon, and Percy Kemish went to Vospers in September 1940 to develop a marine version, detuned to 120bhp for reliability and with two cooling systems: fresh water in harbour and seawater outside. The hull had a multi-step hard-chine design. The day after the first boat was finished the Germans bombed Vospers and they had to start again. Trials of the boat at sea, where it ran at full throttle for hour after hour, showed up a phenomenon which had also occurred at Le Mans: a sudden drop in oil pressure after about two hours. The Admiralty, with more resources than just Percy, eventually found the fault, which was a restriction in the oil system just downstream from the pressure-reducing valve. It was cured by some intricate machining work, which became standard practice for servicing afterwards.

The navy ordered over 100 V12 engines for the boom boats but they were never used. Experiments continued using a Gray "Fireball" V12 which produced 140bhp and was a lot lighter. But the "kamikaze" approach demanded of the crews told against the boats, and the RAF's "earthquake" bomb was the eventual tool of choice to sink the German battleship Tirpitz After the War, with the V12 not after all reintroduced, the navy sold all the engines for scrap.

Throughout the wartime period, at odd moments, the development of the postwar V12 continued, and by an odd quirk the only surviving full-size engine drawing is of this Sanction 3 engine. It featured the smaller inlet valves which had been such a success on the Le Mans engines, and a single oil filter tower instead of the twin ones left over from the abandoned two-pressure system. But the most surprising feature is that the elevation shows the gearbox attached to the flywheel housing and not separate as in Sanctions 1 and 2. The author is inclined to think that this means a Cotal gearbox was intended, since there was no room for a G11 in this position. Bentley

The shape of the radiator cap is repeated in miniature on the headlamps of 1939 cars.

was very keen on the Cotal, and Lagonda, later, in designing the LB6, did a lot of work on speeding up what could be a lethargic up-change. There was even a dummy made up of the 1946 catalogue which showed that the LG6 would have been dropped. But Lagonda's future plans were all changed in 1944 when a V1 flying bomb demolished the block of flats in Stainash Parade where the jigs and tools had been stored. The bomb killed several members of staff billeted there and damaged the works V12 racers housed in the unfinished shops below the flats. So 1944 saw the decision not to revive the V12 but to proceed with the design of a smaller, cheaper postwar car, the LB6, which is another story.

Original factory production record for 1939. Lagonda still couldn't sell cars in the winter.

CHASSIS PRODUCTION ACHIEVED.   2ND SANCTION.   1939.

TYPE	MODEL	W.B.	APR.	MAY	JUNE	JULY	AUG.	SEPT.	OCT.	NOV.	DEC.				TOTAL
V.12	CHASSIS	10'4"			1	2									3
"	SALOON	"		2	2	3	2	1							10
"	COUPE	"		1	3	1	4								9
"	RAPIDE	"			3	1(CN)	1	1							6
"	CHASSIS'	11'0"		1		2									3
'	DE VILLE	"						1							1
"	L.SALOON	"		1	5	1	1								8
"	CHASSIS	11'6"		1											1
V12 TOTALS.			NIL	6	13	9	10	3							**41.**
LG6	CHASSIS	10'7½'													
"	SALOON	"			2	4	1								7
"	COUPE	"		1	1	2		1							5
'	RAPIDE	"		2		1		1	1						5
'	CHASSIS	11'3½'													
"	L.SALOON	"				2	1	1							4
'	DE VILLE	"													
LG6 TOTALS			NIL	3	3	9	2	3	1						**21.**
GRAND TOTALS.			NIL	9	16	18	12	6	1						**62.**

(Vertical notes across right-hand columns: THIS RETURN WAS CLOSED ON 26.9.39. IT SHOWS ALL CHASSIS PRODUCED UP TO OUTBREAK OF WAR. NOTE 2ND SANCTION.)

ISSUED AT THE END OF EVERY MONTH BY PRODUCTION OFFICE.

| MR. NATNEY | MR. WHEELER | MR THORNLEY | W. MANAGER | BUYING X | PROGRESS | MR. LANE. |

V12 SUMMARY STATISTICS

Engine

configuration	60° V12 cylinder, one overhead camshaft per bank
capacity	4480cc
bore	75mm
stroke	84.5mm
RAC rating	41.85hp
compression ratio	7:1 (standard), 8.8:1 (Le Mans spec)
firing order	Sanction 1
	1 2 9 10 5 6 11 12 3 4 7 8
	Sanction 2
	1 12 9 4 5 8 11 2 3 10 7 6
	Number 1 cylinder is on the offside bank, number 2 on the nearside
valve timing	io 12° atdc, ic 33° abdc, eo 40° bbdc, ec 10.5° btdc. Inlet opens for 201°, exhaust for 209.5°
valve clearances	Inlet & exhaust (cold) 0.005in (0.127mm)
brake horsepower	180 @ 5500rpm (standard), 206 @ 5500rpm (Le Mans spec)
crankshaft	
no. of bearings	4
main bearing	2.5in diameter
big end	2.25in diameter
oil capacity	3 galls (13.6 litres)
cooling system	4 galls (18.2 litres)
ignition system	Twin 12-volt coils, twin Delco-Remy distributors
ignition timing	62° btdc maximum
contact breaker gap	0.018in (0.46mm)
spark plug gap	0.015-0.018in (0.38-0.46mm)
carburettors	Two SU downdraught (four at Le Mans), Jets 100, needles WO2
clutch	11in (280mm) Borg & Beck
starter	Bosch
dynamo	Lucas C45HV

Chassis

wheelbases	10ft 4in (3.15m), 11ft (3.35m), 11ft 6in (3.5m)
track	5ft (1.52m)
overall length	Varies with body
overall width	Saloon 6ft 2in (1.88m)
turning circle	37ft 9in (11.5m)
steering box lock to lock	Marles worm & nut, 3.75 turns
wheels & tyres	18in wire spoked, 6.50 x 18 tyres (6.00 x 18, swb 1938 only)
brakes	Lockheed hydraulic, tandem master cylinder. 2LS on 1939/40 models
rear axle	Salisbury hypoid bevel, capacity 3 pints (1.7 litres)
ratios	4.27:1 (11 x 47), 4.45:1 (11 x 49), 4.73:1 (11 x 52)

overall ratios			
Top	4.27:1	4.45:1	4.73:1
Third	5.34:1	5.56:1	5.91:1
Second	7.13:1	7.43:1	7.90:1
First	13.89:1	14.46:1	15.37:1

gearbox	Four speed, capacity 4.5 pints (2.6 litres)
fuel tank	20 galls (90.9 litres)
shock absorbers	Armstrong hydraulic

Prices
(1937 except where noted)

swb	Chassis £1200, drophead £1575, saloon £1550, tourer £1285, Rapide (1938) £1575
mwb	Chassis £1225, de Ville £1625, saloon (1938) £1600
lwb	Chassis £1250

Number built   190

LG6 SUMMARY STATISTICS
All as V12 except

Engine   Meadows Sanction 4 (as Sanction 3 except for minor timing change).

Compression ratio	6.68:1 (Rapide 7.5:1)

Chassis

wheelbases	Short 10ft 7.5in (3.24m); Long 11ft 3.5in (3.44m)
rear axle	Lagonda spiral bevel
ratio	Swb 3.58:1 (Rapide 3.31:1), Lwb 3.82:1

Prices
(1937 except where noted)

swb	Chassis £875, drophead £1220, saloon £1195, Rapide (1938) £1250
lwb	Chassis £895, de Ville £1275, saloon (1938) £1270

Number built   85

Chapter Eight

The V12 in Competition

Having been excluded from the 1938 Monte Carlo Rally as a result of insufficient production, the first appearance of any V12 in serious competition was in the same year's RAC Rally, where Lord Waleran entered a blue V12 drophead, GPG 131 (14029), from the London start. The results were as complicated as ever and he eventually came 28th in class, but won the Palatine Cup in the coachwork competition, awarded to the best drophead in any class. He got much the same result in the RSAC Scottish Rally in June, winning the open class coachwork prize. In August of the same year he drove his V12 in the Paris-Nice Rally but so far the results have resisted all

attempts to uncover them, although the outright winner is known to be Gordini in a Simca-Fiat.

Brooklands was always a busy place in October as manufacturers used to hire it for headline-catching stunts at Motor Show time. Alan Hess had done this for Lagonda in 1937 but was not going to get caught again, and the racing Lagondas had been sold anyway. Instead, Lord Howe and Stan Ivermee took two demonstrators to the track after a bit of tuning and had a go at putting 100 miles into an hour with each. Lord Howe had V12 FPK 550, which we have already noted as being substantially quicker than the common run of V12s, while Stan had an LG6 saloon, FPJ 553

The works cars being prepared in the Spring of 1939. Behind the screen is FPK 550, resting after its Brooklands exploits. This photograph was taken by W O Bentley.

(E3007), subsequently rebodied and sold as a drophead to the trade after its demonstrating days were over. Both cars had already done over 40,000 miles, so were nicely run in. Apart from racing tyres, they were said to be in production trim, but the wheelcases and running boards had been removed. Later inspections when FPJ came to be restored also showed a great many lightening holes drilled in unobtrusive places and a replacement engine.

The October event went off smoothly and successfully. After 21 laps Lord Howe was averaging 105.52mph when Brooklands' notorious bumps punctured a tyre. The car's own jacking system was used to change it, the stop costing 2min 42sec. The attempt then resumed and Lord Howe finished after covering 101.5 miles, timed by Mr Ebblewhite as the RAC had declined to get involved in these unofficial runs. On his last lap Lord Howe opened up and completed it at 108.27mph. The LG6 was slower, as expected, but nevertheless covered 95.87 miles with a last lap at 98.43mph. These were really impressive figures. Had the puncture not occurred, Lord Howe would probably have covered about 106 miles, all while smoking a cigar and listening to the radio, in contrast with Alan Hess's spartan ride of only one year earlier.

At Christmas 1938, when the motoring world was beginning to turn its thoughts toward the Monte Carlo Rally, Alan Good dropped another of his bombshells. He declared that he intended to enter a works team for Le Mans in 1939 and that Dick Seaman had been asked to drive one car. Dick had a soft spot for Lagondas, having owned a 2 Litre for years and driven in the Spa 24 Hours in one. The combination of W O Bentley's record with Dick's talent would make them favourites to win whatever the opposition, but unfortunately Mercedes-Benz would not release him to drive in the middle of the GP season.

W O has recorded his horror at being given less than six months to turn his civilised gentleman's carriage into a Le Mans winner. His protests were strong enough to get Good to agree that the 1939 attempt would be in the nature of experience gathering rather than anything else, the target being to finish. Then an all-out effort could be made in 1940. Nevertheless, with Bentley's five wins and Lagonda the only other British winner, the omens were in place for a Lagonda/Bentley victory.

In 1939 there was no objection to V12s in the Monte Carlo Rally and Alan Good went in a drop-

head specially prepared by the works. This was GPK 564 (14031), an early car but fitted with an S2 engine, a 4.73:1 rear axle and a variety of rallying extras. Special towing and de-ditching gear had been added to the front of the chassis. In addition, a set of Hartford friction dampers had been grafted on to the front suspension, with extended spindles that protruded through the "bosoms" to give instant adjustment by handwheels when required. The usual variety of shovels, pickaxes, etc., were stowed in ingenious places devised by the bodyshop.

Good took with him Charles Brackenbury, obviously a glutton for punishment, "Mort" Morris-Goodall and Rupert Watkins-Pitchford, who filmed the whole event on a 16mm cine camera. They were to start from Tallinn as number 69. Two other Lagondas had been entered, J W Miller and J E P Howey, both starting from John O'Groats. Howey had licence problems but started somehow, and Miller later opted to start from Glasgow. It was a year of favourable weather, resulting in a huge number of finishers. Good came 39th overall but won the convertible class of the confort competition, which was rapidly becoming a Lagonda speciality. First place overall was a tie between Trevoux/Lesurgue (Hotchkiss) and Paul/Contet (Delahaye), who even tied on the timed hillclimb that was supposed to sort everything out.

By March the Experimental Dept, under Stan Ivermee, had got the first four-carburettor Le Mans engine running on the test bed, and it was announced that Arthur Dobson would drive one car, with A N Other, and that the second car would be works prepared but would belong to private entrants, Lords Selsdon and Waleran. It was also stated publicly that 1939 was to be only a rehearsal for a 1940 win. Adding two more carburettors was not a simple exercise and in fact this cylinder head was totally different internally to the normal one. Bentley went to an 8.8:1 compression ratio, the maximum sensible given that the cars had to race on the fuel supplied by the organisers and were not permitted to add anything. But the better inlet arrangements removed some of the oddities in the normal V12 torque curve. Peak torque went up to 224.5lb ft at 4000rpm from the normal 208.5 at 2000, and peak power grew to 206bhp at 5500rpm. With our experience of power claims you won't be surprised to hear that 220bhp was claimed.

With all the works emphasis on Le Mans there were no factory entries in the RAC Rally, but W F Watson drove an H J Mulliner V12 saloon from the Stratford start to come 23rd overall and second in

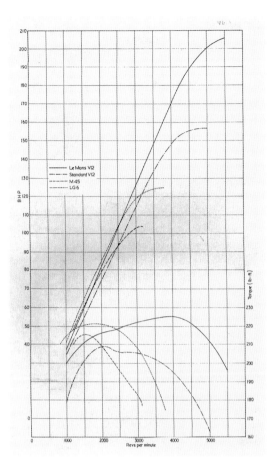

meticulous attention to detail on the cars. The party dragged on for so long that Good eventually got Derek Rutherford, the chief tester, to get out the 1907 Tricar and drive it around to distract the journalists so that Ivermee could get his cars back to carry on working on them, for there was much still to do. So tight was the schedule that only the works car got any testing before setting off for France, and that was confined to one session at Brooklands. The second car had not turned a wheel before they left and was run-in on the drive to the ferry at Newhaven.

The 10ft 4in chassis frame was not only riddled with lightening holes but was also of thinner gauge steel than standard. All the holes but one (for the handbrake cable) were filled with light aluminium discs to cut down drag, including holes in the

The press party on 7 June 1939. Wire mesh has replaced the chrome slats. Le Mans is only a week or so away.

Power and torque curves for the 4½ litre and V12 engines.

First roll-out of Car Number 14089, complete with posh chromed radiator slats and chromed headlamps.

his class of the coachwork competition to Jack Barclay's Rolls-Royce 25/30. Watson followed this by winning his class in the RSAC Scottish Rally coachwork competition, and Lord Waleran won the equivalent drophead class. There was no overall winner, but Lord Waleran was 7th in class 5 and Watson 19th in class 6. You can judge the severity and professionalism of the event by discovering that Lord Waleran took his spaniel with him.

On 7 June Alan Good ensured a lot of publicity for the Le Mans team by throwing a cocktail party for the press at the factory and showing the cars, which looked finished but were not. The two noble drivers were there, with a batch of other racing drivers and some remnants of the "Bentley Boys". Of course the return of W O to Le Mans was bound to attract enormous attention, and despite his protestations that it was only a rehearsal and that the drivers would have strict running instructions, the potential performance of the cars made them candidates for a win anyway. The Experimental team of Ivermee, Percy Kemish, Jack Sopp and Lionel Taylor were all vastly experienced in racing car preparation and this showed in the

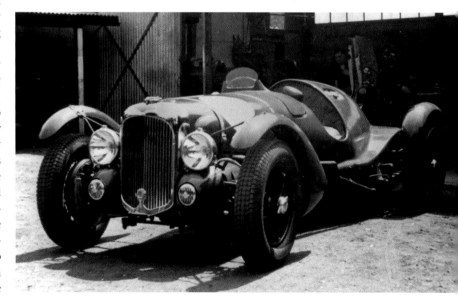

brake drums. Even the suspension wishbones were drilled. Every single component was scrutinised to see if it could be reduced in weight, and it is recorded that 17lb (7.7kg) was shaved off the steering box alone. The suspension was not greatly changed, apart from spring rates, but friction dampers were added at the front and special cooling ducts were arranged for the dampers all round. The front brakes were the newly announced two-leading-shoe Lockheeds, with air scoops on the back plates to cool them. There was no room in the tight-fitting body for the handbrake in its normal right-hand position, so it was transferred to the centre of the car, standing upright. Presumably because the drivers preferred it, the throttle pedal returned to the traditional centre position. The gear lever was much shorter than on a saloon and grew directly out of the top of the gearbox, with the remote control set-up removed and the lever swivelled round to bring the knob close to the steering wheel.

The bodywork was ultra-light and consisted of five major sections, all hand-beaten from aluminium sheet and mounted directly on the chassis, with no framework underneath. They were attached by Dzus quick-release fasteners. The body fitted very closely round the engine and was symmetrical as far as the cockpit, then offset to the offside behind that, with a pointed, raised tail incorporating the fuel tank and its twin fillers. The radiator was cut down in height but had the water capacity restored by extensions to the header tank above the engine. A supplementary oil tank was fastened to the cockpit side of the bulkhead with an access flap above it and, similarly, a small access flap allowed oil to be added to the main oil filler without opening the bonnet. Very light aluminium wings weighed less than 6lb each and were as small as the regulations permitted. The regulation wire mesh windscreen was never erected and lived flat in a special recess in the top of the scuttle, the driver using an aeroscreen in the race. The dashboard was quite fully stocked for a racing car, with an extra-large oil pressure gauge in front of the driver and no speedometer. The rev-counter read to 7000rpm and the oil gauge to 100psi. Fuel capacity was a nominal 38 gallons (173 litres), although in the race they found it possible to squeeze in another gallon. Right at the tail a complicated piece of panel beating made up

Scrutineering at Le Mans in 1939. Arthur Dobson is in the car and Charles Brackenbury (hands in pockets) beside it, with Percy Kemish on the extreme left. Black headlamps are more suited to night driving, with no distracting reflections, but so far the white circles have not appeared around the horn enclosures. This was done in the pits just before the race to aid identification of number 5 at night.

the front. To the same end, the batteries were also as far back as possible.

Charles Brackenbury had been chosen to accompany Dobson in the works car, carrying number 5, and he did get to do the Brooklands test, but the two lords never sat in their car, number 6, until they got to Le Mans. At scrutineering it was clear just how much weight had been saved as each car, complete, weighed 27cwt (1372kg). A normal V12 bare chassis weighed 29cwt (1473kg). Both cars were painted dark green and their lordships had their coats of arms on the sides of their car, but Derek Rutherford felt this was going to be insufficient to distinguish the cars at night and painted white circles on the front "bombs" that faired in the front suspension of number 5.

It is clear that W O's return to Le Mans was a very emotional event for him and he kept every scrap of paper to do with the event, even restaurant bills. All are now part of the Lagonda Club's archives, thanks to the generosity of Margaret Bentley after W O died. Greetings telegrams arrived from practically everyone in the racing world and all key Lagonda staff. Still, there was an immense amount of work to do at the track, most of which fell on Stan Ivermee and Percy Kemish, both demon drivers if given the chance. So much so that the designated drivers had to borrow other cars to learn the circuit. Eventually Brackenbury did manage a lap at 88.51mph and Dobson one at only one second slower.

Bentley's plan was to run at a set speed, ignore

Practice at Le Mans. Stan Ivermee leans reflectively on the refuelling rig above their lordships' car.

Le Mans, 17 June 1939, the start. Dobson has already gone and Lord Selsdon in number 6 gets away a trifle slowly - not surprising since he had only had a few laps to get used to the car.

the detachable spare wheel cover, the wheel lying flat to the rear of the fuel tank.

In developing the engine for racing, Stan Ivermee had managed to convince W O (or withheld from him) that Weslake's ideas on inlet valve sizes were right and those of the V12 were too big. The Le Mans engine had inlets of 1.3125in diameter (33.3mm) compared with the standard engine's 1.4375in (36.5mm). Rather surprising on a racing engine, the hotspot was retained, perhaps with experience of the cool air of the early morning hours at Le Mans. Special camshafts with much higher lift and special valve springs from Eaton in the USA were fitted, the engine being stressed to stand 6200rpm, although the drivers were not told this. Extra oil capacity was added by extending the sump downwards with a plastic spacer, which also lowered it further into the cold air stream.

The gearbox was lightened where possible and higher intermediates meant the car would do 80mph in first and 130mph in top, aided by 7.00 x 19 tyres at the rear and a 4.09:1 (11 x 45) rear axle ratio. The front tyres were smaller at 6.50 x 19 in an attempt to counter the understeer likely to afflict a car lightened by about half a ton at the rear but fitted with an engine slightly heavier than usual at

the opening scramble and any subsequent battles, and to finish at all costs. If all the opposition fell by the wayside, then so be it, but this would not be a reason to speed up in an effort to win. The speed he chose was 1mph faster than the previous year's winning Delahaye, which had averaged 82.35mph. However, substantial changes had been made to the track since last year and the Bugatti people were full of confidence that this year's race was going to be much faster. The opposition was formidable. A blown 3.3 Bugatti for Benoist/Wimille, a 4½-litre Delahaye for Dreyfus/Ralph, seven 3½-litre Delahayes , including one for Rob Walker and Ian Connell, three 4½-litre and two 4-litre Talbots, and a pair of very fast 3-litre Delages. The British contingent, apart from the Lagondas, was at the smaller end of the entry, although there was a 2-litre Aston Martin for Hichens/Goodall.

The weather was bright and fine at 4pm on 17 June when the traditional hush descended, followed by the pattering of feet and the grind of

starter motors. Arthur Dobson went straight into the lead in number 5 as the equally traditional mad blind began. At the end of the opening lap Chinetti's Talbot, a thinly-disguised Grand Prix car, was leading with a standing lap at 88.7mph and Dobson was 6 seconds behind him, leading a bunch of all the faster cars. But Dobson was driving strictly to Bentley's orders and slowly dropped out of this contest, lying sixth on the next lap. Lord Selsdon, who had not made a good start in number 6, was 18th. Louis Gérard got his Delage into the lead on lap 6 and worked his lap speed up to 95mph as he got away from the Bugatti. Dobson stuck to orders, lapping at between 5min 40sec and 5min 50sec and was steadily overhauled, dropping to 12th place, whereas Peter Selsdon, new to the car and the car itself probably rather stiff and new, steadily reduced his lap times from 6min 45sec (74.52mph) to get inside 6 minutes by lap 11. He had a short 20-second pit stop on lap 8 and was lapped by

Le Mans 1939. After the finish. The Lagondas took third and fourth places. The car alongside number 6 is the fifth-placed 2-litre BMW.

Dobson on lap 18, at which point the Lagonda pit controller speeded Dobson up to separate the two cars on the road, mindful of the 1928 debacle, made worse, if not brought on, by running in company. This lap by Dobson at 89.82mph was the fastest in the race by either car.

Refuelling was permitted after 24 laps and Ivermee called both cars in on their 25th lap at a distance of 209.6 miles. Checking the remaining fuel enabled this interval to be extended to every 27 laps, representing a consumption rate of 6 miles per gallon. Both drivers changed at this stop, which was completed in 1½ minutes now that the mechanics – and not just the driver – were permitted to work on the car. At about this time the outright lap record was broken by Mazaud's Delahaye at 96.74mph (5min 12.1sec), locked in a struggle for the lead with Gérard's Delage.

While Dobson and Brackenbury were very evenly matched as drivers and were anyway under strict team orders, it was evident that Bill Waleran was quicker than his team mate. By lap 30 had got down to 5min 40sec and got the slow down signal for his pains. On lap 41 both cars were called in for a warning, but we don't know what this was about. At dusk and the second driver change, done at lap 50 (Brackenbury) and lap 52 (Waleran), there had been enough retirements for the two Lagondas to be placed eighth and eleventh, two laps apart. During the night the two cars ran like clockwork, naturally at slightly reduced speed,

around 6 minutes per lap, with the drivers changing at the set intervals and everyone tucking into the lavish supplies of food and drink provided by the Hôtel Moderne. (W O kept the bills; perhaps in disbelief.) At 2am the leading Delahaye went out after catching fire, leaving Gérard with a lap in hand, and further retirements among the faster cars meant that by 7am Dobson was fourth and Selsdon sixth. Then just before 8am a crash put out both Hug in the second Delahaye and Mathieson in Chinetti's Talbot, so that the Lagondas were now third and fourth.

With the coming of daylight everyone speeded up and Dobson, Brackenbury and Waleran were all lapping at 87mph or thereabouts, with Selsdon slightly slower at around 83mph, fast enough to have won all previous races apart from 1937. When Brackenbury came in to hand over just before 9am he complained that the clutch wasn't freeing. There was a delay of nearly seven minutes while this was investigated, which allowed the other car to take back one of the laps that separated them. By this time 19 of the 40 starters had retired and at least two cars were limping round with less than their normal quota of cylinders functioning, victims of the early mad blind and drivers' volatile temperaments. At the changeover on lap 184 it was Dobson's turn to complain that the clutch was not freeing. This time 17 minutes were spent trying to cure the problem, and this brought the second car on to the same lap. At about the same time the Bugatti began to speed up, reducing its deficit to only one lap by noon. By 1pm it passed the Delage, which was ailing but had been so fast earlier that it still was nine laps ahead of the

The noble drivers of number 6, Lord Selsdon (left) and Lord Waleran.

After a V1 flying bomb demolished the shops at Stainash Parade, the remains of the racing cars were taken to the paddock at "Ironbarks". At least two other cars were damaged at the same time, as neither of the two in this picture is HPL 448, the Dobson/ Brackenbury car.

The asymmetrical body shape is best seen from above, as in this Brooklands shot after Le Mans.

Charles Brackenbury bought HPL 448 from the factory in 1945, made it just about driveable and used it in this bodiless trim as a road car. The tyres were completely bald. The car is capable of 140mph.

first Lagonda. Just after 1pm Brackenbury came in to hand over, when was discovered that the offside exhaust was breaking away, but it only took 3 minutes to lash it up, not enough for the second car to catch up. By 3 o'clock the Bugatti had a three-lap lead and was set to break the distance record. It led the first Lagonda by 10 laps, with the second one a lap down and the first BMW two laps behind that. The last hour was just a case of running to finish, and after a precautionary pit stop at 233 laps Dobson finished third at 239 laps, 2006 miles. Selsdon finished on the same lap at 2000 miles, the two cars' average speeds respectively being 83.61mph and 83.35mph. Both the winning Bugatti and the Delage broke the previous best mileage. The Lagondas won their class, since the Bugatti, being supercharged, was counted as a 5-litre car.

Everyone was delighted at the finish, the French ecstatic at a third French victory in a row and the British at beating everyone else. The race had been faster than predicted and there was a lot of speculation that, had Bentley set a higher target, the Lagonda could have won. We shall never know, but it must have made Bentley wonder, because among his papers is an analysis of the race in which he calculated that the clutch troubles and the exhaust problem had cost 44 miles, which, had they not occurred, would have put number 5 on the same lap as the Delage in second place. For interest, the calculated running averages for each driver were Dobson 85.2mph, Brackenbury 86.78mph, Selsdon 83.28mph and Waleran 85.5mph.

By the end of the race the lightweight aluminium panels of the body had chafed themselves to a very tattered state, but the cars had been running as well as ever, even if the left hands of Dobson and Brackenbury resembled pieces of steak where they had had to ram the gear lever through. It was only years later that Dobson revealed there had been no brakes either by the end. But the crucial test would come when the engines were stripped down to see what state they were in. Not too bad, since the cars were driven back to England, but Percy Kemish discovered that of the 96 special valve springs in the two engines, only three were still intact, although the breakages were such that the engines had continued to run pretty well as normal. (One of the problems with a V12 is determining if all twelve cylinders are functioning, since it feels much the same on ten or eleven). All the heads had cracked at the points where two exhaust valves are adjacent. This was to lead W O, in his next engine, the LB6, to go to twin overhead

camshafts in order to get a bit more cooling to the exhaust valves. There was also evidence of oil starvation, confirmed by the drtvers, who noted that the oil pressure of 80psi at the start dropped off alarmingly after about two hours of racing, although it never disappeared completely, even under braking. As the utmost care had been taken in design to avoid this sort of thing, an investigation was mounted, with little success until during the war the Admiralty discovered the reason, outlined in the last chapter.

In his later years Bentley would not admit any of these findings. In 1954, when someone wrote in the Lagonda Club magazine that the cars had been in a bad way at the end of the race, he wrote in to deny it all and said that the cars had gone straight to Brooklands for the August 1939 meeting without being touched. This must be nonsense, for the purpose of the Le Mans effort was to see what was required to win, and you must strip the engines down afterwards to discover the results. Charles Sewell made a minute examination of the broken Eaton valve springs, finding that they were distressingly badly made, with wide variations between them for the key dimensions. He deduced that they were unnecessary anyway, given the strict rev limit W O had set and which the drivers had adhered to. The clutch problem was confined to number 5 and is unexplained. The author suspects that the normal

method of lubrication had been removed in the process of increasing oil pressure elsewhere and that there had not been time to do this on the second car, but this is pure speculation.

Alan Good was delighted. He was confident of victory in 1940, was considering an entry in the Donington Park GP and later put in a bid for ERA when it ran into financial difficulties, with an idea he could put a V12 into the ERA chassis and make a Formula 1 car. None of this came about, of course.

There was time for one more race meeting before the war clouds obscured everything. Both Le Mans cars were entered for the August Bank Holiday meeting at Brooklands, at the end of which were to be three three-lap Outer Circuit blinds. For once "Ebby" nodded and under-handicapped the Lagondas to such an extent that they were lifting off to avoid embarrassing him too much. Even so Brackenbury won the first race from Selsdon at 118.45mph after a fastest lap at 127.7mph. They were instantly re-handicapped for the next race and didn't bother to try too hard. Both cars showed the hard life the bodies had had, with numerous patches riveted on, but both had new scuttle panels without the wire mesh windscreen needed at Le Mans. They ran without wings or lights, of course, and probably were even higher geared. Lord Selsdon then entered their car for the Liège GP at the end of August, got it there just in

Robert Cowell in the Jersey Road Race of April 1948, showing the new body on HPL 448. He came ninth and was described as "a mobile chicane" by Motor Sport.

Testing at Brooklands prior to the August 1939 meeting, where the cars ran without wings or lamps. Left to right: Percy Kemish, Stan Ivermee and Charles Brackenbury.

Another re-body for 448 and a re-registration to boot, to get the £10 flat rate tax. Tony Crook is at the wheel at the 1950 Brighton Speed Trials in 1950. The nose is from a DB 2.6 Lagonda.

The Selsdon/Waleran car was also rebuilt after the war and sold to Robert Arbuthnot, seen above near the steering wheel. He entered it at Indianapolis in 1946, where this picture was taken.

On the way to practice at Indianapolis, 449 came off the tow rope and crashed. This is what the chassis looked like afterwards, so the car could not run. Arbuthnot was killed that August and the car remained in America for many years, but it is now back in the United Kingdom.

time for the race to be cancelled, and was lucky to get back again with it by 3 September, when all travel was banned.

The Selsdon/Waleran car emerged briefly during the War, still in Brooklands trim, to be displayed at Chessington in 1941 for a fund-raising war effort rally. Both these cars survive, after total rebuilds. Both were badly damaged in the 1944 Stainash Parade V1 attack but were sold after the War. One went to Charles Brackenbury on condition he didn't race it, which of course he threatened to, but eventually he sold it to Bob Cowell (who did). The other went to Robert Arbuthnot, who took it to Indianapolis, where it was unaccountably slow and then crashed when on tow and never started. Their adventures since would fill a small book, and when number 5 was auctioned at Goodwood a few years back it fetched the best part of three-quarters of a million pounds, evidence of the value the world places on the cars. Since the War dozens of derelict V12s have had replicas of the Le Mans cars built on them but none has been particularly successful in competition.

Chapter Nine

On the road today

Listed at the end of this book are the published contemporary road tests of 4½ litre and V12 Lagondas from 1933 to 1941. All are eulogistic, for these were the "supercars" of their day and no more likely to be encountered on an everyday basis than Lamborghinis are now. For example, the *The Autocar*'s road test of the M45 saloon was headed, "A car so fascinating that to overrate its virtues is hardly possible". In addition there were shorter, less informative, articles in the upmarket magazines like *Country Life* and *The Tatler*. *The Daily Telegraph* and *The Times* also carried short descriptive articles of cars thought likely to appeal to their readership.

Conditions today are utterly different, and while none of the contemporary road tests criticised the rearward visibility, as it wasn't considered important at the time, we now find the tiny rear windows in the hoods of the open cars and the not much bigger ones of the saloons a considerable nuisance. The worst period was 1933-34; by 1937 the rear windows were growing, but the blind spots are still large and wing or door mirrors are vital for safety. It was not important in the 1930s. The driver of a big Lagonda had no worries about being overtaken as his car could cruise at speeds in the 80s when the average car rarely exceeded 40, while outside the big towns and cities the roads were virtually empty of other motor vehicles, although there were plenty of bicycles. Nor would he expect to do much reversing, except in the morning, out of the motor house.

These cars are still fast enough not to be an embarrassment in present-day traffic. Modern cars, even the small ones, are theoretically quicker, but are rarely driven that hard. Just as important, Lagonda always fitted remarkably good brakes, to the point of controversy in 1934 when Rapiers on test bettered 1g, denounced as impossible by pundits at the time. These are still just as effective if the car is in good order.

All these models bear some similarity, but they also have enough differences for each type to have its distinctive feel. The M45 was in some ways the last of the Vintage sports cars. It has very high-geared steering which, on the crossply tyres, gives a directness modern drivers, brought up on radials and power systems, will not have experienced before. They will also soon appreciate why the big steering wheel is so close to the chest, for this is the position at which the biceps can be most effective, especially at manoeuvring speeds. Yet the steering lightens up at speed and is delightful on a winding road taken briskly. The M45 also has a very hard ride, made tolerable for the occupants of the front seats by the long wheelbase, but harsher in the rear. In many cases the Telecontrol supplementary dampers will have given up and the only damping is from the friction Hartfords, probably set quite firm.

The Meadows engine in its least tuned form develops enormous torque right from tickover but is very intolerant of high revolutions. That red line on the rev-counter must be obeyed. In deference to 70-year-old connecting rods it is advisable to keep well below it. There is little point in high revs anyway, as a change up will put you into a fatter part of the torque curve. The spark control is there to be used, and drivers in the 1930s, reluctant to change gear, regularly used it to crawl through traffic in a high ratio.

The gear ratios themselves are rather strange, and derive from the habits of the customers of the day. All buyers of a new Lagonda would have been wealthy, so there is a likelihood that they were middle-aged and had learned to drive in the Edwardian era or before. As a consequence they tended to be terrified of changing gear and did it as little as possible. On anything but a mountain they would start in second and quite possibly go straight into top as soon as they could, using the spark control thereafter. If top proved too high for a given hill they would like a high third, easy to get into from top. A gearbox designed round these habits would have first gear about right, but rarely used, a very low second for starting from rest, and then a yawning gap to a high third, close to top, followed by a top gear again about right. The Meadows T8 gearbox in the M45 follows that pattern exactly. It had the merit of an easier change than Lagonda's admittedly tricky Z 'box.

At the same time the sporting driver hated the wait on upward changes for the unsynchronised cogs to slow down before engaging the next gear. Hence the presence of the clutch stop, which was in essence a disc brake mounted on the shaft which joins clutch to gearbox. It was operated by the clutch pedal and slowed down the input side to make engagement quicker. It could be adjusted both for its timing and for how hard the braking effort was, so that at full bite the gearlever could be pulled straight through

on an upward change, although it has the opposite effect on a down change, making it harder instead of easier. How it is adjusted is a matter of personal taste - and the author prefers to slacken it right off so that it doesn't work at all, but not everyone agrees. The geometry of the device is none too clever and it will wear rapidly if set very fierce. An odd feature of the M45 Rapide was that it had a freewheel, which permitted clutchless upward changes, but retained the clutch stop.

Lagonda had a succession of tall men in charge and there is never a shortage of legroom in any of the cars, in front at least. There was also a tradition of flat floors, achieved by placing the body on top of the chassis frame and aided by the right-hand gear lever and handbrake, ideally positioned to go up the driver's trouser leg, especially on T7 tourers with no driver's door. The seats sit directly on the floor and originally had pneumatic cushions, mostly now replaced by springs or foam. The rear pneumatic ones, even when new, were rather disconcerting in that a second person sitting down projected the first one upwards, as the air chambers were linked across the car. Although there is no adjustment for the angle of the backrest, most people find the seats very comfortable, and are prepared to undertake a long run. Even on a car as long as this there isn't room for the rear passengers' legs to be as horizontal as the front ones and footwells were provided for the back seats, with an access in one to a concealed toolbox below the floor. Once installed, the rear passengers find they

M45 tourer cockpit. The Bluemel sprung steering wheel was normally of the flat-spoked, celluloid covered, variety, rather than the wire-spoked type shown here. The unlabelled rectangular object next to the glove compartment is a cigarette lighter, not a standard fitting, although common.

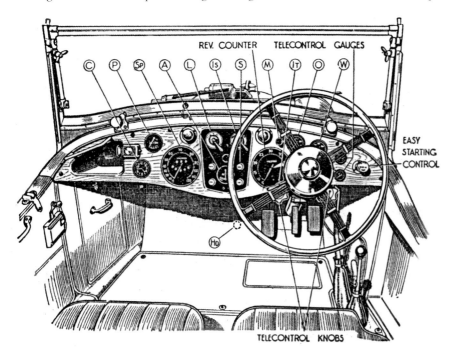

REV. COUNTER   TELECONTROL GAUGES

C P Sp A L Is S M It O W

EASY
STARTING
CONTROL

TELECONTROL KNOBS

KEY

A.—Ammeter.
C.—Clock.
D.—Direction signals, switch.
H.—Horn button.
Hd.—Dip-switch headlamp control.
Is.—Ignition switch.
It.—Ignition timing control.
L.—Lighting switch.
M.—Mixture control or strangler.
O.—Oil pressure gauge.
P.—Petrol gauge.
S.—Starter button.
Sp.—Speedometer.
T.—Hand throttle setting device.
W.—Water temperature indicator.

NOTE.—Other special fittings are named in full. In cars provided with Startix the one unit embodies the ignition switch and starter button.

LG45 tourer dashboard, with only four dials instead of seven but the same amount of information. Black instrument bezels were an option, as here.

are sitting higher than the front ones and if the hood is down, are not protected by the windscreen. Headgear is obligatory and suddenly a flying helmet does not seem to be an affectation.

Although the instruments and their layout are shared between tourers and saloons, the shape of the dashboard is quite different in each model. The saloon's has a flat top with an oddment shelf immediately next to the windscreen, whereas the tourer's dash follows the scuttle shape. Both windscreens open upwards, hinged at the top. Immediately in front of the driver the large rev-counter and the oil pressure gauge are clearly the important items, with all the other instruments rather scattered. The fuel gauge will be reading zero, since it only indicates when its button is pressed. The ignition switch is a Lagonda special with four positions: Off, Coil, Magneto, Both. One normally runs on "Both" but the separate switching is valuable for testing. On the saloon, another of Lagonda's special features is the quick-drop driver's window. The 1933 and 1934 cars had no indicators, and since the driver might need to drop his window quickly to make hand signals, the window was spring-loaded down, controlled by a long vertical lever which lowered it instantly and also served to raise it again, against considerable resistance. But the window could be left in any intermediate position by returning the lever to the vertical. This feature had been invented for the 12/24 and remained until indicators became common and standard. All other windows had ordinary winders.

For as long as mechanical brakes were fitted,

Lagonda made the brake pedal the right-hand one. This simplified the layout a great deal, since the pedal could then operate longitudinal rods directly and be mounted in a strong position directly on the chassis side rail. The idea of having the pedals the "wrong" way round tends to alarm newcomers to old cars but the driver soon gets used to it. In the author's experience over 50 years of Lagonda motoring it has not once proved to be a hazard. It certainly makes "heel and toe" actions (simultaneous braking and throttle opening) a great deal more natural, which is the reason, I am sure, that the 1939 works drivers had their Le Mans car set up this way.

The M45's braking system was exactly as its 3 Litre predecessor's but with a Clayton-Dewandre vacuum servo added. The handbrake, of Lagonda's normal fly-off pattern, where the ratchet only engages when the knob is pressed, acts directly on the main rods, and although there is a slipping link which in theory means it only operates on the rear wheels, in practice it applies all four. A driver accustomed to the dead modern pedal will find the lively reactions of the pedal of an M45 a new sensation, and the really testing moment comes if the car runs up a diagonal ramp while under braking, with first one wheel and then the other kicking back on the pedal. The servo gives a very good assistance to the driver's foot and tends to make hissing and panting noises like a heavy goods vehicle. There is an easy test to see if it is working, important in cold weather when the diaphragm may go hard, but the car can be stopped quite adequately if it isn't, given more effort by the driver.

The forward view is excellent, with the top of the nearside sidelamp just visible, giving off a small red signal at night to confirm that the bulb has not failed. But the driver sits about six feet from the radiator cap and, when emerging from a gateway or side road between walls, it is rather alarming that the car has to stick out about eight feet before the driver can see if it is safe to proceed. On the tourer, with the hood down, you have of course a 360-degree clear view, but it is a different story with the hood up. The original rear view windows were small metal-framed glass ones about nine inches by two, while saloon ones, also a pair, were not a great deal bigger. Reversing either involves great reliance on wing mirrors or ideally, outside assistance. When ordering a new hood the tourer owner has the dilemma of deciding whether to increase the visibility or not. Most nowadays opt for plastic, but the size is a matter of personal taste. A huge plastic window may be practical but it makes the car very non-original looking.

Now we have to start the engine, not simply a matter of turning a key. For a start, there isn't one. The first operation is to turn the ignition switch to the "Both" position, which energises the fuel pumps. Then wait until the clicking stops, as it will when the float chambers are full. One then sets the spark control to about half advanced (say 9 o'clock on the steering wheel hub) and operates the Ki-gass pump. This is a little hand-operated fuel pump, mounted at the extreme right hand end of the dash, and is needed because these SU carburettors have fixed jets which cannot be lowered for starting. Six pumps is normally enough, counting from when the Ki-gass starts to pump petrol and not air. One quickly learns to distinguish the different feel, and an old, worn pump will probably leak petrol on to one's fingers to confirm it. The inlet manifold will now have a little pool of petrol in it and pressing the starter button will usually result in a first-compression start. In very cold weather one may have to "catch" the engine on the Ki-gass if it falters, but soon the Ki-gass can be screwed home and won't be needed again.

Immediately after a cold start the oil pressure needle will whiz round the dial and in winter may go right round to the back of the zero stop, but it soon drops back to around 20psi. Once on the road it should stay at this figure but the novice may be alarmed to find it registering zero under heavy braking, when all the oil rushes forward, away from the oil pickup which is right at the back of the sump. Many Meadows engines run rather hot, a feature brought on by the successive enlargements from 3 litres to 4½, which inevitably reduced the water passages at the same time as increasing the heat output. They are also great sludge producers, a characteristic not unconnected with all the dissimilar metals they contain leading to electrolytic interactions. Worse still, some clown may have used tap water in the cooling system, a habit forbidden by Lagonda in the 1930s to avoid chalky or limescale deposits. The radiator shutters are thermostatically controlled and should open at the right moment as the engine warms up, a very slow process by modern standards. Once they are open the extraordinarily powerful Lagonda fan draws a lot more cold air in (and probably costs a horsepower or two in the process).

Driving at night reveals that the huge Lucas P100 headlamps were designed for pre-war French Routes Nationales, lined with poplar trees. The lamps will light up about half a mile of these but have very little spread. The original set-up for dipping was that both P100s went out and a centre lamp with a flat-top beam came on. This is now illegal and all M45s will (should) have been altered so that both lamps stay on in the dipped beam. Similarly, at the rear the pre-war rear lamp on one side matched by a reversing lamp on the other is also illegal, and all cars must have been converted to two rear lamps. The foot dipswitch can prove elusive for someone more accustomed to steering column switches, and pre-war dynamos don't always take kindly to the modern custom of driving with the headlamps on at all times after dark. A good battery is essential, along with a battery charger in the garage.

All the above relates to the M45 and M45 Rapide, and there are many similarities when the LG45 is considered. The performance is nigh on identical – there is more difference between good and bad cars of the same model than there is between models. The LG is more refined, the engine mounts are more sophisticated and there is more hardware between the engine and the crew. An odd subjective feeling creeps in that the LG feels higher and narrower. It isn't, the dimensions being almost the same, but the impression is caused, I think, by the M45 having broad flat front wings while the LG has the first of Frank Feeley's trademark "gothic arch" section curved ones The Girling brakes, with no servo, are just as efficient as the M45's but do need a stronger push on the pedal.

W O's civilising changes are apparent on the LG45. The tourer body sides have no cutouts for the

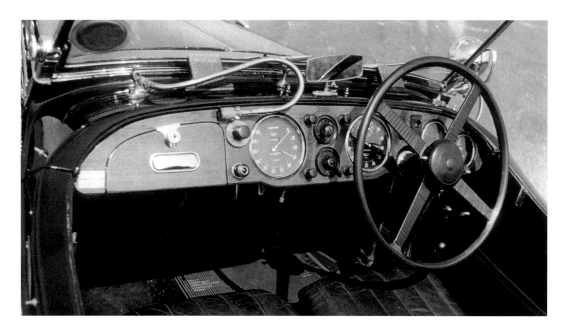

LG45 Rapide interior, much the same as the tourer's, but squeezed up a bit by the narrower body. The owner has added a modern map-reading lamp on a bendy stalk

driver's elbows, simply because there was no need. The body sides are further away and the lower-geared steering does not require the driver to put so much effort into it. Occasionally one comes across an LG needing superhuman strength to manoeuvre; the cause is nearly always that non-standard front springs have been fitted which have increased the castor angle to such an extent that the lower-geared steering hasn't helped. As the only control over castor angle is the spring shape, the cure is to fit wedges between spring and axle to sort things out.

The dashboard layout is less scattered than the M45's, with the four minor instruments joined together into two pairs in front of the driver. There is no Ki-gass pump as the SUs now have adjustable jets for starting, controlled by a steering-column lever. The black or chromium-plated bezels for the instruments are set into the dash panel and internally lit, so the earlier pull-out dash lamps have gone, and the layout is more symmetrical. One oddity of the dash is that there is no ignition warning lamp now that there is only magneto ignition. Owners have to watch the ammeter to check that the dynamo is charging. The standard wheelcases were soon discovered to be ideal places for wing mirrors and very many LGs have these, nearer the driver's eyeline than a door mirror, and less remote than one at the front of the wing.

In driving the LG45, the increased smoothness is at once noticeable; it goes with the "City gent" atmosphere of the whole car, but performance is effectively unchanged. There is much less noise, with triple silencers on the exhaust and an air cleaner that removes the prominent sucking noises from under the bonnet. The clutch stop was removed, so the owner is relieved from coping with that, but the contrast between the upper two and lower two ratios feels all the greater now that third and top have synchromesh. Later cars with the G10 gearbox usually, but not always, have a centre change. The lever is very long and memories of Ford Populars make one expect it to be willowy, but it isn't. Far from it: the lever is very sturdy and the movements it controls much more ponderous. The whole gearbox is immensely strong and this shows in the action. On the plus side, the ratios are much more rational, with second further from first and nearer third, doing away with the yawning gap found in the Meadows 'box.

In an LG45 tourer, with the hood down, the rear-seat passengers find themselves not quite so exposed as in the M45, but headgear is still vital. The detachable aero screens fix to the sides of the windscreen to make efficient wind deflectors for front-seat passengers. The drophead is another matter, for the hood here is an elaborate padded affair if original or a correct replacement. When folded it stands much higher than the tourer hood, which Frank Feeley contrived to fold away completely out of sight. The saloons seem much closer to the M45 in their interiors, but Sanction 3 saloons are visibly lower at the rear after the space formerly occupied by the batteries became available for passengers' bottoms. There was an embarrassing moment when an S3 saloon was being assessed by the Metropolitan Police for their use. The car was a high-mileage demonstrator and the combination of this and heavyweight constables caused the rubber diaphragm supporting the seat to give way, depositing the official blue serge on to the road. Metal bars were put in afterwards to prevent a recurrence.

The boot space hardly changed, but since the spare wheel had now permanently gone to live on the offside wing it was possible to make its lid open out flat to take a large trunk if needed. On the M45, if the spare was on the bootlid - and it nearly always was - it prevented the lid opening totally flat and there had to be spring assistance upwards to take some of the weight. Without these springs, opening the lid tended to hit the owner in the pit of the stomach with the considerable weight of the spare wheel.

The handling of the LG45 is very little different from the M45, although, with the weight distribution a touch more nose-heavy, the initial understeer may be a bit more pronounced as one enters a corner. This soon gives way to roll oversteer, like most "cart-sprung" cars with a flexible chassis. The LG45, unlike its predecessors, had an anti-roll bar mounted on the rear dampers, linking them across the car, with the aim of stiffening up the outer spring when weight was transferred to it in a corner. Unfortunately the mechanical advantage is not great, and although it has some effect it isn't much. The LG45 was Lagonda's first model to be fitted with a front bumper as standard. The design chosen claimed to aid roadholding in that it prevented both chassis frame and axles vibrating at the same frequency. It is difficult to know whether this claim means anything The Rapide is of course a deal faster, but feels very similar, since the chassis is identical, the extra performance being the result of more power with less weight and a reduced frontal area.

When we come to consider the V12 there is a complete transformation. It is believed that not a single part was carried over from the preceding models. Experienced Lagonda tinkerers learn to recognise the various parts that were progressively beefed up as the cars grew bigger and more powerful. They may be stronger but there is a family resemblance. Not so with the V12; it really was designed from a clean sheet of paper. It is not surprising, given the Rolls-Royce background of Tresilian and his companions, that there are some items that look absurdly complicated. The hand-brake, for example. On the LG45 it was coupled to the brake rods directly. With hydraulic brakes, the law said it had to be separate, but the system actually installed allows for scores of different adjustments and balancing mechanisms, when the

law would have been satisfied with a cable and a pulley. Along the same lines, the anchorages of the brake shoes are immensely complicated to allow for all the possible movements, both radial and circumferential, so that there are 11 separate components, all without lubrication, where most firms would have specified an oversize hole and left it at that.

The first thing one notices on the V12 is the pedal arrangement, with the accelerator now on the right and with the pedal arms coming up through slots in the floor rather than horizontally through the bulkhead. The second thing is that for the first time the driver can get in without colliding with the handbrake lever, now nearly horizontal on the floor to the right of the seat. Although the whole car is lower, Lagonda almost managed to retain their flat floor in the front, but the gear lever is noticeably shorter and the dash tidied up even more. Only short chassis cars got a rev-counter as standard, although many buyers of the longer ones ordered one as an extra. The driver is faced with four large dials, all the same diameter, comprising the rev-counter, speedometer, a single unit with all four minor gauges contained within it and, over on the left, a multiple switch panel which contained the key lighting and other functions surrounding the ignition switch, now key-operated (Lagonda's first). This multiple switch panel had a very long life, featuring on all the David Brown post-war Lagondas and even on his Aston Martins. As Lagonda were known for never throwing anything away, one concludes there had been an immense original order. An odd change was the removal of the clock, which on the LG45 shared the rev-counter dial, to the glove locker lid. The V12 Rapide had a slightly shallower dash, on which the same instruments were rearranged since there wasn't room on the extreme right for the minor gauges.

One change that might be thought a backward step was the lack of boot space. The V12's shapely tail did not contain the same boot volume as the squarer LG45, made worse by the lid being top-hinged and therefore not available as an additional platform when opened. The Rapide was even worse, as there were no wheelcases in the front wings, so the spare wheel had perforce to retreat to the boot and occupied very nearly all of it. Lagonda's insistence that the Rapide was a four-seater, which presumes three abreast in the front, is largely ignored today and many cars have been rebuilt to have two bucket seats in front and the sideways one behind.

Charles Sewell was responsible for the changes

LG6 drophead dash, identical to the V12's apart from the rev counter. Lagonda's traditional flat floor has gone, compromised by the gearbox remote control. The circular switch panel was found on postwar Lagondas throughout the David Brown era, and on Aston Martins.

needed to make the Rapide (aside from the coachwork) and his notes have survived. One such reads, "Must make more noise". This was about the extent of the mechanical changes, the Rapide being otherwise completely standard. It is a shame none was ever road tested before the War to give us comparable figures.

Once on the move, the contrast with the earlier "cart sprung" cars is immense. The LG45 had a markedly softer ride than the M45, but the V12 was much softer again. The driver could control the damping effort on the rear axle, but not the front dampers which, it has to be admitted, don't do much because of the way in which they are attached. In the early postwar period there was a lively trade in converting V12s to telescopic front dampers, but purists resist this. If it were possible to drive a car blindfolded, a person placed in a V12 would date it as a car of the 1960s, never a pre-war design. The engine is as smooth as a 12-cylinder ought to be, and the rev-counter needle shoots round the dial in the lower gears. Modern drivers are accustomed to using these, and the lack of bottom-end torque so commonly cited is of little consequence. Again, it was the tendency of 1938 drivers to hang on to top gear that probably generated this accusation. The independent front suspension does rather understeer initially, but the travel is limited compared to more recent designs and as on the earlier cars, roll oversteer cancels it out later in the corner.

As it was intended to be, the LG6 is a compromise. It looks and feels exactly the same as a V12,

but the engine is much more of a lugger, much higher geared and less frenetic at cruising speed. For an owner wary of the complications of the V12 the LG6 offers a splendid compromise, with Meadows ruggedness allied to the soft ride and hydraulic brakes of its companion. One possible drawback that hydraulics introduce is that they deteriorate with time, not wear, so that a car off the road will probably need attention to its brakes as regularly as one in constant use. This does not apply to the earlier mechanical systems.

Throughout the period 1933-40 you will notice from the tables how the extra power extracted from the engines is matched by the extra weight, so that performance remained very nearly the same (LG45 Rapide excepted, of course). Much of this extra weight comes from the steadily increasing equipment that customers were demanding, such as a radio, in those days a heavy piece of kit. To our eyes, carrying four jacks about permanently looks over the top since punctures now are so rare. But they weren't then, and the well-dressed Lagonda customer had no desire to wreck his suit climbing under the car to fix a jack, hence the Jackall system. In addition, customers had enormous freedom to specify extras, and although most had only modest requests, there were some hyper-fussy individuals who covered sheets of paper with what are sometimes very odd requirements indeed. By today, though, the majority of cars have been rebuilt in one way or another and most restorers work to standard designs extracted from catalogues, so the really weird cars are disappearing.

Chapter Ten

Ownership Today

One hopes that some readers of this book will be contemplating buying a Lagonda and that they may never have owned a pre-war car or, if they have, it was of another make. Lagondas have the common characteristics of most pre-1939 cars, plus a few specific to the make, such as the centre throttle pedal, covered in the last chapter. The first piece of advice one can give is to join the Lagonda Club. It is not necessary to own one to do this, and when cars come on the market members are encouraged, not least by our minimal advertising rates, to first offer their car through the club's monthly newsletter. By joining, one can take advantage of the accumulated experi-

ence of over 800 members worldwide, have access to the "Workshop Manuals" produced by expert club members, and make use of the spares service, which manufactures virtually all components to either the original design or, where appropriate, in improved modern materials if there was a problem with longevity. An example of the latter is the various aluminium water pipes found on the Meadows engine, which are prone to corrosion from the inside. The replacements are made in a modern alloy which resists such corrosion.

First of all, the choice of model and body type. It is a sad fact that open cars fetch about twice the price of closed ones, so that when a saloon needs

Mark Walker's V12 Rapide drophead coupé is the very image of a mile-eating supercar, and with around 200bhp under the bonnet this example would not disappoint.

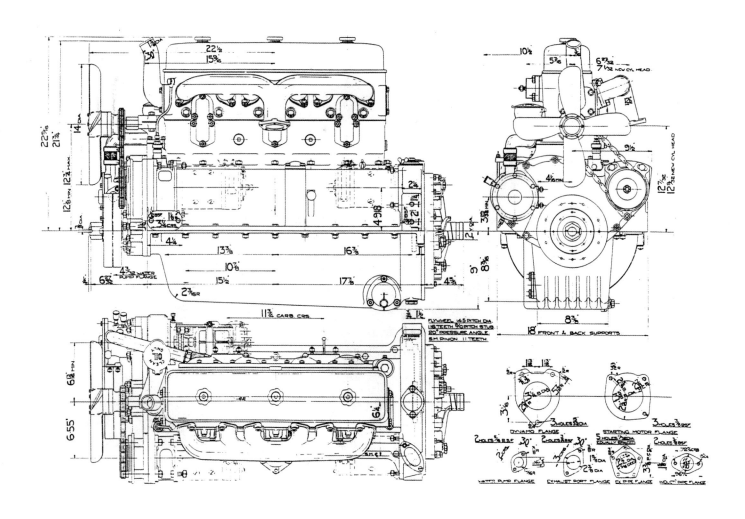

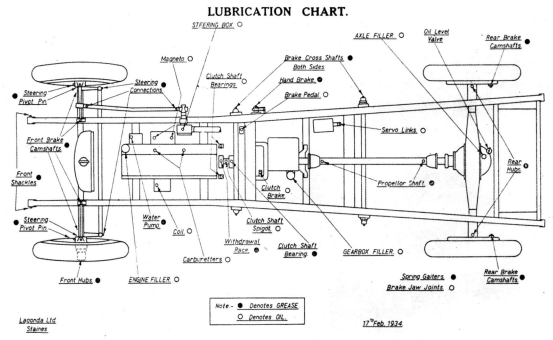

LUBRICATION CHART.

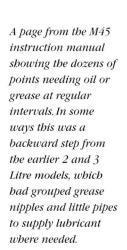

A page from the M45 instruction manual showing the dozens of points needing oil or grease at regular intervals. In some ways this was a backward step from the earlier 2 and 3 Litre models, which had grouped grease nipples and little pipes to supply lubricant where needed.

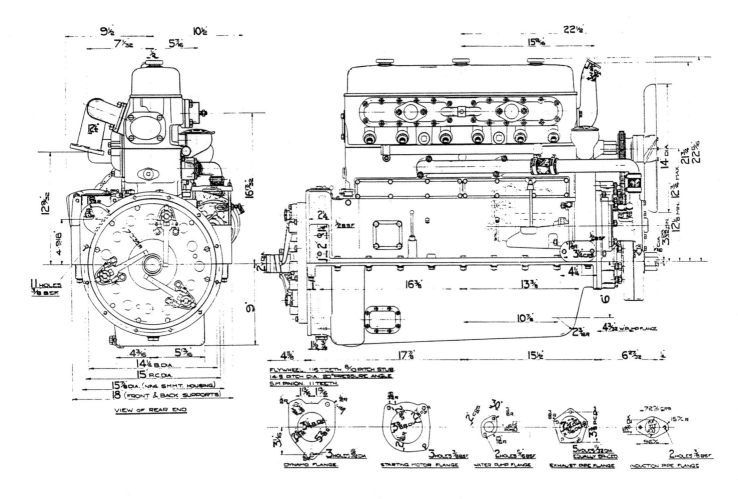

LUBRICATION CHART.

Meadows' own drawings of the 6ESC (M45) engine show only a single offside magneto, but two sets of sparking plug holes. Lagonda steadily introduced more and more modifications up to 1939.

The M45 Rapide returned to the grouped nipples for centralised chassis lubrication. It meant that the owner was less likely to leave one out.

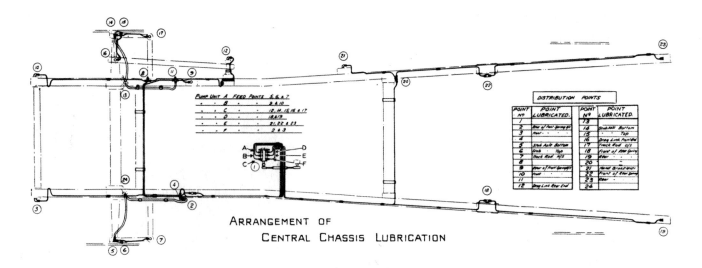

ARRANGEMENT OF
CENTRAL CHASSIS LUBRICATION

SCREW DOWN
TO DECREASE
SCREW UP
TO INCREASE
FLOW

SPRING
LOADED
GLAND

OIL
CONTAINER

ROCKER
SHAFT

DELIVERY
UNION
CONTAINING
VALVE

OIL
INLET

ADJUSTING
BUSH
LOCKNUT
LEATHER
WASHER
GUIDE
PIN
CROSSHEAD
ROCKER
STOP PIN
PISTON
PLUNGER
WASHER
5/32 BALL
VALVE
SPRING
FIBRE
WASHER
VALVE
PLUG

SECTION THROUGH CHASSIS LUBRICATION OIL PUMP.
It is attached to the rear end of the sump and is provided with
adjustments. To increase flow, screw out adjuster. To decrease,
screw it in.

Recommended Lubricants

Engine and Gearbox ... Castrol XXL, Mobiloil D, AeroShell.

Rear Axle   ...   ... Castrol Hi-Press, Mobiloil E.P.,
                      Shell E.P. Spirex.

Water Pump   ...   ... Stauffers Special Centi Grease.

Fan and Universal Joints Mobiloil C 200.

Steering Gear Box   ... Castrol Hi-Press.

CHASSIS LUBRICATION. This is automatically controlled
by the clutch pedal, there being a device incorporated which insures
the pump's operation, even provided the pedal is not pushed fully.

OIL PRESSURE IN ENGINE. This should register 20 lbs.
gauge pressure after the oil has had a chance to get warm, at
30 m.p.h. The pressure will obviously rise just after the engine
has been started and may vary slightly in summer or winter, or
after prolonged hill climbing. Any undue drop in oil pressure
should be immediately investigated.

Possible causes of low engine oil pressure are :—

Insufficient oil in sump.	Choked filter element.
Dirt under relief valve.	Clogged suction filter.
Broken relief valve springs or plunger sticking.	Loose oil union inside engine.
	Worn main bearings.

The comparable page from the LG45 book. Lagonda had now abandoned castor-based oils in the transmission. All these little pipes are fine provided the oil stays clean and free of sludge. At least there was a proper filter now..

bodywork attention it has been very common for an owner of the philistine persuasion to scrap the body, replace it with a tourer or even a primitive "boy racer" and then sell at a profit. As a result, good saloons have become very scarce. The author's view is that the saloons, which changed annually, are more interesting than the tourers, all much of a muchness, and carry a lot more period charm in their fittings. It will, of course, depend on what is available on the market and how long the buyer is prepared to wait for the right car. All 4½ litres and V12s, if they are any good, will be quite expensive. The cheap "barn find" may not be such a good buy if it requires expensive professional attention, but might well attract a

person able to do it him/herself.

The six-cylinder cars have the attraction of good, simple and rugged engines, easy to understand and work on. The V12 is a different animal altogether, and some parts of the car, not only on the engine, seem to have been designed to discourage the amateur. The first requirement will be a set of Whitworth/BSF spanners. These are no longer stocked by mainstream tool merchants but are available at the larger autojumbles. The open-end variety will do most jobs on the Lagonda but there are one or two places where a tubular spanner, rare nowadays, was originally employed. Mostly a modern socket set will replace it. On both the Meadows and V12, spark plug access has its problems, for different reasons. On the Meadows some of the plugs are very close to the manifold and Lagonda originally supplied a special thin-walled spanner for these. For a time, the club was able to supply special plugs with a 14mm hexagon on the 18mm body, but these seem to be no longer available and it may be necessary to grind down the walls of a normal plug spanner to suit. On the V12 the plug spanner has to have a universal joint in it and in 1938 this was so unusual that the firm supplied one in the car's extensive toolkit. They went further and added a rubber disc to grip the top of the plug to aid in extracting it after it had been loosened. This was regarded as very high-tech then but it is easy to find such a spanner today. For dealing with the electrical side, should you feel competent to do so, you will also need a set of BA spanners, chiefly the even number sizes, 2BA, 4BA and 6BA. Imperial feeler gauges for setting valve clearances are still easy to find and it is safer to use these than to attempt to convert to the nearest metric equivalent.

Where should your car come from? Undoubtedly the best source is directly from a fellow club member. He will have the history of the car in his ownership and will of course let you drive it to sample its performance and listen for unwanted noises at the same time. The Meadows engines are renowned for being easy to start from cold, so I would be a bit alarmed if the car is nicely warmed through when you arrive. The starting handle will enable you to check if all the compressions are there and if two are missing and they are adjacent cylinders, suspect gasket failure. As a result of its design, on the Meadows this does not let water into the oil, a useful guide on other makes. If you are unsure, it is prudent to take with you an experienced club member who is familiar with the model, but buy him a decent lunch for his trouble.

Buying from a dealer may be a more high-pressure experience, but you may be able to screw some sort of guarantee from him to justify the higher price. Again, a test drive is vital and possibly an RAC or AA inspection, although expertise on old cars in their ranks must be getting rare now. Auction prices are the lowest, but you rarely get much chance to drive the car.

Having bought your Lagonda, some choices regarding maintenance become immediate. If leaded petrol is available locally, use it as the cars were designed for it. If not, the unleaded-plus-additive route is recommended, provided the additive is one approved by the Federation of British Historic Vehicle Clubs, who test them at regular intervals to make sure the formulation hasn't changed. The choice of oil is very subjective and depends on engine history. The old "straight" oils, ie non-detergent, tended to deposit carbon in all sorts of nooks in the engine, which is why pre-war motorists decarbonised so regularly. When detergent oils came in, they dissolved this carbon, carried it round the engine and, if you were lucky, deposited it in the filter. But Meadows M45s and V12s don't have much in the way of filtration, only enough to keep out the larger rocks. Those of us who converted to detergent oils found them turning jet black after only a few miles. Several changes later, it all sorted itself out, but the conversion was messy and expensive in oil. You need to know the engine history before deciding on which oil to use, and if in doubt use the straight one. Detergent oil is fine if the engine has been fairly recently dismantled or if you are prepared to go through the conversion process. Synthetic or semi-synthetic oils are a waste of money in a Lagonda.

Chassis lubrication is another debatable issue. The M45 has straightforward greasers and oilers which require quite frequent attention (see the diagram). But as owners became richer or less inclined to have a chauffeur, each successive model grew more sophisticated automatic chassis lubrication systems, worked by a pump activated by first the clutch and later the brake pedal. But the problem was that the engines of the day produced large quantities of sludge which found its way into the tiny pipes and blocked them. So the modern owner can either connect the pump to a source of clean oil, not that stuff in the sump, or do away with the whole thing and revert to greasers. The V12 and LG6 have a problem here with the front suspension, where the original system pumped oil to the uppermost part and hoped it would drain by gravity to the rest. Grease is not so accommodating.

Access to the working parts was always a Lagonda priority. In the days of the 16/65 great play was made of the fact that the oil filler held a quart, so the owner could open a tin, dump it in and go off and do something else while it drained. The beam-axle cars, within limits, follow this philosophy and most operations can be carried out without access problems, although the new owner must beware of the weight of the bigger components. If dropping a Meadows sump, for example, one must support the weight with a jack; nobody is strong enough to hold it up unaided. But the

Lubrication Diagram

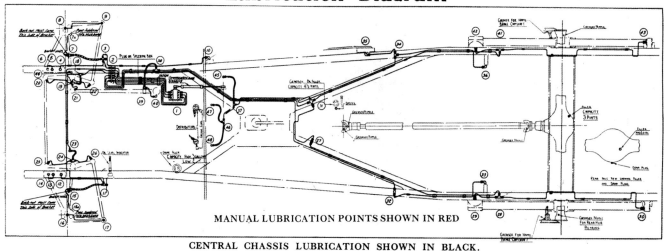

MANUAL LUBRICATION POINTS SHOWN IN RED

CENTRAL CHASSIS LUBRICATION SHOWN IN BLACK.

1. Chassis lubrication pump.
2. Junctions from pump to chassis.
3. 4-Way branch.
4. Upper Wishbone Bearing, Rear, O.S.
5. „ „ „ Front, O.S.
6. Lower „ „ O.S.
7. Flexible pipe connection (upper wishbone arms), O.S.
7a. Upper wishbone arm (outer pins). O.S.
8. King Pin—Offside.
9. Offside steering lever and outer track rod ball joint.
10. Accelerator pedal spindle.
11. 3-Way junction.

12. Upper wishbone bearing, Rear, N.S.
13. „ „ „ Front, N.S.
14. Lower „ „ N.S.
15. Flexible pipe connection (upper wishbone arms, N.S.)
15a. Upper wishbone arm (outer pins), N.S.
16. King pin—nearside.
17. Nearside steering lever and outer track rod ball joint.
18. 3-Way connection.
19. 4-Way connection on tie rod arm (offside).
20. Inner track rod—offside ball joint.
21. Steering drag link—front ball joint.
22. Outer track rod (offside), inner ball joint.

23. 2-Way connection.
24. 3-Way connection on tie rod arm (nearside).
25. Inner track rod—nearside ball joint.
26. Outer track rod (nearside) inner ball joint.
27. Pipe junction.
28. 3-Way connection.
29. Rear spring—front eye (nearside).
30. Rear spring shackle—nearside.
31. 4-Way connection.
32. Pipe junction.
33. Hand brake swinging lever—nearside.
34. 3-Way connection.
35. Hand brake lever.

36. Hand brake swinging lever—offside.
37. 3-Way connection.
38. 3-Way connection.
39. 2-Way connection on steering drag link.
40. Steering drag link—rear ball joint.
41. 3-Way connection.
42. Rear spring Front eye (offside).
43. „ „ shackle (offside).
44. Offside tie rod arm spindle.
45. Pedal shaft.
46. 3-Way connection.
47. Clutch withdrawal—offside.
48. „ „ nearside.

More complicated still: the V12/LG6 book needed two colours to distinguish between automatic and manual lubrication points. The automatic system is a total-loss one, of course, in that the pump forces oil to the chassis point, whence it leaks on to the road. If your engine stops losing oil, suspect that the lubrication system has given up or become blocked.

V12 is a different matter and some of the operations required seem extraordinarily complicated. In the club's Workshop Manual, three whole pages are needed to explain how to set the camshaft timing. And why, when moving the oil filler to the cambox, was the offside one chosen when the oil level float is on the left?

One striking feature of Lagondas which will be immediately noticed by someone with experience only of modern cars is the quality of the materials and engineering. Rust is very rarely a problem, wings, even steel ones, were rolled round wire on their edges and welded up, while much of the bodywork was aluminium. Mind you, there may be a problem with woodworm or moth. On the engineering side, consider the fit of the brake drums. Having removed the road wheel and the eight bolts that fasten a brake drum to its hub, one still cannot move it by hand. Two holes tapped 5/16in BSF are provided in the base of the drum and two matching bolts in the tool kit. Screwing the bolts into the holes forces the drum off. Putting it back only involves a soft-faced hammer, also in the toolkit.

One last "beware" item before I stop criticising the V12 is the fatigue life of the duralumin connecting rods, now heading for 70 years old. The V12 thrives on revs but the number of stress reversals these rods can survive is not known and

even if it was, could not be established for any particular engine. Cautious owners rarely exceed 3000rpm and these low speeds do not do justice to the rest of the car (it represents only about 60mph in top gear). For serious motoring it is strongly recommended that the engine be fitted with modern steel connecting rods. There is a choice, but XK Jaguar ones are common. They are longer than the originals, so require a piston with a lower crown. There is a sad history, and it has happened far too often, of an impetuous enthusiast discovering a V12 in a barn where it has lain for decades, buying it from the widow, getting it to start with new plugs and petrol and promptly taking it up the motorway to see "What she'll do". The result is always the same: a loud bang and a rod through the crankcase. Some of the oil passages are tortuous and old oil turns to toffee. Result: zero lubrication. If a V12 has been unused for years it requires a lot of attention before one can safely start it up.

From all the foregoing the reader may be put off considering a V12, but that was not the intention. For the opposite side of the coin is that once set up properly a V12 will run for many thousands of miles with no more than routine attention and will give a far more comfortable ride than its predecessors. Just don't think of the fuel bills.

ROAD TEST COMPARISONS

Date	Model	Price	Weight (cwt)	0-50 (sec)	0-60 (sec)	0-70 (sec).	Maximum (mph)	Mean (mph)	Mpg	Source
M45										
14.11.33	Tourer	£795	32.5		14.2			92	16	Motor
22.12.33	Tourer	£795	32.5	10	15.8	20		95.74	16	Autocar
Jan 34	Tourer	£795	32.5	11	16	22.5		91	15.5	Motor Sport
13.4.34	Saloon	£950	35.5	10.4	15.8	22.2	92.78	90	17	Autocar
M45 RAPIDE										
26.11.35	Tourer	£1000	33.1	9.4	14.6	21	100.56	98.36	15	Autocar
May 35	Tourer	£1000	32	10	14	19		94	12.5	Motor Sport
LG45										
18.2.36	Tourer	£1000	35.3	11.2	15.5		97.7		16	Motor
10.4.36	Tourer	£1000	35.6	12.6	17.2	24	96.77	93.02	16	Autocar
May 36	Tourer	£1000	35	12	15	21		94.7	13	Motor Sport
9.4.37	Saloon S3	£1125	39.2	11.7	17.3	23.4	93.75	91.14	14-16	Autocar
22.5.37	Saloon S3			11.2					15	Practical Motorist
LG45 RAPIDE										
10.11.36	Tourer	£1050	32	9.4	13.2		108.2		16	Motor
4.6.37	Tourer	£1050	31.75	10.3	12.9	18.4	103.45	100.28	14-16	Autocar
LG6										
3.5.38	Short Saloon	£1195	38.5	10.4			94		13.5	Motor
17.6.38	Short Saloon	£1195	38.5	11.3	16.4	23	95.74	91.37	12-14	Autocar
17.3.39	Short Saloon	£1225	39.5	11.3	16	21.5	94.74	91.14	15-17	Autocar
V12										
11.3 38	Short Saloon	£1550	39.5	9.7	12.9	17.9	103.45	100.28	12-15	Autocar
17.5.38	de Ville	£1625	39	10.1			101		12.5	Motor
27.9.38	Short Saloon	£1550	38.5	9.9			103		12.3	Motor
7.10.38	de Ville	£1625	41.5	11.1	14.8	21.5	100	96.77	12-14	Autocar
30.6.39	Medium Saloon	£1600	40.7	10.7	14.6	20.8	100	95.74	13-15	Autocar
15.3.40	DHC	£1575	39	10.2	13.1	18.4	94.74		13-15	Autocar
Sept 41	Medium Saloon	£1600	39.2	12	14.3	20			c11	Motor Sport

The Lagonda Club

The Lagonda Club AGM is always well attended and is the big social event of the year, held each September.

The Lagonda club was formed in 1951 by the amalgamation of the Lagonda Car Club, itself a reformed pre-war club, and the Two Litre Register. It has three main objectives:

First, to preserve and develop interest in all types of Lagonda vehicles from the motorcycles to the latest models. Second, to promote the sport and pastime of using Lagonda cars by various activities – social, sporting or just fun. The club publishes a monthly newsletter, a high quality quarterly colour magazine and a worldwide register of members and their cars. The club also reprints and publishes the original instruction books for each model, plus amplified "Workshop Manuals" prepared by club experts on most models.

Thirdly, the club operates a comprehensive "in-house" spares section, which holds and manufactures virtually a complete range of spares for the pre-war cars. Also, there is a range of high quality regalia, ties, badges etc.

For the new member, the club can provide a wide range of general, technical and historical information from the club's archives. It offers the opportunity to meet like-minded people and make new friends. We pride ourselves on being non-stuffy and approachable. For those seeking a car, advertisements are published monthly in the newsletter.

For more information, please contact the Hon. Secretary, Colin Bugler at Wintney House, London Road, Hartley Wintney, Hants. RG27 8RN.

Tel/Fax: 01252 845451

e-mail: lagclub@tiscali.co.uk

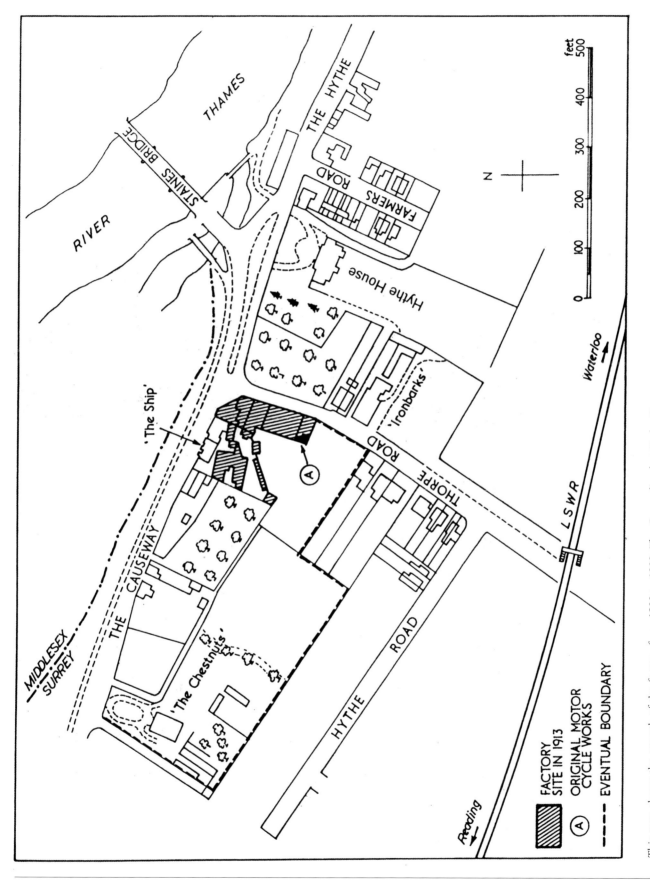

FACTORY
SITE IN 1913

Ⓐ ORIGINAL MOTOR
CYCLE WORKS

— · — EVENTUAL BOUNDARY

This map shows the growth of the factory from 1900 to 1939. The Gunns lived at Hythe House and during the Second World War Lagonda/Wyndham Hewitt took over "Ironbarks" as well.